Islam in Sau

'In the popular imagination, Saudi Arabia is a monolithic and static relic from an earlier age, wedded to a reactionary interpretation of Islam and led by an authoritarian monarchy whose alliance with a retrograde religious establishment has assured its survival. David Commins challenges this view by tracing the origins and evolution of the Saudi state from its eighteenth century roots through the present day. For Commins, Saudi Arabia's contemporary social and political order is the product of dynamic historical and ongoing struggles, both internal (pitting dynasts against religious traditionalists, Wahhabi true believers against non-Wahhabis and their more liberal Wahhabi allies, and an old guard against a younger generation habituated to a world of social media, cable television, and consumerism) and external (including threats from imperial powers in the nineteenth and early twentieth centuries, Arab nationalists in the 1950s–60s, Saddam's Iraq in the 1990s, and, currently, Iran and al-Qaeda). Commins tracks the Al Saud's efforts to balance and overcome these challenges, in the process creating a system whose defining characteristics are contradiction and ambiguity. An eye-opening account, clearly written, subtly argued.'

James L Gelvin, Professor of History, UCLA, author of
The Arab Uprisings: What Everyone Needs to Know
and **The Modern Middle East: A History**

Islam in
Saudi Arabia

David Commins

Foreword by Malise Ruthven

CORNELL UNIVERSITY PRESS
ITHACA, NEW YORK

For Susan

Originally published in Great Britain in 2015 by I.B. Tauris & Co Ltd

First published in the United States of America in 2015 by Cornell University Press
First printing, Cornell Paperbacks, 2015

Typeset in Garamond by JCS Publishing Services Ltd, www.jcs-publishing.co.uk
Printed and bound in Great Britain by T.J. International, Padstow, Cornwall

Library of Congress Cataloging-in-Publication Data

Commins, David Dean, author.
  Islam in Saudi Arabia / David Commins ; foreword by Malise Ruthven.
    pages cm
  "Originally published in Great Britain in 2015 by I.B. Tauris & Co. Ltd."-- Title page verso.
  Includes bibliographical references and index.
  ISBN 978-0-8014-5411-0 (cloth : alk. paper) —
  ISBN 978-0-8014-5691-6 (pbk. : alk. paper)
  1. Islam--Saudi Arabia. 2. Islam and state--Saudi Arabia. 3. Wahhabiyah-- Saudi Arabia. I. Ruthven, Malise, writer of introduction. II. Title.

  BP63.S33C66 2015
  297.8'1409538--dc23
                  2015004964

Cloth printing   10 9 8 7 6 5 4 3 2 1
Paperback printing   10 9 8 7 6 5 4 3 2 1

Contents

Illustrations

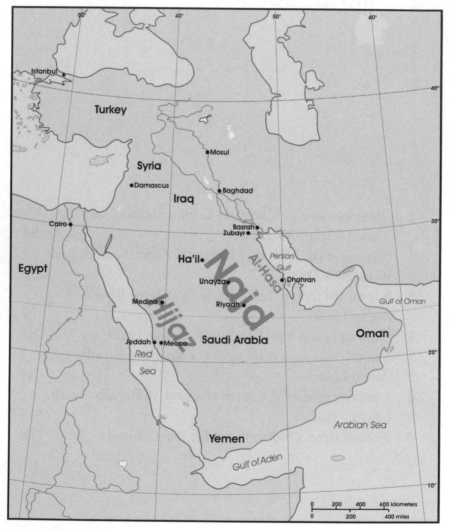

Map of Saudi Arabia

Foreword

In October 1939 after Joseph Stalin had signed his infamous pact with Adolf Hitler, Winston Churchill famously described Russia as 'a riddle, wrapped in a mystery, inside an enigma'. Today Churchill's richly pungent phrase instantly invokes the Kingdom of Saudi Arabia. Since the collapse of the Soviet Union in 1991, it can hardly be doubted that the world's largest oil producer is also one of the world's most enigmatically powerful states, a land of contradictory polarities where the pre-modern codes of desert and oasis – puritanical, patriarchal, frugal, and austere – coexist and frequently clash with lavish displays of wealth and such emblems of modernity as air-conditioned shopping malls, designer boutiques, and four-lane highways flashing with super-charged vehicles driven exclusively by males. Saudi Arabia has the rare distinction of being the only country in the world where women are forbidden to drive by law. As David Commins shows in this admirably lucid, balanced yet scholarly account of Islam in the kingdom, the consequences of this law, which is rooted in tribal prejudice rather than Islamic teachings, are fraught with contradictions: for example, a woman who employs a chauffeur, or travels in a taxi, must find herself in close physical proximity with a male who is not a *mahram* (relative forbidden in marriage), in direct violation of the *sharia* rules that are supposed to govern male–female interactions.

The faith tradition that holds the Saudi system together – and sometimes threatens to tear it apart – is Wahhabi Islam, the iconoclastic creed of the eighteenth-century Islamic reformer Muhammad ibn Abd al-Wahhab (1703–92), whose pact with the Al Saud family, revived after two abortive attempts in the nine-teenth century, led to the creation of the modern Kingdom of Saudi Arabia in 1926. Though easily dismissed as a retrograde obstacle to progress, the Wahhabi discourse is not so much 'an unchangeable essence but rather a tradition in motion, subject to interpretation and reinterpretation' in accordance with circumstances.[1]

As David Commins explains, the mission to wipe out idolatry, fundamental to Ibn Abd al-Wahhab's teaching, 'required continuous expansion under the banner of jihad'. Saudi Wahhabi ambitions were global. Their military offensives were not mere raids in the tradition of the tribal warfare that was endemic in the uplands of Najd, the Saudi homeland. They were 'an instrument for reviving Islam. Beyond Najd, neighboring lands such as Hijaz, Syria, Iraq, and Oman were legitimate objects of warfare and plunder because their inhabitants were idolaters, not Muslims.'

The practice of pronouncing *takfir* (excommunication) on Muslims who did not share Wahhabi tenets was the rationale for the regime of conquest and plunder commanded by the warrior king, Abdulaziz ibn Saud, from 1906 until the mid 1930s. An important casualty, in addition to many thousands of victims, was the religious and cultural diversity that characterized the Arabian Peninsula prior to the Saudi conquests. One example is the southwestern province of Asir, a mountainous region bordering on Yemen, where local customs were obliterated in the cause of counter-idolatry. Asiri men had been known as the 'flower men' from the flowers they wore in their hair (an indication perhaps of their status as cultivators rather than nomads). Even their turbans were adorned with flowers, grasses and stones. Asiri women were clothed in spectacular explosions of color, their headdresses glittering with coins and jewelry. Following the region's annexation in the 1930s the Wahhabi clerics forced young males to remove their 'un-Islamic' locks and headgear as well as the traditional daggers that symbolized their masculinity. The women were obliged to adopt the *niqab* (full facial veil) in place of the traditional headscarf. Typically, the Yemeni and Asiri tribesmen who eventually drifted to cities in search of work could only find low-paid jobs as cooks, gardeners, or drivers; and after guest workers arrived from South Asia and the Philippines, even these menial positions were hard to come by. It is no accident that 12 of the 19 hijackers who attacked the World Trade Center in New York and the Pentagon near Washington on 11 September 2001 came from this region, with its long history of resentment and neglect.[2]

The conquest of the Hijaz – the Islamic holy land, containing the cities of Mecca and Medina – though brutal, brought the Al Saud respectability as guardian of the holy places and overseer of the *hajj* or annual pilgrimage which Muslims are required to perform at least once in their lives. Before the discovery of oil made Saudi Arabia one of the world's richest countries, the hajj was the principal source of revenue. In today's more sophisticated world, it is real estate values, as much as pilgrim revenues, that make the guardianship of Mecca an asset for the Saudi rulers. A vast and garish complex with hotels and shopping malls, topped by a giant clock tower modeled on London's Big Ben, and five times its size, now dominates the skyline surrounding the Grand Mosque, which has been enlarged to accommodate up to two million worshipers. New developments adjacent to the Haram area will feature two 50-story hotel towers and seven 35-story apartment blocks. As Commins relates, the redevelopment by the Bin Laden construction group included the demolition of an eighteenth-century Ottoman fort, drawing protests from the Turkish press and government. Far from discouraging such architectural vandalism, the Wahhabi discourse may have facilitated it by relentlessly attacking religious practices that have grown up over centuries on the ground that they are 'innovations' of the original practices enjoined by Muhammad, and therefore idolatrous.

Paradoxically, the Prophet himself is not immune from the corrosive effects of Wahhabi iconoclasm: after the conquest of Hijaz the new Saudi rulers demolished shrines at his birthplace and the house of his first wife Khadija, as well as the tombs of his Companions at Medina, on the grounds that the veneration of the Prophet (as distinct from the worship of God) was a form of idolatry. Celebrating the Prophet's Birthday – a festival widely honored in other parts of the Muslim world – was suppressed or actively discouraged, so much so that the name 'Muhammad' is now used disparagingly, as a catch-all nickname for despised expatriates who make up a quarter of the kingdom's working population.[3]

Commins shows how up till now the Al Saud family has managed to ride the tiger of Wahhabism by a shrewd combination of appeasement, repression, and co-optation. The policy of appeasement is manifested in the 5,000-strong religious police force known as the *mutawaeen*, controlled by the Commission for the Promotion of Virtue and Prevention of Vice, who patrol cities in four-by-four vehicles enforcing prayer times, sexual segregation, female dress codes and the prohibition of non-Wahhabi religious worship. Co-optation and repression are made easier by the absence of an overarching institution, comparable to the papacy, that 'speaks for Islam'. The formidable Sheikh Abdulaziz ibn Baz, who died in 1999, possessed a quasi-papal authority, despite inviting international ridicule for his pre-Copernican insistence that the sun revolves around the earth. But his *fatwa* (legal ruling) allowing the stationing of infidel US troops in Saudi Arabia to protect the country, following the 1990 invasion of Kuwait by the Iraqi dictator Saddam Husain, proved much more controversial, provoking widespread resistance and demands for reforms. These included a strong Islamic army inspired by the call of *jihad*, an increase in social spending, and the right of preachers to raise political questions in their sermons in addition to morals and rituals.[4]

The Sahwa ('awakening') movement embracing political-cum-religious opposition to the Saudi regime's pro-Western policies had been strongly influenced by the Islamist ideology of the Muslim Brotherhood. The Brotherhood's leading intellectuals (including Muhammad Qutb, brother of Sayyid Qutb, who was executed by the Egyptian Nasser regime in 1966) had been given refuge in Saudi universities during the 1970s, when King Faisal led the conservative opposition to Arab nationalism. While there were significant differences between the ritualistic and literalist approach of the Wahhabi scholars and the Brotherhood's political radicalism, there was enough common ground to make this collaboration highly dangerous to the Saudi rulers and their Western protectors. The Wahhabi habit of pronouncing takfir on other Muslims, suppressed by the Saudi regime in pursuit of Islamic unity, meshed neatly with Sayyid Qutb's use of the term *jahiliyya* (the era of barbarism and ignorance prior to Islam) to describe the Muslim world's incumbent regimes, whether liberal or socialist in orientation.

The Saudi regime was able to contain the Sahwa challenge with a classic combination of divide and rule. Its leading dissident preachers were imprisoned. A loyalist faction reaffirmed the Wahhabi imperative of purifying the creed, leaving the task of governance to the princes. In effect they endorsed the power of the state by reaffirming the de facto separation between religion and politics that had prevailed in the past, when the *ulama* (religious scholars) had restricted their concerns to areas of morality, ritual, and belief. Saudi support for the Egyptian Salafist al-Nour party in the 2012 parliamentary elections at the expense of the Muslim Brotherhood seemed to confirm this trend. When in July 2013 the

Egyptian military responded to popular demonstrations by arresting the Muslim Brotherhood's Muhammad Morsi – the only president of Egypt ever to have been elected by a relatively honest ballot – and by clamping down on the Brotherhood, killing hundreds of its supporters, many observers saw the hand of Saudi *realpolitik* at work.

The most radical manifestations of the Sahwa spirit emerged in the 1990s, when Saudi and other *mujahedin* (holy warriors) who had expelled the Soviets from Afghanistan with funding and arms from Saudi Arabia and – covertly – from the CIA turned their sights on their homeland, and its principal foreign sponsor. The atrocity of 9/11 that killed almost 3,000 Americans was the logical outcome of an Islamist ideology that challenged the Saudi regime, using its own takfiri ideology, by attacking its principal ally, America. As Commins explains, Osama bin Laden, the Saudi dissident who funded al-Qaeda and oversaw the attacks on New York and Washington from his lair in Afghanistan, had been influenced by the Muslim Brotherhood during his youth in Jeddah. The jihadist movement he headed found a ready cause after the American-led invasion of Iraq in 2003. Its prospects in Saudi Arabia, however, were blunted by the loyalist counter-movement and the closing of ranks between Wahhabi clerics, Sahwa sheikhs, and the government. In 2003 the al-Qaeda franchise in Saudi Arabia, al-Qaeda in the Arabian Peninsula (QAP), executed a string of attacks in Riyadh and other places in which Americans and others were killed, but the movement was quickly contained. As Commins explains, 'a fundamental problem for QAP was its failure to attract new recruits to replace the men lost to gun battles and arrests.'

It is far from clear, however, if Saudi tiger-riding will prove sufficiently skilful to preserve the regime indefinitely. To the contradictions between Wahhabi fundamentalism and the regime's *raison d'état* – namely, the preservation of family power – must be added the tensions in the system of heredity whereby the throne passes down the line of brothers, rather than directly from father to son. With the death of King Abdullah in January 2015 the problem of the succession may have been deferred, rather than solved. The new King Salman (b. 1935) will be succeeded by his younger brother Prince Muqrin (b. 1945), the youngest surviving son of the great Abdulaziz. In a move that shrewdly demonstrates the dynasty's collective will-to-power, King Salman appointed his nephew Prince Muhammad in Nayef as deputy crown prince, making him the first of Abdulaziz's grandsons in line for the throne. Through his father, the late Crown Prince Nayef, the US-educated Prince Muhammad belongs to the powerful Sudairi gruop, the seven sons and numerous grandsons of Hassa bint Ahmad al-Sudair (1900–69), the highly influential widow of King Abdulaziz and mother of the present King Salman. As a Sudairi prince, Muhammad belongs to a powerful group within the royal family. But as the father of two daughters and no sons, he may be spared any suspicion of from having dynastic ambitions of his own.

A darker cloud on the Saudi horizon remains the sectarian conflict arising from its rivalry with Shiite Iran and the civil wars in Syria and Iraq. Anti-Shiism is fundamental to the Wahhabi religious outlook. The change in Iraq from Sunni minority to Shiite majority rule occasioned by the US occupation has profoundly affected the sectarian balance of power in the Fertile Crescent, with the leaders of Sunni states, including King Abdullah of Jordan, fearing that it is now becoming a Shiite Crescent, extending from Iran by way of embattled Iraq and Syria to Lebanon, where the Shiite Hezbollah movement is the dominant political force.

Shiite solidarity has been demonstrated in Iran and Hezbollah's support for the embattled Asad regime in Syria: the Asad regime is dominated by the Shiite Alawi sect who are generally regarded as heretics by the Saudis and their allies. Although some of the restrictions on the Saudi Shiites who reside in the oil-bearing Eastern Province were lifted after 9/11, when the government responded to the challenge posed by al-Qaeda by making small moves in the direction of pluralism, geopolitical logic suggests that advances towards toleration will be slow in coming.

In March 2011 the Saudi government sent 1,200 troops across the causeway into Bahrain to assist the Sunni minority, led by King Hamad bin Isa al-Khalifa, in repressing the movement of popular protest that erupted in the wake of the uprisings in Tunisia and Egypt. At this writing, the Saudi government claims, unconvincingly, to be 'unable' to prevent volunteers from joining the al-Qaeda affiliates in Syria and Iraq who are fighting what they see as a legitimate jihad against infidel Shiites backed by Iran. These young men, many of them from well-connected families, are motivated by the same ideology that brought the Al Saud to power in the 1920s: Muslims not subscribing to the Wahhabi version of Islam – even children – are infidels deserving of death.[5]

As Commins puts it, 'Royal support for moderation through national dialogue and revising school textbooks may not be enough to uproot the spirit of intolerance firmly entrenched with much of the population.' As in early modern Europe, that spirit of intolerance is exacerbated by the sectarian conflict being promoted, deliberately or otherwise, in neighboring states. In their hostility to Shiite Iran the Saudis have even formed a de facto accommodation with the traditional enemy, Israel. There is a perverse religious logic here: Jews, though regarded as being in error for having 'corrupted the scriptures', are nevertheless 'peoples of the Book' entitled to recognition and protection as a religious community. In the original Wahhabi canon, Shiites have no such rights. Like the Trotskyites anathematized by Stalin prior to his pact with Hitler, they are infidels pure and simple.

Saudis, along with others who share their mindset, have yet to learn the painful lessons of the religious wars in Europe: toleration of religious pluralism is the prerequisite, the *sine que non*, for peace.

Malise Ruthven

Acknowledgments

When I first exchanged ideas with the publisher about writing a survey of Islam in Saudi Arabia, the topic struck me as boundless and I felt that it would require so much pruning that the result would truncate whatever facets I included while omitting much else that is worth mention. I also thought it presumptuous for an American scholar to undertake the task of describing Saudis' daily habits and customs. Four years on, I have the same misgivings but, with the benefit of a lot of help from others, I think I have drawn a portrait that does justice to two essential truths. One is that Saudi society, and hence the role of religion in the kingdom, is far more complex than is often realized in the West. A second is that the ways Saudis understand religion and what it obliges or forbids are not immune to change.

At I.B. Tauris, I thank Minna Cowper-Coles for getting me started on the project and Maria Marsh and Alex Wright for seeing it through. I am grateful as well to series editor Malise Ruthven for suggesting that I take this on. His writings about Islam are a model of how to explore the complexities of Muslim societies without sacrificing engaging style. Regarding the topic at hand, what merit this book may have owes much to hospitality I have found in Saudi Arabia. For sponsoring and giving me a Riyadh research base, I am grateful to Dr. Yahya al-Junaid and Dr. Awadh al-Badi and the King Faisal Foundation for Research and Islamic Studies. There I had the good fortune to share an office with Mark Thompson and to gain from him a more nuanced understanding of the King Abdulaziz Center for National Dialogue. Friends and colleagues in Saudi Arabia enriched my experiences there and generously shared their insights. Of them, I wish to mention Abdulrahman al-Shuqir, Abdullah al-Muneef, Sohail Sapan, Saud al-Sarhan, and Rakan Alsheikh. I am particularly indebted to Abdullah al-Askar, Khalid al-Dakhil, Abdulaziz al-Fahad, and Abdulrahman al-Shemlan for reading parts of the manuscript to clarify some points and to correct me on more occasions than I wish to remember. Where there remain shortcomings by way of emphasis, omission, and error, the fault is mine.

I am grateful to Michele Hassinger for composing the map of Saudi Arabia and the Middle East. Saudi Aramco World granted permission to use photographs from the very rich collection gathered on its Public Affairs Digital Archive.

I can always rely on my family for support, and for keeping it real when I get a little too immersed in distant times and places – thanks to my daughter Marcia Zakeeya Commins, mother Marcia Faye Commins, Aunt Rosemarie Goodbody, and brothers Steve, Gary, and Neil Commins. Much of the material in this book is gleaned from visits to Saudi Arabia with my wife Susan Lindt. Possessing the curiosity of a reporter and the intrepid soul of an explorer, she is an essential partner in my search for ways to make sense of the unfamiliar.

1 Introduction

In the early years of American oil exploration in Saudi Arabia, word reached King Abdulaziz that a preacher in one of the southern oases was denouncing him for 'selling the land, and his people, into bondage of unbelievers'. The king summoned the sheikh to his court, where the preacher boldly argued with the ruler and senior religious scholars, insisting that Islam forbids reliance on unbelievers, in this instance, American engineers drilling for water and digging irrigation canals to raise agricultural production. The defiant preacher backed down only when the king gave up on persuasion and threatened to punish him.[1]

Royal power, oil, and puritanical Islam are primary elements in Saudi Arabia's rise to global influence. The Saudi dynasty has supported the religious establishment for 200 years. The accession to the throne of Salman ibn Abdulaziz upon the death of King Abdullah in January 2015 is sure to continue that tradition. Oil is the reason for Western interest in the kingdom and the foundation for commercial, diplomatic, and strategic relations. Were it not for oil, the government of Saudi Arabia would lack the resources to construct a modern economy and infrastructure, and to thrust the kingdom into regional prominence. Were it not for oil, Saudi Arabia would not be able to fund institutions that spread its religious doctrine to Muslim and non-Muslim countries. That doctrine, commonly known as Wahhabism, is a puritanical form of Islam that is distinctive in a number of ways, most visibly for how it makes public observance of religious norms a matter of government enforcement rather than individual disposition and social conformity, as it is in other Muslim countries.

To understand the roles that religion plays in Saudi Arabia, it is essential to have in mind five elements: Wahhabi doctrine, the Saudi dynasty, government institutions, the diversity of society, and relations with the Muslim world. Since the formation of the alliance between the founder of Wahhabi doctrine and Al Saud (the House of Saud) in the 1740s, the first two elements have remained fairly constant while the last three have undergone profound change.

Wahhabi doctrine is rooted in a theological position upheld by its namesake Muhammad ibn Abd al-Wahhab in his preaching and writings from around 1740 until his death in 1792. One thousand years after the rise of Islam, 500 miles west of his native region of Najd, Muslim religious practice had evolved a variety of forms, some of which involved venerating holy men believed to possess spiritual powers. Sheikh Muhammad considered such practices to signal a lapse to idolatry and viewed his mission as nothing less than the revival of Islam. Other Muslims naturally found his view of their practices as idolatry objectionable and utterly unwarranted, giving rise to a theological controversy that persists to the present.

The controversy moved from sermons and writings to the political realm when Sheikh Muhammad found a patron in Muhammad ibn Saud, chief of a minor oasis town. Their pact committed them to support each other so that Al Saud's political and military endeavors acquired religious legitimacy as *jihad* against infidels, which is how Wahhabi doctrine branded Muslims who did not conform to its outlook, and at the same time Sheikh Muhammad's mission gained the backing of an ambitious ruler. In the course of Saudi expansion through conquest, Sheikh Muhammad's doctrine was established and his theological opponents were either silenced or chased out of Najd. By 1800, when the first Saudi emirate reached its peak, Wahhabi doctrine was dominant in most of Arabia, enforced by religious judges and propagated by preachers appointed by Wahhabi clerics in the capital. With every conquest, they were closer to realizing their vision of purging idolatry from the world, a program that put them at odds with Muslims outside the Saudi domain.

Indeed, hostility and tension were the hallmark of Saudi and Wahhabi relations with the rest of the Muslim world, as illustrated by two events in the early 1800s. In the first, a Saudi raid on the Shiite shrine city of Karbala in southern Iraq, Wahhabi warriors massacred several thousand men, women, and children, and plundered the shrine. Today's propaganda war between Saudi Arabia and Iran's Islamic Republic – an officially Shiite government and a champion of Shiite interests – has deep roots. The second event that made the Wahhabis notorious among Muslims was the Saudi conquest of Islam's holy cities, Mecca and Medina. In the millennium since Islam's founding, these places had, in a sense, belonged to all Muslims, regardless of theological and sectarian difference. Under Saudi-Wahhabi rule in the early 1800s, zealous puritans razed domes erected over tombs, prohibited vices such as tobacco, and barred pilgrim caravans unless they agreed to perform pilgrimage rites in accordance with Wahhabi doctrine.

The Saudi reign in the holy cities lasted but a decade before the Ottoman Empire expelled the invaders in order to regain the luster of its role as guardian of Islam's foremost shrines. A few years later, the first Saudi emirate lay in ruins, crushed by Ottoman–Egyptian forces. But enough members of the dynasty and Wahhabi religious personalities survived to recoup power when the invading army withdrew a few years later. The second Saudi emirate did not quite replicate the conquests of the first, but for roughly half a century it dominated Central Arabia and provided shelter for the consolidation of Wahhabi doctrine as the sole expression of religion in that region. Sheikh Muhammad's descendants and fellow Wahhabi clerics handed down his teachings, planting them deep in the soil of Najd, becoming so firmly associated with the region's towns and oases that by 1900, they commonly referred to their revivalist movement as the 'Najdi mission'. As for the rulers of the second emirate, they were chastened by demonstrations of superior military power; consequently they refrained from expansionist war. That did not mean that Wahhabi hostility toward other Muslims abated; it merely took a new form – an attempt to minimize contact in the name of prohibiting travel to infidel lands, by which Wahhabi *ulama* (religious scholars) meant Iraq, Syria, and Egypt, not Europe or the United States. The second Saudi emirate disintegrated in princely power struggles in the late nineteenth century and the ruling family was ousted from Riyadh in 1891.

The contemporary Kingdom of Saudi Arabia is the third incarnation of Al Saud–Wahhabi power, achieving unification of its territories through conquest between 1902 and 1932. While the kingdom's historical roots were essential foundations of political power and religious authority, the contemporary face of Saudi Arabia – social life, government institutions, economy, and relations with the outside world – took shape during the reign of its founder, Abdulaziz ibn Saud. In three decades of political expansion, he blended deft diplomacy toward foreign empires (Ottoman and British) and warfare against rival Arabian principalities while harnessing the energies of nomadic tribes and Wahhabi warriors. Toward the end of his conquering days, Ibn Saud was forced to choose between dynastic consolidation and perpetual religious warfare, which was threatening to put him on a collision course with Great Britain, the guardian of his neighbors in Transjordan and Iraq. His decision to pursue normal relations with London spurred a rebellion in the name of religious purity, which he put down. That was just the first step in putting relations with the outside world, Muslim and non-Muslim, on a new footing. At the same time, Ibn Saud did not dilute the Wahhabi monopoly in defining correct religious practice, enforcing prayer attendance and public morality, teaching at mosques, and issuing legal rulings based on Islamic law.

At the time of Ibn Saud's proclamation as the King of Saudi Arabia, he ruled a poor, thinly populated realm. The Great Depression diminished his treasury's main source of revenue, the annual pilgrimage. In a bid to develop a new stream of funds, in 1933 he signed an oil concession with American oilmen. It was the genesis of Saudi Arabia's emergence as a petroleum producer and of its close relationship with the United States. There is little record of Wahhabi opposition to the new stage in relations with the outside world, perhaps because Western oilmen were confined to isolated residential compounds, an arrangement that achieved two purposes. First, it spared them the need to be mindful of local sensibilities. Second, it made the infidel presence less visible to the faithful. The export of oil, starting in 1946, gave Ibn Saud abundant revenue to co-opt tribal leaders and ensure the loyalty of their fellow tribesmen. By the early 1950s, oil income afforded Al Saud a measure of affluence in its palaces, but, except for the oil-producing Eastern Province, barely affected the rest of the kingdom.

The transformation of Saudi Arabia's economy and political institutions took place during the 1960s, a period of intense regional rivalry pitting conservative kingdoms against revolutionary republics led by Egypt's Gamal Abdul Nasser, whose anti-Western rhetoric resonated with young Arabs, from Morocco to Arabia. The challenge to Saudi stability was amplified by an 11-year succession struggle that followed the death of King Abdulaziz in 1953. His sons, King Saud and Crown Prince Faisal, headed rival princely factions wrangling over precedence and policy. Faisal proved more adept at political maneuvering and took on the role of *de facto* ruler even before Wahhabi ulama endorsed the decision of senior royals to depose Saud. As king, Faisal then took decisive steps to shore up the kingdom against Nasser's meddling by laying down the framework of a modern state.

In the 1960s, Saudi Arabia formed ministries for defense, foreign affairs, commerce, petroleum, and so forth. The project of creating bureaucratic administration extended to the religious realm. Consequently, the sphere of clerical authority was given formal definition. The Ministry of Justice became the center for appointing judges to religious law courts and devising regular procedures for the courts. Staff at the Ministry of Education designed a uniform curriculum and wrote textbooks that turned Wahhabi doctrine into a national catechism. Other government bodies organized and defined the scope of clerical authority. The upshot for Wahhabi clerics was their incorporation into government-funded institutions that allowed them to maintain theological dominance through mosques, schools, and law courts – all of which had been under their control since the first Saudi emirate – and to censor media and enforce their conceptions of rectitude in public behavior. The most obvious signs of the latter include limits on the mixing of men and women, compulsory veiling, the prohibition against women driving motor vehicles, and the closure of shops, businesses, and offices during prayer times, all enforced by a government body, the Commission for the Promotion of Virtue and Prevention of Vice.[2]

Were the perpetuation of Wahhabi authority in Saudi Arabia's religious and social life a purely domestic affair, it would matter little to outsiders. But since the 1960s the kingdom's rulers have used Wahhabism as an instrument of foreign policy, working through transnational Islamic institutions, private charities, and Saudi embassies to proselytize. Such missionary work is a natural extension of Wahhabism's foundational impulse to erase idolatry. Backed by formidable resources of oil wealth, the modern Wahhabi mission's network of mosques, libraries, and schools has made inroads throughout the Muslim world; at the same time it has perpetuated theological controversies with other Muslims who are convinced they do not need 'rescuing' from idolatry. In addition to outward proselytizing, the kingdom's Islamic University in Medina draws thousands of Muslims from abroad, many of whom return home imbued with Wahhabi doctrine. Finally, the annual pilgrimage brings millions of Muslims to Mecca and Medina. The Saudi government created a special ministry to organize the logistics of the sudden massive influx of visitors as well as to oversee proper performance of the pilgrimage rites. Much as Muslim rulers in previous centuries garnered prestige from assuming the role of guardian of the holy cities, Saudi Arabia holds a special place in the Muslim world, amplified by modern communications, with broadcasts of pilgrims at the Haram – the Grand Mosque – in Mecca on television and the internet, fostering the identification of Islam's cradle and symbolic spiritual center with the solicitude of Al Saud and the rectitude of Wahhabi clerics.

In contemporary Saudi Arabia, public conformity with Wahhabi doctrine gives the impression of uniform belief and practice. In fact, beneath the surface, Saudi society exhibits more diversity than meets the eye. There are three basic reasons for this. First, beyond Najd, the regions conquered by Al Saud had different religious traditions. Second, the kingdom's integration with the global economy affords exposure to outside influences. Third, oil wealth altered the basic conditions of daily life as scarcity gave way to affluence, turning many Saudis into avid consumers.

In the early Islamic centuries, different parts of Arabia developed distinctive patterns of religious loyalty. Oman, for example, became the scene for a series of dynasties rooted in the Ibadi tradition that is distinct from both Sunni and Shiite traditions. The Arabian shore of the Gulf has always had a diverse population, not only in terms of mixing Sunni and Shiite

Muslims, but also in ethnic terms: Arabs, Persians, Baluchis, South Asians, and Africans rubbed shoulders in busy port towns, a sign that the Gulf was as much part of the Indian Ocean world as the Arabian world. In medieval times, the people of the eastern coastal region known as al-Hasa and the islands of Bahrain across a small bay became primarily Shiite, adhering to the same branch of Islam's second sect as Shiites in Iraq and Iran, and therefore forming part of a broader zone of Twelver Shiism. The first and second Saudi emirates ruled al-Hasa intermittently between 1790 and 1870 but were unable to convert its folk to Wahhabi doctrine. Abdulaziz ibn Saud wrested the region from Ottoman rule in 1913, and in doing so not only incorporated a large Shiite population but also annexed the richest oil reserves in the world, although at the time that was not known. Initially, the acquisition of al-Hasa caused tension between Ibn Saud's wish for the smooth integration of the area's inhabitants and Wahhabi desires to convert the Shiites, or at least suppress public celebration of their ceremonies and close their teaching circles. Since their absorption into the Saudi realm, they have endured neglect, even though their home region sits on top of the oil, and their religion has been consistently defamed by Wahhabi clerics. Frustration with inferior living conditions boiled over when demonstrations broke out in late 1979, spurred in part by the example of the Iranian Revolution across the Gulf. The government responded with pledges to improve public services such as sanitation and water, but the stream of anti-Shiite sermons in Wahhabi mosques and media remained relentless.

Much of Arabia's western coast forms the region known as Hijaz, where the holy cities are located. By the eighteenth century, the bulk of the population was Sunni, with a sprinkling of Shiites around Medina. The Sunnis of Mecca and Medina followed all four of the historical law schools that determined the bounds of orthodox belief and practice. Various Sufi brotherhoods had branches in the holy cities, and popular saint cults coexisted with clerics who regarded such practices as illegitimate innovations. When Ibn Saud conquered Hijaz in the 1920s, he was careful to avoid actions that would cast his rule in an unfavorable light before the broader Muslim world. He was eager to acquire recognition as the legitimate guardian of the holy cities so he followed a lenient policy that tolerated practices that were at odds with Wahhabi doctrine as long as they were kept quiet. Beyond the pan-Islamic dimension of the shrines, Hijaz was Ibn Saud's window on the Middle East and Europe, as Jeddah became the headquarters for diplomatic representatives. Moreover, the merchants of Hijaz, in particular in Jeddah, were essential for the nascent kingdom's long-term commercial prosperity. Considerations of economic interest, diplomacy, and religious legitimacy outside Arabia therefore governed the king's light touch in Hijaz, which was not incorporated into a national system of government until the early 1960s.

The religious traditions of al-Hasa and Hijaz resisted Wahhabi pressures to conform to the puritanical doctrine, but they could not challenge the domination of the kingdom's official religious establishment. Starting in the 1950s, however, a new strain of Muslim thought entered Saudi Arabia, carried by religious activists seeking refuge from persecution by Arab nationalist governments in Egypt and Syria. The activists belonged to the Society of Muslim Brothers, an organization founded in Egypt in the late 1920s for the purpose of rejuvenating Muslim societies through religious revival. The Muslim Brothers held that Egypt and other Muslim countries had come under European domination because believers failed to fuse personal piety with social and political engagement. Consequently, Europeans were able to attain political, economic, and cultural supremacy. For Muslims to reclaim their independence, they had to cultivate the inner strength of each individual believer through daily practice and they had to overcome divisions in order to unify their ranks to confront European power.

In the early 1950s, the Muslim Brothers collided with Arab nationalist rulers in Egypt and Syria over the latter's secular leanings and endured fierce persecution. Saudi Arabia became the refuge for many Muslim Brothers, in spite of differences on points of doctrine that were set aside for the sake of political considerations. On the matter of defining one's standing as a believer, Muslim Brothers took a broad view because of their emphasis on unity, as opposed to the Wahhabi propensity to label non-conformity as idolatry. On the other hand, the two tendencies shared alarm at the popularity of secular and leftist ideas in the Muslim world. The Wahhabis viewed the Muslim Brothers as allies in combating those influences. For the Saudi rulers, the Muslim Brothers offered an additional advantage. As oil revenues rose, the government took steps toward modern national development with a program that included education and health, but very few Saudi nationals had the professional training to staff schools, universities, and hospitals. Because the Muslim Brothers had attracted a large following in the ranks of modern professions, quite a few refugees were able to supply their hosts with much-needed expertise. Hence, they struck deep roots in the kingdom and over the next few decades quietly spread their views about the need to fuse religion and politics to the younger Saudi generation. The partnership between Muslim Brothers, Wahhabis, and Saudi government proved fruitful for all three until 1990, when Riyadh invited the United States and other Western powers to station military forces to defend the kingdom against the threat of Iraqi invasion. By then, the Muslim Brother outlook was too firmly established among Saudi nationals to uproot; one might even say it had become naturalized to the point that it became the main challenge to the Wahhabi tradition in the twenty-first century.

Another facet of the kingdom's modernization is the alteration in basic living conditions. In the early 1950s, the population was small, under five million, and dispersed in towns, oases, and the desert. By 2000, the country's population was over twenty million and increasingly concentrated in three large metropolitan areas: Jeddah, Riyadh, and the Dhahran–Dammam–Khobar region. The oil boom of the 1970s was the pivotal period when urban expansion took off, affluence came within reach of Saudis outside royal circles, and the expatriate population rapidly increased, to supply technical expertise and abundant cheap labor for construction projects. Forty years later, Saudi Arabia is very much a consumer society, in part because there is little to do for leisure apart from browsing global brand merchandise in malls and dining out since the religious establishment prohibits cinemas, theatre, and other public entertainment. The arrival of satellite television in the 1990s, then of the internet and cell phones in the 2000s boosted consumer culture. They also made it impossible for Wahhabi censors to control the flow of images and texts, with their implicit impact on values and ideas. The upshot is that there is a split between the appearance of conformity with official norms and evasion in private. That is not to suggest that Saudis are abandoning faith. Rather, it seems that, like Muslims elsewhere, they are adjusting their conception of religious rectitude to the habits and values of a society suffused with technical modernity and mass consumption. This does not mean shirking daily prayer or not fasting during Ramadan, but it does mean the spread of a skeptical if not contemptuous regard for Wahhabi officialdom bent on perpetuating a doctrine and mindset that are unconvincing to a sizable, if immeasurable, segment of society.

2 The Establishment of the Wahhabi Tradition

In the blazing summer heat of southern Iraq nearly three centuries ago, a wayfarer came across a bedraggled traveler on the verge of dehydration. The kind wayfarer strapped the exhausted man to his donkey and took him to the nearest town, where his charge regained strength for the journey to his home in Central Arabia. The incident, reported in an early Saudi chronicle, suggests the difficult circumstances surrounding the genesis of the Wahhabi tradition. The forlorn traveler was Sheikh Muhammad ibn Abd al-Wahhab. He had gone to Basra for religious studies but he fell foul of local opinion when he preached against the cult of holy men. His reward for chastizing popular practice was expulsion from town. It was the first of three such incidents indicating that fellow Muslims found his preaching offensive. That he persevered in the face of persecution is testimony to the strength of his conviction, a trait that has not diminished among his followers today.

Religious controversy has a long trail in Islamic history. Wahhabism is part of the boisterous debates over political, theological, and ritual issues that have engaged Muslims since the seventh century. Some of the most divisive questions took shape in the decades after the Prophet's death in 632. Two questions that preoccupied his followers were: who had the right to lead them? and did the leader possess religious as well as political authority? Hammering out a consensus proved impossible and Muslims became divided into three main camps that evolved into distinct sects – Sunni, Shiite, and Kharijite.

Given the imperative to justify worldly action in religious terms, the sects developed distinctive theological positions. One vexing question emerged in the wake of the assassination of the third rightly guided caliph Uthman (r. 644–56) in Medina, when some argued that because he committed major sins, he was an unbeliever, therefore his killing was justified. This position was adopted by the Kharijites, a group that rebelled against Muslim rulers they regarded as sinners. In the eight century, the caliphs of Damascus and Baghdad stamped out the Kharijites in the central lands of the Middle East, but they survived in outlying regions such as Oman and the northern Sahara. They also survived as straw men in theological debates as archetypes of extremism. When a group adopted a strict view on belief, its opponents would characterize it as Kharijite, which is how the Wahhabi mission's adversaries labeled it in the 1700s.

The Kharijite position on belief was not the only enduring religious consequence of early political conflict. One party of Muslims fervently supported the Prophet's cousin and son-in-law Ali in his bid for leadership. This faction evolved into the Shiite branch of Islam (from the term *shi`at Ali*, or the party of Ali). A central tenet in Shiism is that the Quran and the Prophet established the special standing of Ali and his descendants, creating a line of leaders, or imams, to lead Muslims through the ages. Because it was not always obvious which descendant of Ali in a given generation was the imam, Shiites divided into rival factions that nevertheless concurred on the privileged position of Ali's line, seen as possessing unique esoteric knowledge of the secret meaning of God's revelation in the Quran. Veneration for the imams was a religious duty that signified a believer's gratitude to God for providing them as guides and exemplars. In the Sunni view, and in Wahhabi doctrine, such veneration not only had no basis in revelation, but was tantamount to idolatry.

In the early Islamic centuries, Shiite imams failed to gain power. Ali's bid for leadership was thwarted by his chief rival and he was murdered by a Kharijite. His son Husain was killed by enemy Muslim forces. The Shiite record of failed revolts and assassinations nurtured a feeling of persecution by wicked Sunni rulers and their misguided backers. In the Shiite view of early Muslim history, the first three caliphs of Medina were usurpers who plotted to deny Ali his rightful position as leader, from the moment of the Prophet's death. Eventually, Shiites gave ritual expression to that view by cursing the first three caliphs, a ritual that infuriates Sunnis. Shiites also looked to the graves of their imams as holy sites where believers could obtain blessings. Hence, Ali's shrine in Najaf and Husain's shrine in Karbala, both located in southern Iraq, are sacred pilgrimage destinations.

Political feuds were not the only source of religious controversy among early Muslims. Muslims enjoyed remarkable military success that spread Islam from Spain to India and brought them into contact with other religions and philosophies as colonies of Muslim settlers rubbed shoulders with Christians, Jews, and Zoroastrians. In the course of time, non-Muslim subjects of the caliphate converted to Islam, contributing to the formation of a new civilization that blended Arabian, Hellenistic, Persian, and Indian legacies. Encounters with multiple intellectual and religious currents generated debates over the nature of God and his revelation, which in turn spurred questions about free will and predestination. Several schools of thought emerged in the eighth and ninth centuries. Some borrowed methods of reasoning and logic from Hellenistic philosophy and Christian theology to develop and defend theological positions regarding God's attributes described in the Quran, such as his knowledge, speech, and power.

The incorporation of rational methods spurred a response from men who insisted that only a literal reading of the Quran and the Prophetic Tradition was allowable. The literalist position became identified with a ninth-century Baghdad scholar named Ahmad ibn Hanbal, an assiduous student of the Prophetic Tradition. With regard to theology, Ibn Hanbal and his followers claimed that their method of understanding the Quran and their conception of God preserved the way of the earliest Muslims, dubbed the Pious Ancestors, in Arabic, *al-salaf al-salih*, the term from which derives 'Salafi' – one who follows the Pious Ancestors in belief and practice. In the Hanbali view, any concept or practice that cannot be traced to the Pious Ancestors is an illegitimate innovation, citing a Prophetic Tradition that says, 'The worst of all things are novelties (*muhdathat*); every novelty is innovation (*bid'a*); every innovation is error (*dalala*) and every error leads to hell.'[1]

Establishing the category of illegitimate innovations might seem a straightforward matter of referring to the Prophetic Tradition, but applying it to a multitude of beliefs and actions was very complicated. For instance, early Sunni Muslim scholars concurred that the second caliph Umar had introduced a minor change to evening prayers during Ramadan. Apparently, not every innovation is error (and Shiites considered Umar's innovation illegitimate, perhaps because they viewed Umar as one of the men who usurped Ali's right to leadership). The great ninth-century jurist al-Shafii drew a distinction between something new that contradicts the Quran and the Prophetic Tradition on one hand, and something new that does not, which is harmless. Judging what is and is not consistent with authoritative sources turned out to depend on who did the judging: innovation is in the eye of the beholder. Charges of innovation became a polemical weapon wielded in debates between Sunnis and Shiites, theological rationalists and literalists.

Enumerating deplorable innovations became a preoccupation for generations of scholars across the spectrum of Sunni learned opinion. Catalogues of innovations in specialized works established categories of innovation. One covered new ways of reciting the Quran. For instance, some Muslims performed musical recitations that innovation-fighters rejected not only because they were new but also because the melody could distract the listener from grasping the meaning of the words and because it resembled the custom of non-Muslims. Another category dealt with innovations in mosques: setting up a box to collect alms, fanning oneself, speaking in a foreign language, cutting nails or hair, sitting on cushions (but mats and carpets were allowed), killing fleas, and spitting. Forms of worship and the wording of prayers also came under the scrutiny of innovation-fighters. They listed raising one's hands and speaking in a loud voice as blameworthy innovations because they resembled Jewish custom. Using a rosary was condemned but gained such widespread acceptance that some scholars decided it was permissible (Wahhabis view it as a blameworthy innovation). In general, it seems that scholars who admitted that not all innovations were bad kept a sharp eye out for anything that looked like imitation of Jews and Christians, keeping in mind the Prophetic Tradition that says, 'Do not imitate the unbelievers.' Given the emphasis in Wahhabi doctrine on condemning veneration of holy men at their tombs, it is striking that older treatises on innovation seldom mention it. Even more striking is that the earliest works do not justify attacks on innovation by citing the imperative to follow the Pious Ancestors.[2]

Ahmad ibn Hanbal's reputation in his time and later centuries owed much to his defiance of an inquisition instituted by the powerful Abbasid caliph of Baghdad. If only to avoid a whipping, most scholars went along with the caliph's demand that they embrace a controversial theological doctrine that the Quran is the created Word of God. Ibn Hanbal refused and paid a heavy price, enduring both lashings and prison. His compelling personality and firm convictions inspired loyalty in his disciples. In the generations after his death, they developed a distinctive approach to Islamic law that they attributed to him, so that one of the four historical Sunni law schools, in the sense of a tradition of interpretation, became known as the Hanbali School. Support from rulers led to the establishment of one law school or another as the major tradition in particular regions. For instance, the Maliki School became dominant in North Africa while the Hanafi School took root among Turkish rulers in Iran and Iraq. The Hanbali School remained confined to Baghdad, Damascus, and a few towns in Palestine. Exactly when it spread to Najd is not entirely clear, but Hanbali scholars were present by the mid 1400s.

Najd is the vast expanse of Central Arabia that stretches from the borders of Iraq and Jordan to Oman and Yemen, and from the fertile coastal region along the Persian Gulf to the mountainous district of Hijaz along the Red Sea. The region's arid climate shaped its economy, society, and politics. The population was divided between roving nomadic tribes grazing flocks of camels and sheep, and oasis dwellers tending date groves and gardens. Caravans traversing the desert occupied nomadic and settled folk. Nomads served as guides and provided camels to transport merchandise while oasis dwellers refreshed provisions at rest stops.

The Muslim dynasties that rose and fell in Egypt, Syria, Iraq, and Iran had no sway in Najd. From their vantage point, Central Arabia was too poor to be worth the trouble to conquer and hold. As a result, Najd was its own political zone where the balance of forces among nomads and settled folk was roughly equal. Each tribe and oasis was self-governing, making the political map a patchwork of extensive, thinly populated tribal domains in the desert with enclaves of autonomous oases under their own ruling clans. Smaller oases came under the power of nomadic tribes that compelled their inhabitants to pay a tax, essentially to buy protection from tribal raids. Politics consisted of incessant power struggles within oases among factions in ruling clans and Bedouin clashes for control over grazing grounds.

Long-distance trade networks were channels of outside cultural and religious influence. The primary zones of contact lay in Iraq, Syria, and Hijaz. Their urban centers – Baghdad, Damascus, Mecca, and Medina – provided models of Islamic culture, including traditions of religious scholarship. By the 1400s, the Hanbali tradition of Baghdad and Damascus had thrown out shoots to Najdi oases, where chieftains, traders, and cultivators supported a small number of scholars. At the dawn of the eighteenth century, religious learning in Najd had two characteristics related to the emergence of Wahhabism. One was the tendency for particular clans to become associated with religious learning. A second was the tendency for pupils to begin their studies with family members and then pursue advanced learning outside Najd in Hijaz, Syria, and Iraq. One of the most prominent clans known for scholars, religious judges, and teachers was Al Musharraf. The most renowned judge of the early 1700s, Sheikh Sulaiman ibn Ali, came from Al Musharraf. His son, Abd al-Wahhab, likewise became a judge and teacher in the oasis settlement of al-Uyaina, where his own son Muhammad, the founder of the Wahhabi mission, was born in 1702.

The son of Abd al-Wahhab followed the family tradition of religious study with focus on the Quran, Prophetic Tradition, Arabic grammar, and Islamic law. Then, as a young man, Muhammad ibn Abd al-Wahhab did what other ambitious Najdi pupils sometimes did – he went to Medina for specialized studies. According to some accounts, it was there that he came under the influence of a teacher immersed in the innovation-fighting tradition. His next destination was the eastern Arabian province of al-Hasa, home to a mixed population of Shiites and Sunnis. From there he went to Basra, where he became mired in controversy over the permissibility of popular rituals related to veneration of holy men and their tombs. His preaching sparked a strong backlash and he was chased out of town.

Upon his return to Najd, Sheikh Muhammad found his father had relocated to Huraimila to take up the post of judge. By this time Muhammad had formulated his theological views, but he did not declare them in public until after his father's death in 1740, perhaps because they were not in agreement. At that point, Muhammad issued his manifesto, *The Book of God's Unity*, which set forth his central concepts about correct belief and worship and the many forms of polytheism that, in his view, had corrupted Muslim life. Controversy quickly erupted as word spread of his preaching a revival of Islam in a land whose inhabitants, including its scholars, thought they were practicing Islam perfectly well. The first Saudi chronicler, writing about fifty years after these events, described the kinds of popular customs that Sheikh Muhammad found abhorrent. Tombs of the Prophet's Companions drew men and women seeking their intercession with God. Particular trees were believed to possess special powers. In one village, young women put their arms around the trunk of a palm tree to make a wish for a husband. In another village, people tied rags to a tree after the birth of a baby boy to ensure his health. The chronicler also mentioned sacrifices made before a blind sage.[3]

The call to wipe out idolatry gained a following in the cluster of small oasis settlements of Sheikh Muhammad's native region, Wadi Hanifa. His mission also triggered hostility and his foes were able to have him expelled from Huraimila. He then resettled in his hometown of al-Uyaina, whose emir backed Sheikh Muhammad's program for religious purification. On one occasion, the emir led townsmen to the nearby tomb of an early Muslim hero, Zaid ibn al-Khattab, and leveled it. On another, Sheikh Muhammad gathered his followers to chop down sacred trees. The most dramatic episode related in the Saudi chronicles about the mission's early years relates not to Sheikh Muhammad's campaign against polytheism but his firm resolve to implement Islamic law. One day a woman came to him to confess an act of adultery. Sheikh Muhammad seemed reluctant to impose the punishment of stoning her to death, but the woman repeated her confession and others attested to her sound mental state, so he ordered the grim sentence.[4]

His adversaries responded to his growing influence in two ways. They reached out to religious scholars in the holy cities, al-Hasa, and Iraq to lend their prestige to a campaign to discredit him by composing epistles attacking his views. Contrary to the common notion in Western scholarship that his doctrine was merely an expression of the Hanbali tradition, some of his harshest critics were Hanbali scholars. This included his own brother Sulaiman, also a religious scholar, who composed a detailed treatise to prove that Sheikh Muhammad was utterly misguided because he lacked the scholarly training to understand the texts that he believed justified his views. His foes also worked at undermining the al-Uyaina emir's support for him. Here they succeeded in persuading the emir's overlord in al-Hasa that Sheikh Muhammad was a dangerous troublemaker. The emir who had welcomed him yielded to pressure from his overlord and told Sheikh Muhammad he had to leave. It was 1744, the turning point in the history of his mission. His next refuge was the oasis ruled by Al Saud, the emirs of al-Diriyya.[5]

According to one of the early chronicles, it was the wife of Muhammad ibn Saud, Mudi bint Sultan Abu Wahtan, who paved the way for his meeting with Sheikh Muhammad. However the encounter was arranged (another account credits the sheikh's local disciples), it led to the alliance between the Wahhabi call for reviving Islam and Saudi political power that has endured to the present. Sheikh Muhammad told the emir that he would attain worldly dominion if he supported the call to worship God alone.[6] The compact elevated the emir's clashes with rivals from petty contests over the meager resources of Najdi oases to a universal religious cause. The Saudi-Wahhabi realm expanded very slowly at first, but in the course of 30 years its warriors conquered one oasis settlement after another, fueled by the certainty that they were true believers waging war against infidels.

Without question, the most controversial facet in Sheikh Muhammad's campaign to eradicate idolatrous customs was his position on belief. In letters and treatises, he repeatedly affirmed that failure to renounce such customs or to combat them made one an unbeliever, a *kafir*. The Arabic word for pronouncing somebody an unbeliever is *takfir*. The judgment of takfir approximates excommunication but has weighty political connotations because it means that the protection against attack afforded by affiliation with the community of Muslims falls away: in the language of Islamic law, one's life, honor, and property are open to attack in the just struggle (jihad) to spread Islam. According to Sheikh Muhammad's interpretation of Islam's authoritative religious texts, Muslims had lapsed into idolatry, as foretold by the Prophetic Tradition: 'Islam began as a stranger and will return as a stranger.' And, just as the Prophet Muhammad had resorted to warfare to defend and advance Islam in the seventh century, so would Sheikh Muhammad justify Saudi warfare against neighboring chieftains in the name of spreading God's word. In a sense, Sheikh Muhammad and his Saudi backers saw themselves as re-enacting the drama of the first community of believers a thousand years earlier.

Of course, other Muslims saw things differently. They noted that it was not enough for Sheikh Muhammad to agree with him that seeking a holy man's intercession was contrary to the imperative to direct all worship to God. He also insisted that you had to take his side in his fight for true belief, and that if you did not, then you were an infidel too. His adversaries composed treatise after treatise condemning him for departing from well-worn consensus, in essence, inventing a blameworthy innovation. One argument commonly directed again him, and therefore found in anti-Wahhabi writings to the present, held that the criterion for determining belief is reciting the testimony of belief, the *shahada*, professing one believes in no god but God and in Muhammad as his messenger. Some asserted that anyone who recites the shahada, performs the five daily prayers, and pays alms must be counted a believer. Even if such a person contaminates his belief with sacrifices and vows to holy men, living or dead, it is wrong to consider him an infidel.[7] Because of Sheikh Muhammad's broad grounds for takfir, his foes categorized him and his supporters as latter-day Kharijites, misguided fanatics who threatened to tear apart the fabric of Muslim society.

As the religious controversy raged, Saudi forces achieved a breakthrough in 1773, by subjugating the nearby oasis of Riyadh. Its proud Emir Diham ibn Dawwas had been a perennial thorn in al-Diriyya's side, repelling Saudi assaults and allying with powerful nomadic tribes to launch counterattacks. But while Riyadh stood its ground, the Saudi realm absorbed one oasis settlement after another. It became clear that the balance of power in Wadi Hanifa was tilting in Al Saud's favor. Rather than surrender, Emir Diham left with his family and allies, including Riyadh's chief religious scholar, who had written some of the first tracts against the Wahhabi call.[8]

When Sheikh Muhammad died in 1792, half a century after starting his mission, much of Arabia was under the control of his political allies. The logic of his campaign to purge all traces of idolatry required the silencing, expulsion, or elimination of opponents. Consolidating a domain of purified monotheism also required the training and appointment of cadres devoted to teaching and preaching. Whenever Saudi forces absorbed an oasis settlement, Sheikh Muhammad would install a teacher and judge there, either from among his pupils in al-Diriyya or from a local figure who embraced his doctrine. Clearing Najd of idolatry, then, meant implanting a network of proselytizers. It also meant suspicion toward the outside world, now viewed as an abode of unbelief. As a result, religious pupils no longer left Najd to study in Iraq, Syria, or Egypt. Instead, al-Diriyya became the focal point for religious studies to ensure doctrinal correctness. Over the course of the first Saudi state's 70-year existence, dozens of Wahhabi cadres were trained under Sheikh Muhammad's direction, ensuring the perpetuation of the mission.

The mission to wipe out idolatry required continual expansion under the banner of jihad. From the Wahhabi perspective, Saudi military offensives were not mere raids in the tradition of Najdi fighting but an instrument for reviving Islam. Beyond Najd, neighboring lands such as Hijaz, Syria, Iraq, and Oman were legitimate objects of warfare and plunder because their inhabitants were idolaters, not Muslims. Of course, Muslims targeted by Wahhabi proselytizing and Saudi warfare regarded both as utterly illegitimate and they fought back. Initial responses by the major Muslim power of the age, the Ottoman Empire, were feeble because Istanbul lacked the resources to mount counteroffensives on the distant Arabian frontier. A couple of military campaigns organized by the governor of Baghdad failed to blunt Saudi offensives in eastern Arabia. The Saudi danger materialized in a particularly bloody assault on the Shiite shrine town of Karbala in 1802, when Saudi-Wahhabi warriors plundered the shrine of Imam Husain and massacred thousands of townspeople.

The high point for the first Saudi state came with the takeover of Hijaz. In 1803, Mecca fell without a struggle and Wahhabi leaders set out to purify the holy city, razing domes over mausoleums and banning tobacco. In a pragmatic vein, the Saudi commander designated a local dignitary to serve as governor. A few months later, an outbreak of disease thinned the Saudi garrison's ranks and left it unable to face an Ottoman relief force, so the Saudis withdrew. But the threat to Istanbul's control over the holy places did not go away. Nearby Bedouin tribes jumped on the Wahhabi bandwagon and helped Saudi forces take over Medina in 1805. The following year they regained Mecca from the Ottomans but allowed the town's traditional leader, known as the *sharif*, to retain his position in return for loyalty to al-Diriyya. For the Wahhabi ulama, control over Mecca meant they could ensure that the annual pilgrimage rites would no longer be blemished by illegitimate innovations. To that end, they blocked the Ottoman-led pilgrimage but allowed the caravan from Morocco to proceed because its leader agreed to adhere to Wahhabi guidelines.

From the Ottoman perspective, the Saudi takeover of Mecca demanded a response for two reasons. First, Ottoman sultans had ruled the holy cities for nearly three centuries and derived much of their religious prestige from the claim to ensure the safety of caravans and the annual pilgrimage rites. Second, Wahhabi clerics rejected the Ottomans' legitimacy, charging them with idolatry. But political turmoil in Istanbul prevented the Ottomans from taking any steps in the immediate aftermath of losing the holy cities. In 1807, mutinous soldiers rose up to depose the sultan. When stability was restored a few years later, the sultan directed the pasha of Egypt, Muhammad Ali, to expel the Saudis. An Ottoman–Egyptian military campaign set out in 1811 and regained the holy cities by the end of 1813. After further inconclusive skirmishes, Muhammad Ali and the Saudis agreed on a truce.

The Ottoman–Egyptian recovery of Hijaz put pressure on the Saudi domain in Najd, where several emirs threw off allegiance to al-Diriyya. Wahhabi sheikhs regarded switching sides as more than a political tactic. It was choosing idolatry over monotheism. One of Sheikh Muhammad's grandsons, Sulaiman ibn Abdullah, composed a treatise making the case against befriending or giving loyalty to infidels, in this instance referring to the Ottomans. He cited Quranic verses commanding believers to hate infidels and to avoid any contact with them because it could lead one away from belief. The Arabic shorthand for that principle is *al-wala' wa al-bara'*, a phrase translated either as befriending Muslims and hating infidels, or giving loyalty to believers and disavowing infidels. In a separate treatise, Sheikh Sulaiman argued that Muslims might travel to the infidel lands only if they avoided friendly interaction with their infidel hosts. He drew on a Prophetic Tradition that says, 'Whoever associates with the idolater and lives with him is like him.'[9] The founder of Wahhabism had given these issues cursory attention in his writings, but his grandson's two treatises gave them a prominent place in Wahhabi doctrine, accentuating its xenophobic streak.

The end for the first Saudi state came soon after the collapse of the truce in 1817. A large Ottoman–Egyptian force invaded Najd, methodically overwhelmed one town after another and put al-Diriyya to siege, forcing its surrender in September 1818. The Saudi emir was dispatched to Istanbul for public execution, and leading Wahhabi clerics were deported to Cairo, but some Saudi emirs and Wahhabi clerics escaped to remote parts of Arabia. After a few years, Muhammad Ali found the cost of maintaining garrisons hundreds of miles inland too high and he ordered a withdrawal in 1824, but only after thoroughly demolishing al-Diriyya. As Egyptian soldiers departed, fugitive Saudi emirs rushed back. The founder of the Saudi second state, Emir Turki ibn Abdullah, found the old capital in ruins, so he made nearby Riyadh the new seat of power. Wahhabi clerics rallied support for the revival of Saudi rule and regained religious authority.

The second Saudi state possessed the same urge as the first to expand the domain of true belief through jihad, but the political situation had changed in the early nineteenth century with the arrival of a new power in the Gulf – Great Britain. In the later years of the first Saudi state, its political ambitions collided with Britain's interest in protecting Indian trade passing through the Gulf. In striving to annex southeast Arabia, the Saudis allied with the sheikhs of Ra's al-Khaima (in present-day United Arab

Emirates). These sheikhs commanded fleets of nimble vessels that preyed on merchant ships heading into and out of the Gulf. British officials regarded their assaults as piracy. After warnings and a bombardment failed to stop attacks on maritime trade, the British dispatched a naval squadron in 1819 to bombard Ra's al-Khaima and nearby ports into submission. The Arab sheikhs suffered a decisive defeat and the British squadron commander forced them to sign a truce that inaugurated a century and a half of Pax Britannica in the Gulf. By the time the second Saudi state turned its attention to the Gulf, it found a firm British determination to back allied sheikhs and repulse Saudi advances.

The first Saudi state lasted 70 years without dynastic infighting. The second Saudi state was not so fortunate. Emir Turki's rule was cut short when a relative assassinated him as he was leaving Friday prayer. At the time, Turki's son and lieutenant, Faisal, was leading an expedition in the eastern districts but he rushed home, defeated the assassin, and took over. Emir Faisal had little time to settle affairs before Muhammad Ali mounted an invasion in 1837. Some years before, the pasha of Egypt had rebelled against Istanbul by invading Syria and annexing it to his realm. The addition of Arabia may have been a prelude to expansion into Iraq to complete the construction of a vast Arab kingdom. As the pasha's forces advanced, Emir Faisal withdrew to a southern redoubt, where he held out for a time before surrendering. He was then transported to Cairo, where he lived under house arrest while Muhammad Ali installed a rival member of Al Saud, Emir Khalid, as his agent in Riyadh.

Central Arabia's subjugation to Egypt was brief, thanks to Great Power intervention against Muhammad Ali to shore up the Ottomans. He gained international recognition as hereditary governor of Egypt in return for withdrawing from Syria and Arabia. With the departure of Egyptian forces, Saudi emirs rushed to get rid of Emir Khalid. One of his cousins, Emir Thunayan, took control in Riyadh. Somehow Emir Faisal made his way back as well: some accounts relate that he made a dramatic escape from captivity, others suggest the Egyptians allowed him to leave. One way or another, he rallied loyalists to his banner and wrested power from Emir Thunayan in 1843.

At that point, the internal situation was fairly settled and Emir Faisal recognized the limits on expansion. He tested British resolve in the Gulf and found them determined to shield Bahrain's emirs against his efforts to turn them into vassals. In Oman, the British did not get involved with power struggles occurring in the rugged interior districts, so they did not object to the Saudi takeover of the Buraimi region. When it came to the coastal zone where maritime trade was under British protection, Saudi raids triggered warnings and retaliation sufficient to keep them at bay.

Outside powers put limits on expansion by the second Saudi state, but within Arabia it was the strongest independent power of the nineteenth century. Under its auspices, Wahhabi clergy consolidated their position as a religious establishment akin to a church in the sense that a central leadership – largely descendants of Sheikh Muhammad – exercised authority to appoint judges, teachers, and preachers, and to ensure doctrinal uniformity by subjecting suspicious scholars to interrogation and suppressing dissident views. The turmoil surrounding Emir Turki's assassination and the Egyptian occupation did not reverse the growing identification of Najd with Wahhabi doctrine. In fact, it was during the second Saudi state's rule that Wahhabi clergy began referring to their movement as the 'Najdi mission', suggesting an emergent regional identity rooted in a religious orientation that transcended attachment to tribe and town.

This is not to say that maintaining a uniform religious outlook was always easy. The second Egyptian occupation, of 1837–41, revived the issue of loyalty to believers and disavowing unbelievers that had come to the fore 20 years earlier. This time, Wahhabi clerics debated whether to emigrate or stay put. Advocates of emigration argued that to live under the Egyptians was prohibited because it entailed loyalty to unbelievers. The other side held that it was allowed to live under the Egyptians as long as one did not make a formal declaration of allegiance and loyalty. The immediate problem went away when Egyptian troops departed, but the question of contact with infidels took other forms.

After the second Egyptian occupation, Emir Faisal lowered political tensions with the Ottomans by professing loyalty to Istanbul, but doctrinal hostility between Ottoman and Wahhabi religious scholars did not abate because the Wahhabis did not water down their view of other Muslims as idolaters. Since jihad was not possible, Wahhabi leaders strove to minimize contact with idolaters in order to prevent contamination with their customs. Outsiders had no reason to spend much time in Najd; caravans traversed its inhospitable terrain as fast as they could. Najdi merchants, however, had a long history of travel to surrounding lands to buy and sell. For them, applying the Wahhabi prohibition on travel to the lands of idolaters – the Wahhabi term for Iraq, Syria, and Egypt – would mean giving up their livelihood. The towns of Qasim, the northern part of Najd, were the centers of long-distance trade and the scene of resistance to the concept of banning such travel. Merchants engaged in trade with Ottoman towns allied with local emirs whose allegiance to Riyadh was a matter of bowing to superior power, not heartfelt loyalty. Consequently, the autonomous leanings of Qasim's traders and emirs turned the area into a pocket of resistance to Wahhabi doctrine. The town of Unaiza, in particular, was home to several religious scholars who openly disputed the prohibition on travel to infidel lands. (Qasim is now a stronghold of Wahhabi purists, but that was not the case before the early twentieth century.)

Wahhabi leaders adopted a defensive posture to hold the line against idolatry, discouraging contact between believers and unbelievers for fear that daily association would result in unbelievers' ways rubbing off, and awaiting opportunities to spread the mission through conquest and persuasion. Openings for Wahhabi proselytizing appeared in the late nineteenth century, when new religious trends took shape in Syria, Iraq, and India. In Damascus and Baghdad, Arab theologians responded to the rise of secular ideas in the Ottoman Empire by calling for a reinterpretation of Islamic law to allow adaptation to modern science, technology, and political institutions. While they did not see eye to eye with Wahhabis on the critical question of belief, they did share an interest in purifying religious practice of innovations, including the widespread practice of venerating saints. The Arab reformers and the Wahhabis forged contacts through Najdi merchants trading with Damascus and Baghdad, sowing the seeds of a network between Arabia and the rest of the Arab world.

In the same period, India was the scene of religious ferment in response to Britain's abolition of the Mughal Empire in 1858. A group of Muslim scholars emphasized the need to return to the Prophetic Tradition as a foundation for communal revival. Their movement, known as Ahli Hadith (the Folk of Prophetic Tradition), became enmeshed in controversy with other Indian Muslims, but their drive to erase innovations gave them common cause with the Wahhabis. In the 1890s, Ahli Hadith teachers attracted pupils from Najd. The relationships between reformers in India and the Fertile Crescent were modest in scope but foreshadowed the spread of Wahhabi influence through persuasion rather than jihad. When Saudi Arabia's political significance grew in the twentieth century, these narrow channels of religious comity broadened and multiplied.

As the outlook for the Wahhabi mission improved outside Arabia, its political foundations began to crumble. After Emir Faisal died in 1865, his sons became embroiled in civil war for the next two decades. Early in this period of dynastic strife, a Saudi emir triggered a crisis for the Wahhabi ulama when he requested military assistance from the Ottoman governor of Baghdad. According to Wahhabi doctrine, it was forbidden to seek assistance from an infidel. The ulama became divided over how to respond. Some of them supported the emir because Faisal had designated him as his successor. Others condemned him as an unbeliever for allying with the infidel Ottomans. The controversy drew on the same theme that animated debate over disavowing infidels and travel to infidel lands: namely, the imperative to draw a sharp line between believers and unbelievers to preserve the purity of believers. The practical outcome of the request to Baghdad horrified Wahhabi ulama: Ottoman forces occupied al-Hasa in 1871 and claimed Najd as a dependency, even though Istanbul never made a serious bid to establish authority there.

The Ottoman occupation of al-Hasa had little effect on the Saudi civil war, which continued unabated. Indeed, dynastic strife sapped Saudi power and paved the way for a capable vassal in the northern Arabian town of Ha'il to extend his sway even though he was careful to declare his loyalty to Riyadh until its final subjugation was within reach. Muhammad ibn Rashid combined military leadership with tribal diplomacy in a gradual campaign to establish himself as the supreme chief of Najd. In 1887, he intervened in a bout of Saudi feuding, chasing off one faction, bringing the head of another to his court for 'protection', and installing a deputy in Riyadh. Ibn Rashid crushed a last-gasp effort by Saudi emirs in 1891 to regain power. Rather than accept his rule, the Saudis moved to Kuwait, where they were granted refuge.

The self-destruction of the second Saudi state did not imperil the Wahhabi mission. One hundred and fifty years after the Saudi–Wahhabi compact, it had deep roots in Najd. Furthermore, the Rashidi emirs of Ha'il supported Wahhabism, unlike the Ottoman–Egyptian invaders at the beginning of the century, who viewed it as a heretical movement. How it would have fared in the long term without Saudi backing is an interesting question. Barely ten years after evacuating Riyadh, a young Saudi emir recaptured it.

In January 1902, Abdulaziz ibn Saud struck out from Kuwait with a band of 60 men. The small Saudi force took a circuitous route to Riyadh in order to spring a surprise attack. Under cover of darkness, Abdulaziz and his men approached the town walls and breached them in the early morning hours. After a brief fight, he was master of Riyadh. In the next 30 years, Emir Abdulaziz, commonly referred to as Ibn Saud, regained his patrimony through war and diplomacy. Keenly attuned to the broader political dynamics surrounding Arabia, he avoided conflict with the British in the Gulf, where London was committed to protecting the rulers of Kuwait, Bahrain, Qatar, and the Trucial States (today's United Arab Emirates). At first, Ibn Saud concentrated his energies on the contest with the Rashidi emirs for supremacy in Najd. In 1913, an opportunity to seize al-Hasa arose when Istanbul redeployed forces for a war against Balkan powers. The province fell without a struggle.

When the Ottoman Empire entered World War I as an enemy to Great Britain, the Arabian potentates responded by aligning with London or Istanbul for leverage in their rivalries. The Rashidi emirate allied with Istanbul, Ibn Saud signed a treaty with Britain, and Sharif Husain of Mecca enlisted British support for the Arab revolt against Istanbul. The sharif and Ibn Saud received money and arms from London, but the military balance among the three Arab rulers was roughly equal, and when the war ended the northern half of the peninsula was divided among them.

World War I was a political watershed for the Middle East. The collapse of the Ottoman Empire resulted in the division of its Asiatic Arab provinces: Iraq, Palestine, and Jordan came under British rule, while Syria and Lebanon came under French rule. In Arabia, the Ottoman defeat left the Rashidi emirate without a patron. Ibn Saud was able to conquer it in 1921. That left Ibn

Saud and Sharif Husain, now ruler of the Hashemite Kingdom of Hijaz, as the two main Arabian powers.

One of the keys to Ibn Saud's military success after the war was the emergence of the Brethren, known by their Arabic name, the Ikhwan. They were Bedouin tribesmen who agreed to abandon their nomadic way of life and settle in agricultural colonies, where they became avid pupils of Wahhabi clerics. We do not know who conceived the idea of creating the Ikhwan. The first mention of an Ikhwan colony dates to 1912. The term for such a colony was *hijra*, a place of emigration, here meaning not merely geographical relocation but religious movement from infidelity to belief. There is a common misconception that Wahhabism was the product of Arabian nomads, but in fact Wahhabi clerics had long regarded nomads as idolaters and poor candidates for conversion because their desert wanderings left them out of the reach of proper religious instruction. In the hijra colonies that sprouted up in Najd, however, the Ikhwan became fervent adherents to Wahhabism and ferocious warriors for jihad against infidels. As a military asset, they were the most reliable corps of tribal warriors the Saudis ever had, so long as the Saudis continued to wage jihad. At times, though, they embarrassed Ibn Saud by committing massacres against unarmed men, women, and children, a blatant violation of well-established rules in Islamic law governing jihad. The Ikhwan could be a potent force for expansion, but also a wild card for a ruler striving to stabilize his realm and anxious to avoid collision with the British.

In the struggle between Saudi Najd and Hashemite Hijaz, Sharif Husain expected London to support him in return for his revolt against the Ottomans. Instead, the British adopted a neutral attitude toward its wartime allies. After a series of skirmishes along the ill-defined frontier between Hjiaz and Najd, Ibn Saud figured that Britain would not interfere in the Saudi–Hashemite struggle. He seized on the sharif's refusal to permit members of the Ikhwan to perform the pilgrimage in 1924 as a pretext to mount an invasion of Hijaz. The darkest episode in the Hashemite–Saudi conflict took place in July when Ikhwan warriors attacked Ta'if, a town near Mecca. The sharif's forces withdrew without a fight, leaving the townspeople defenseless against the Ikhwan, who carried out an awful massacre, slaying men, women, and children. Sharif Husain abdicated the throne in October; two weeks later Saudi forces met no resistance upon entering Mecca. The sharif's son, Ali, then retreated to Jeddah, which came under siege for nearly a year before he abandoned the effort and left the town notables to hand it over to Ibn Saud at the end of December 1925.[10]

Eager to avoid a repeat of the Ta'if atrocities and gain international acceptance of his rule over the holy cities, Ibn Saud kept the Ikhwan presence in Mecca to a minimum. The enormous religious significance of the hajj made sovereignty over the holy cities and responsibility for the safety of pilgrims perennial sources of legitimacy for Muslim rulers. It was natural that when Abdulaziz ibn Saud conquered Mecca he paid close attention to the first pilgrimage to take place under his rule to shore up his position as guardian of the holy places. Foreign Muslims were alarmed when Wahhabi clerics ordered the destruction of tombs associated with the Prophet's family and his Companions. To allay such concerns, the first Saudi newspaper, which was published in Mecca, carried articles detailing measures designed to improve conditions for pilgrims. Overland travelers no longer feared Bedouin raids thanks to Ibn Saud's pacification of the desert (not quite complete at the time). The guild of pilgrim guides came under strict regulation to end their notorious gouging and sharp practices. The introduction of quarantines and public hygiene brought an end to the peril of epidemic disease that used to ravage the ranks of pilgrims.[11] But Saudi rule in Mecca hit a bump during the hajj of 1926.

For centuries, the ceremonies surrounding the annual pilgrimage included the replacement of the *kiswa*, a black cloth embroidered with Quranic verses, which covers the Kaaba at the center of Mecca's Grand Mosque. A company of Egyptian soldiers would lead a camel caravan bearing the freshly made kiswa into the city, handing out food and money to beggars and announcing their arrival with bugle calls. The custom was offensive to Wahhabi doctrine which forbids music, especially on such a solemn occasion as the hajj. Ibn Saud was quite aware of this issue and he took the precaution of contacting the Egyptian authorities to work out a deal that allowed the customary delivery of the kiswa if the soldiers refrained from bugling. Everything went according to plan until a few days after the new kiswa was draped over the Kaaba. An Ikhwan patrol in the sacred precinct detected the bugle call of an Egyptian pilgrim and tried to make him stop. A scuffle broke out and Egyptian soldiers fired on the Ikhwan to break it up. Although no casualties were reported, the incident led to a decade-long rupture in Egyptian–Saudi relations and harmed, but did not ruin, Ibn Saud's bid for international respect.

Ibn Saud's drive for international legitimacy collided with the Ikhwan's jihad against tribesmen in Iraq and Transjordan. The Ikhwan viewed national borders as an infidel fiction, but Ibn Saud knew that British power was quite real, and incursions against London's protected realms were likely to backfire. He was trapped between the Ikhwan's commitment to jihad, completely justified under Wahhabi doctrine, and the compelling need to avoid a clash with Great Britain, then at the height of its imperial power. When the Ikhwan forced the issue with raids into Iraq, Ibn Saud tried to rein them in and assert his sole authority to declare jihad. Several Ikhwan leaders, powerful tribesmen who thought of themselves as Ibn Saud's peers rather than subjects, launched a revolt that threatened to plunge Arabia back into incessant strife. Coordinating plans with the British, Ibn Saud suppressed the revolt in a series of engagements in 1929–30. It was a critical moment in Arabian history, marking the definitive ascendance of Saudi dynastic interest over unbridled Wahhabi idealism.

The modern kingdom's founder managed to establish his supremacy over the religious estate by virtue of his achievement of reconquering most of Arabia, including the holy cities. After Ibn Saud suppressed the Ikhwan, he encountered a protest or two to opening the kingdom to Western infidels and modern inventions such as the telegraph, but for the last quarter century of his rule it was clear that he was in full control of political decisions. At the same time, he announced that his actions were guided by religious principles and that the purpose of his rule was to serve Islam. Pacification of the desert, improvements in the pilgrimage, dissemination of Wahhabi treatises to Arab lands, and negotiating the oil concession could all be justified as being part of a program to advance the interests of Muslims within and outside his realm. Ibn Saud staked his legitimacy on a blend of the mundane and the religious that his successors have perpetuated: the dynasty unified and pacified a lawless domain, raised living standards, and supported the spread of Wahhabi teachings.

Whether the Wahhabi ulama approved all of Ibn Saud's policies is not clear. Saudi sources give little indication of dissent over his decision to allow non-Muslims into the kingdom. Stories have been passed down about clerics bold enough to object to allowing Americans to explore the desert for water and oil, only to back down when the king delivered a thinly veiled threat to imprison the dissenter. Or as another desert legend has it, the king got so fed up with grumbling by clerics over his dealings with Americans that he told them if they did not like it, they could leave, and he would assist by sending them drivers to escort them out of the kingdom. What we do know is that he left the clerics in control of education, law, and public morality, and for them that seems to have sufficed as proof of his commitment to preserving the Wahhabi character of the kingdom.

By the time Abdulaziz ibn Saud proclaimed his realm the Kingdom of Saudi Arabia in 1932, almost two hundred years had passed since his ancestor received the father of Wahhabism. Remarkably, the Saudi–Wahhabi alliance had survived two invasions, a civil war, and subjugation to a rival Arabian power. Ibn Saud did not have a blueprint for consolidating his kingdom, but through trial and error he developed a pragmatic approach whose elements included not only force, but also diplomacy and compromise. How to square political realism with Wahhabi aspirations to eradicate idolatry is a question that has loomed large in Saudi Arabia's modern experience.

3 Wahhabism and the Modern Saudi State

Wahhabi doctrine has much to say about matters of creed, ritual, and individual conduct, but offers little guidance on governance, beyond a few principles commonly found in Sunni treatises: Muslims must have a ruler in order to provide unity, carry out religious duties, enforce Islamic law, and wage jihad. As long as the ruler performs those roles and does not command believers to violate *sharia* (Islamic law), subjects owe him obedience. In order to fulfill his obligation to implement sharia, the ruler depends on the expertise and advice of the ulama (clerics, or religious scholars). Accordingly, Saudi rulers and Wahhabi ulama observe a division of labor whereby Al Saud ensures the security and welfare of the population and upholds a moral public order defined by Islamic principles. The ulama counsel the rulers on the details of Islamic principles, and if they see the rulers deviating from or violating those principles, they offer private advice; they are not to denounce rulers in public, for to do so could cause disorder and division.

Given the limited scope of Wahhabi political principles, we must look elsewhere to explain the development and configuration of Saudi Arabia's government institutions. The answer lies in a drive for security and stability that eluded the first two emirates. Under King Abdulaziz and his successors, the dynasty delegated education, law, religious life, and morality to the religious establishment while retaining control over foreign relations, defense, internal security, the treasury, economic development, and petroleum affairs. Basically, the royal family kept sources of material power and wealth while handing off symbolic and discursive authority to the clerics. As formal government organizations evolved, senior princes in charge of ministries treated them as personal fiefdoms, hampering coordination among government offices, impeding implementation of new policies, and perpetuating royal power from one generation to the next by appointing junior princes to deputy minister posts.

The division of labor between Al Saud and the religious estate has had complex effects, but one clear consequence is an accumulation of royal wealth through various means for leveraging political power and influence. The most obvious of these are the princely allowances that rose with and for a time exceeded oil revenue in the 1950s. Members of the royal family have also used control over government offices to take exorbitant commissions on contracts for construction projects, arms sales, import agencies, and the like since the first oil boom. Putting a figure on royal allowances is a matter for speculation since they lie beyond the purview of the Ministry of Finance. In the mid 1990s, the United States embassy estimated allowances amounted to about 5 percent of the annual government budget. In addition, the embassy noted that the most powerful princes appropriated more than 10 percent of oil revenue and confiscated privately owned land to resell to the government, while lower-ranking princes traded in permits to sponsor foreign workers.[1] That members of the dynasty have continued to exploit their position for financial gain in recent years is suggested by the frequency of complaints about unfettered corruption and its debilitating effects on economic performance, not to mention the sheer waste and inequity.

Even though Saudis know that members of the ruling family exploit their political domination for financial gain, leading Wahhabi ulama keep silent because of the concept that public criticism is divisive and harmful to Muslim interests, and perhaps because they have vested interests in the political system as officeholders themselves. How those offices evolved is part of the longer story of Saudi Arabia's opening to the outside world due to its pursuit of security and stability. Starting under the second Saudi state in the 1800s, accommodation to Ottoman and British power marked the first breach in the barrier Wahhabi ulama had erected against outside influence in the conviction it would inevitably lead to the infiltration of idolatrous beliefs and habits. Then Ibn Saud opened the door when he admitted foreign Arab advisors and American oil prospectors, which was a prelude to the flood of expatriates during the oil boom.

The Opening of Saudi Arabia

In its first century, the Saudi emirate's relations with its neighbors reflected the Wahhabi doctrine's vision of a world sharply divided between believers and infidels. Warfare against towns and tribes that did not accept Saudi authority was not merely a struggle for power but jihad in the path of God, in which truces served as pauses between expansionist military campaigns. The primacy of religious idealism did not expire with the Ottoman–Egyptian conquest of al-Diriyya in 1818. The second Saudi emirate renewed expansionist jihad until the second Ottoman–Egyptian invasion in 1838. Only after Emir Faisal regained power in 1843 did strategic calculations outweigh Wahhabi doctrine in regard to relations with the outside world. He kept a distant but correct relationship with the Ottomans, occasionally sending tribute to ensure they did not meddle in his domain. He also had maintained contacts with Britain's resident for the Gulf, particularly when Saudi claims on Bahrain and Oman veered too close to London's sense of its prerogatives and interests. Riyadh's relationship with adjacent imperial powers was informal but sufficiently defined to ward off the sort of attacks that had jeopardized the emirate in the early 1800s.

A new turn in Saudi Arabia's relationship with the outside world came during World War I, when Abdulaziz ibn Saud signed a treaty with Britain in 1915. In this first formal diplomatic engagement, Abdulaziz received a guarantee of British protection and a modest supply of arms and funds. In return, London incorporated the Saudis into its network of allied Gulf sheikhs and firmed up Riyadh's opposition to the Ottomans. In a second diplomatic initiative, the 1927 Treaty of Jeddah, Britain granted official recognition to the independence of Saudi Arabia. At the same time, Ibn Saud's diplomatic skills encountered their severest test due to Ikhwan raids against tribes in Transjordan and Iraq. In the 1850s and 1860s, Britain had leaned on Emir Faisal to blunt campaigns against Bahrain and Oman, but the Ikhwan were a new element in the political mix whose allegiance to Wahhabi doctrine now collided with the dynasty's mundane interests. The revolt and its suppression marked the definitive assertion of royal control over religious ideals.

Until the early 1930s, engagement with the outside world arose from the need for security, whether through Emir Faisal's informal contacts or Ibn Saud's formal treaties. The next big step arose from the need for internal stability. At the time when Ibn Saud rounded out his conquests and declared the Kingdom of Saudi Arabia in 1932, the country's major economic resource – the annual pilgrimage – was in decline due to the global depression, cutting into the funds he needed to ensure the loyalty of tribal leaders. The 1933 oil concession negotiated with a consortium of United States companies came at just the right moment to restock the treasury, even if it took another decade before petroleum revenues could do more than ease the immediate fiscal crisis. Implementing the concession posed a challenge to Wahhabi doctrine because it meant allowing American geologists and engineers to roam the domain of belief, violating the perennial ban on infidels, whether they were nominal Muslims from the Ottoman lands or European Christians. The residential compounds set up by American companies served two purposes. They created a space inside the Wahhabi domain where foreigners did not have to observe local rules, and the ulama also presumably preferred to keep contact between foreigners and Saudis to a minimum to avoid cultural contamination. The early trickle of foreign workers foreshadowed the later torrent of expatriates that inundated oil fields, construction sites, and business offices. If today one in four residents of Saudi Arabia is an expatriate, it is due in part to the kingdom's lack of technical expertise when its oil industry first developed.

The influx of oil revenue provided the means to expand government services for the population. In the 1950s and 1960s, however, few Saudis were qualified to staff new hospitals and schools, s the government recruited foreign Arabs. Some of these foreign Arabs belonged to the Muslim Brotherhood.[2] The Egyptian government banned the Brotherhood in the early 1950s and persecuted its members and sympathizers; Syria and Iraq put pressure on local branches as well. In Saudi Arabia the Brotherhood found a congenial climate for its political and religious views. The foreign Arabs represented a different sort of external cultural influence that shared with Wahhabis the view that religious principles must occupy a central place in public life but differed in significant details on how to implement those principles as well as on matters of creed.

A third strand of outside influence became a bridge between Arab and Western residents and local society, namely, the growing number of Saudis traveling to the West for university education. By the early 1970s, several thousand Saudis had spent at least a few years in the United States and returned to fill positions in the expanding number of government offices as well as the oil industry. Exposure to Western culture inclined many of them to a more relaxed religious outlook that put them at odds with Wahhabi norms. At the same time that Western-educated Saudis were lending their newly acquired skills and knowledge to national development, the ulama were cementing control over law and education. As a result, there evolved two distinct administrative spheres, one for Saudis with technical skills and another for Saudis with religious expertise. The latter dominates law, education, and public morality through government bureaus.

The significance of these bureaus has been twofold. First, they incorporated religious authority as a component of modern Saudi government. Second, they represented the religious establishment's claims to preside over particular spheres of life. Those claims are not formally embedded in a constitutional order but the outcome of gradual bureaucratic evolution. In law and education, for instance, religious and secular camps coexist, but sometimes spar for primacy and resources. Under King Abdulaziz there developed a set of statutory courts to enforce regulations for matters that did not have clear guidelines in sharia, but in recent decades the ulama have tried to extend their sway over such courts. Higher education is also divided between religious and secular institutions that compete over resources and positions for their graduates. Areas clearly reserved to the ulama include supervision of the annual pilgrimage, the kingdom's thousands of mosques, and public morality, supervised by the Commission for the Promotion of Virtue and Prevention of Vice, commonly known in the West as the religious police.

The Legal System

In March 2008, Human Rights Watch issued a report itemizing what it called deficiencies in Saudi Arabia's criminal justice system: arrests without warrants, arbitrary detention, confessions extracted through coercion, trials where defendants did not know the precise charges or evidence against them, and violations of due process. Punishments include flogging, amputation, and beheading. To top it off, the kingdom's lack of a penal code means it is impossible to know when one is breaking the law. To illustrate some of these transgressions of Western legal norms, the report described the case of a young Saudi man put on trial for violating the ban against gender mixing. Apparently, a young woman had been stranded by another Saudi man and the defendant gave her a ride home. After arrest, the police beat him and held him in solitary confinement. His trial consisted of a short hearing, less than half an hour, before a judge, with no witnesses or attorneys present. The judge found him guilty and sentenced him to 90 lashes and six months in prison, reduced to 50 lashes thanks to a general royal amnesty. The Human Rights Watch report noted that the criminal procedure code promulgated in 2002 brought some clarity to the legal system but its provisions fell short of international standards for the protection of defendants' rights. The Saudi government is not impervious to criticism and in the past decade has instituted steps to bolster individual rights through the promulgation of a criminal procedure code and a civil procedure code to govern sharia courts as well as establishing the practice of appointing public defenders.[3] The amelioration of procedure, however, will not stem Western condemnation of Saudi Arabia's legal system as long as swordsmen carry out public executions not only for murder but for offences such as drug smuggling, armed robbery, and sorcery.[4]

The Saudi legal system is a frequent target for Western critics because safeguarding individual rights is not a fundamental objective of the state. Rather, the guiding principle is the application of sharia in order to fulfill the duty of obeying God's will, expressed through the Quran and the Prophetic Tradition, as interpreted by religious jurists and judges. Apart from the different assumptions of Islamic and Western law, Saudi Arabia is distinctive among Muslim countries, in the view of human rights groups, for the yawning gap between its legal system and modern international norms. That gap has roots in the kingdom's modern historical experience. Whereas most Muslim countries endured Western domination during the nineteenth century, the Saudi domain's isolation put it on a different path compared to Egypt and the Ottoman Empire, which ruled most of the Arab world and undertook sweeping institutional reforms that included legal systems and law.

The impetus for institutional overhaul in those places arose from the need to cope with European aggression. In 1798, France invaded Egypt, at the time an Ottoman province. Istanbul lacked the military prowess to retrieve its possession but regained control thanks to Great Britain's desire to oust the French, who could use Egypt as a base to challenge London's valuable commercial interests in the Indian Ocean. In the 1820s, European powers intervened in the Greek rebellion against Ottoman rule and forced Istanbul to grant independence to Greece. In 1830, France invaded Algeria, planting the seeds of domination over North Africa that would last until the mid twentieth century. Meanwhile, Russia was pressing on the Ottoman northern frontier from the Caucasus to the Balkans. If the empire was to survive, it had to change by borrowing from its enemies. Starting in the 1820s, Istanbul and its nominal vassal in Cairo, Muhammad Ali Pasha, embarked on the path of institutional reform, remaking military forces, founding bureaus to translate scientific and technical works from European languages, setting up schools, expanding the role of government, and organizing nascent ministries. All this was accompanied by new regulations to rationalize procedures and operations within and among the fast-growing government offices.

It was impossible for law to stand apart from the tide of change. Istanbul issued regulations for the reorganization of the judiciary, drafted new law codes, and established special courts to address disputes between Ottoman subjects and European merchants that inevitably accompanied the increase in trade stimulated by Europe's economic and population growth in the nineteenth century. The crowning achievement of these developments was the compilation of the Mecelle, a partial codification of Islamic law completed in 1870, later supplemented by a code of Islamic family law. In subsequent decades, as European imperialism swept over the Muslim world from Indonesia to Morocco, whether in the form of protectorates, mandates, or colonies, it deepened the hold of Western legal norms and procedures that took root and persisted after the achievement of independence. Because Saudi Arabia was independent of Ottoman rule and escaped European imperial domination, modern institutional change came much later.

We have few details about the administration of sharia in the first two Saudi states, but we do know that most Wahhabi judges followed the Hanbali School, although a few judges from the Maliki School served Saudi rulers as well. The criteria for appointment included expertise in sharia and adherence to Wahhabi doctrine. While the Saudi emir had the formal power of appointing judges, responsibility for vetting credentials rested with the leading members of Al al-Sheikh (the descendants of Sheikh Muhammad ibn Abd al-Wahhab), who were familiar with the small pool of men with the requisite expertise acquired in lessons at al-Diriyya and Riyadh. If a judge's allegiance to Wahhabi doctrine came under suspicion, Al al-Sheikh leaders could summon him to the capital for a kind of inquisition. The historical record on the activities of judges is scant, but they probably handled family affairs such as marriage, divorce, custody, and inheritance, property transactions, and contracts. In addition, as representatives of the Wahhabi leadership, judges appointed local religious functionaries such as prayer leaders, preachers, and teachers. Most judges served until they retired due to old age or died.

In the twentieth century, we can see the effect of political calculation on the development of law and legal institutions. When Abdulaziz ibn Saud annexed Hijaz in the 1920s, he had three constituencies to keep in mind: the dynasty's perennial Wahhabi allies, residents of the holy cities, and foreign Muslims. Rather than impose Najdi institutions on the townsmen of Hijaz, he tinkered with the administration inherited from Sharif Husain's short-lived kingdom, dispatching Wahhabi judges to preside over the law courts in the holy cities and Jeddah but preserving separate administrations for Hijaz and Najd. His agents in Hijaz were the first to cope with the challenge of assimilating inventions such as the automobile since sharia had little to say about driving laws and liability insurance. Ibn Saud's advisors began to issue statutes on a variety of matters that Wahhabi judges were reluctant to take on, and there emerged a system of parallel courts – one set to adjudicate statutes and one to address matters falling under the auspices of sharia – tacitly observing a division of legal authority between dynastic and clerical spheres.

In the 1950s and 1960s, King Saud and King Faisal took steps to organize the Saudi government into formal ministries, but left the legal realm alone due to the towering prestige and authority of the leading Wahhabi cleric, Sheikh Muhammad ibn Ibrahim Al al-Sheikh. A staunch traditionalist, he stood up for clerical autonomy and expressed his firm opposition to new-fangled ways, like the codification of laws, as subversions of sharia. As a result, the clerics continued to function as jurists finding solutions to new cases and as judges adjudicating family and commercial law.

The autonomy of religious law courts is not just a matter of powerful personalities and essentially political calculations. It is rooted in the political theory formulated by Ibn Taymiyya, the fourteenth-century Hanbali thinker whose writings Wahhabi clerics most frequently cite to buttress their views. He assigned to the ulama exclusive authority to interpret sharia, without interference from the ruler. Consequently, Saudi religious judges not only possess independence in arriving at verdicts but also in how they manage judicial procedure. According to Hanbali legal theory, each case has unique circumstances, so judges may choose to follow precedent in a similar case or to ignore it. Furthermore, when they decide a case on the basis of their own independent legal reasoning (*ijtihad*) rather than an explicit text in the Quran or the Prophetic Tradition, the verdict may not be overturned. Dissatisfaction with judges' decisions led to the establishment of the Board of Review (in 1962), which may overturn a verdict and refer the case to another judge for retrial.[5]

The kingdom's bifurcated legal organization began to change after Sheikh Muhammad ibn Ibrahim died in 1969. By that time, the government had created ministries for foreign affairs, defense, education, health, and so forth. King Faisal had issued a royal decree establishing the Ministry of Justice some years before mufti Ibn Ibrahim's death, and with the powerful cleric no longer standing in the way, the moment had arrived to put the decree into effect.[6] In 1971, the king issued a decree for the formation of a new body – the Council of Senior Ulama – to serve as the official representative of the religious establishment and supreme authority for issuing religious legal rulings (*fatwas*). While this was certainly an innovation in Saudi Arabia, it did not elicit clerical protest. Other Muslim countries had set the precedent of establishing a collective religious leadership body, appointed by the government. Saudi clerics, including Sheikh Muhammad ibn Ibrahim, had participated in the formation of collective international bodies in the Muslim World League. The Council of Senior Ulama consists of 20 or so clerics who meet twice a year to issue fatwas on issues ranging from cornea transplants (permitted) to Mother's Day (prohibited). The Council supervises the Committee for Scholarly Research and Legal Opinions, comprised of experts in religious law who prepare briefs on questions relating to ritual, social relations, business transactions, medical procedures, and so forth.

Assessments of the effects of King Faisal's reorganization of the judiciary vary. Some regard it as the formal subordination of the religious estate to royal authority that Sheikh Muhammad ibn Ibrahim had strenuously avoided. Others see it as enhancing clerical influence by giving the ulama control over government offices, staffs, and budgets. The opposing assessments may both be correct in the sense that we can see instances that vindicate each one. They are estimates of political preponderance between royal and religious power. A more accurate picture of the place of religious law in the kingdom would take into account variation in political dynamics according to the gravity of legal cases and principles. Briefly, the more an issue affects Al Saud's core interest in dynastic survival, the more likely it is that the rulers will lean on the religious leadership.

For example, the 1990 Gulf Crisis revealed the willingness of senior Wahhabi clerics to give ground on a well-established principle of Islamic law, the prohibition against seeking the assistance of infidels. That was the same principle that bedeviled Emir Abdullah during the Saudi civil war in the early 1870s when he summoned Ottoman forces to back him against his rebellious brother. The leading Wahhabi sheikhs denounced him for daring to deal with the infidel Turks, as they viewed them. In August 1990, the prohibition on soliciting aid from infidels was on the minds of the Council of Senior Ulama when King Fahd asked it for a ruling on his decision to seek military intervention by the United States to deter Iraqi forces that had occupied Kuwait. Members of the Council initially balked at giving their stamp of approval to a massive influx of infidel soldiers but ultimately caved under intense political pressure and delivered a carefully phrased fatwa that skirted the prohibition on infidel assistance by renaming it the introduction of 'qualified forces with equipment that bring fear and terror to those who wish to commit aggression against this country'.[7] By providing political cover for the massive foreign military build up, the Council earned the king's gratitude, but the verbal dodge was too transparent to escape the notice of purists less beholden to royal power. In subsequent months and years tensions racked the ranks of religious conservatives, and charges of hypocrisy targeted senior ulama enmeshed in the web of powerful institutions spawned in the 1971 royal decrees.

When it comes to less critical matters, the fatwa-making bodies deliberate unencumbered by royal arm-twisting. Broadly speaking, their fatwas fall into two categories. They cling to well-established doctrine on ritual practices, gender segregation, and public morality but bend to accommodate change on mundane issues such as medicine and media. Their hard line on ritual stems from the Wahhabi position on the problem of bid`a, innovation. A well-known Prophetic Tradition says, 'The best words are the Book of Allah and the best path to follow is the path of Muhammad, and the worst things are innovations and innovation is a deviation from the straight path.'[8] Classical Muslim jurists are divided on the Tradition's practical implications. Some read it in the light of a statement ascribed to the second caliph Umar who referred to a special prayer during Ramadan as a 'blessed innovation'. Accordingly, they concluded that there are good innovations and bad innovations. But other jurists, among them Ibn Taymiyya, argued that any innovation in the realm of religious belief and practice is bad and therefore forbidden. They also made a fine lexical distinction by noting that when innovation refers to mundane affairs, it has a different meaning and does not come under the prohibition. That is the position of Saudi jurists.

The large influx of Muslims from Arab countries and South Asia made Saudis familiar with different ways of practicing their faith, ways that Wahhabi doctrine has condemned as tokens of polytheism. A question that arose due to the presence of Muslim expatriates was whether it was allowed to perform prayers in a building used by Sufis. Not surprisingly, the answer was negative and the questioner was warned against even mingling with Sufis to avoid the danger of embracing their misguided beliefs.[9] In contrast to their firm position on religious practices, Saudi jurists exhibit flexibility on modern medical procedures. Cornea transplants are a sensitive issue because of the prohibition against mutilation. Nevertheless, a fatwa from the Council of Senior Ulama approved them, citing the legal principle of seeking benefit and avoiding harm. In the case of a cornea transplant, the benefit to a living person outweighs the harm to the deceased. Similar reasoning lay behind fatwas approving organ transplants, even from a living donor, as long as they do not harm the donor and the donated organ is freely given without pressure or monetary inducement.[10] Flexibility on this and other matters indicates more suppleness than is evident in reports by Western governments and non-government organizations (NGOs) on abuses of due process and individual rights.

Education

For centuries, the purpose of religious education in the Muslim world has been to preserve, transmit, and defend God's guidance, the key to eternal reward. Conversely, anything that leads one away from God's guidance is to be avoided, if not attacked. Since the first Saudi state purged Central Arabia of rival Muslim viewpoints, Wahhabi clerics have dominated education, giving lessons on religious subjects at mosques according to long-established practices observed throughout the Muslim world. A child's first task was to memorize the Quran as a foundation for learning to read and write Arabic. If a child managed to navigate the twists and turns of classical grammar, he would move on to treatises on Quranic exegesis, Prophetic Tradition, creed, and law. For each text mastered, the pupil received a license to teach it to others. There was no diploma to mark the completion of studies, just the accumulation of licenses from one's sheikhs. The curriculum required no acquaintance with natural sciences and just enough arithmetic to handle calculations of intricate inheritance cases, where the division of an estate's fractions among former wives and their children can be complex.

The kingdom's integration into the global political and economic systems created pressure for a modern education system in two ways. First, the rulers needed a cadre of administrators and civil servants to staff the offices of government departments handling foreign relations, national budgets, and economic development projects. The handful of non-Saudi Arabs in King Abdulaziz's entourage were glad to bring in more of their countrymen, but the princes and their Saudi clients viewed government positions as the natural preserve of Saudi nationals. In the 1940s and 1950s, the problem was that very few Saudis had the training to implement policies and manage public offices, so the establishment of schools that offered more than the customary religious curriculum assumed importance. Second, the petroleum sector, the kingdom's primary source of revenue, required engineers, geologists, accountants, and managers. The American oil company Aramco initially provided such expertise, but in the late 1940s and early 1950s came under pressure from workers to train Saudis for technical and administrative positions. In response to these twin pressures, one of King Saud's first acts in 1953 was to establish a Ministry of Education, which absorbed the provincial directorate of education that Ibn Saud had created for Hijaz in 1926. Expenditures on education were modest in the 1950s and 1960s but the kingdom made some strides in building schools throughout the country, gradually raising enrolment and making progress on raising the literacy rate, particularly among boys.

Getting girls into public schools posed a daunting challenge, given the widespread feeling that no good could come from allowing girls out of the house, where mothers could teach them everything they needed to know since their purpose in life was to become mothers themselves. Supporters of girls' education pointed to the history of women scholars of the Prophetic Tradition giving lessons in the holy cities. A few Arabian families engaged sheikhs to teach their daughters the basics of reading and writing at home. The first step to educate Saudi girls came during the 1930s, when affluent families began to spend extended time in Egypt and Lebanon, where they would enroll their daughters in school. In the 1950s, pressure for opening girls' schools came from two directions. First, educated Saudi men had a difficult time finding a suitably literate mate in their country and began to seek wives among non-Saudi Arab women. Second, Princess Iffat, the wife of Crown Prince Faisal, emerged as an influential voice in royal circles for educating girls. She had grown up in Istanbul, where schools for girls were well established and women were working in the health and education professions. In 1956, she established a private girls' school in Jeddah called Dar al-Hanan, initially enrolling orphans and servants of the royal family.[11]

When Crown Prince Faisal announced plans to set up public schools for girls, he encountered opposition from religious leaders who objected to the prospect of girls leaving their homes without their families. Faisal stood his ground and asked the clerics to show him where the Quran prohibited education for girls. The two sides settled on a compromise expressed in a royal decree issued in 1959 placing the education of girls under a special government body, the General Presidency for Girls' Education, headed by the leader of the Wahhabi establishment, Sheikh Muhammad ibn Ibrahim

Al al-Sheikh, who took responsibility for hiring female teachers and checking their religious credentials. The royal decree also stipulated that girls would study subjects suitable to their roles as future mothers: the Quran, religious subjects, homemaking, and childrearing. One more provision to allay conservative sensibilities was to grant families the right to keep their daughters at home if they wished. Even with these concessions, the establishment of a girls' school in Buraida in 1963 triggered violent demonstrations and Faisal had to send the National Guard to protect it.[12]

The opening of schools for girls had far-reaching social and cultural significance in Saudi Arabia, especially in Najd. Girls no longer spent most of their time at home, occasionally going out to visit relatives, but went to school every day, where their social horizons expanded by mingling with other girls and interacting

1. Classroom in a girls' school

with teachers.[13] By 1965, around 50,000 Saudi girls were attending schools – a solid achievement, even if much of the curriculum focused on wifely skills such as cooking, sewing, and childcare. A decade later, the number leapt to nearly 300,000 and more than doubled again by the mid 1980s. The normalization of girls' education increased the literacy rate but since many families refused to send their daughters to school – more because of social conservatism than religion – a gender gap opened that has not yet closed. In recognizing the problem, the government established adult literacy classes for women (and for men as well). Many students are women whose fathers barred them from school but whose educated husbands encourage them to learn basic reading and writing. Nowadays, illiterate mothers push their daughters to excel in school. And, while families still arrange marriages for daughters enrolled in high school, they often insert clauses in marriage contracts stipulating that brides have the right to continue their education, a sign of the pride many families take in a university degree earned by their daughters.[14]

By quantitative measures, the Saudi educational system has done quite well at getting children into schools and universities. The national system of boys' and girls' schools has raised the literacy rate close to 80 percent, although there remains a substantial gender gap: 70 percent of females compared to 85 percent of males. Major gains in literacy were achieved during the first oil boom, thanks to multibillion-dollar budgets. For example, during the Five-Year Plan for 1976–80, education received $28 billion. Nevertheless, in qualitative terms, there were shortcomings such as high rates of attrition at lower grades – as much as 20 percent in the mid 1980s – despite lax standards for passing to higher grades.[15]

It is understandable that a national system built from scratch in a rush would have deficiencies arising from hasty design of the curriculum, hurried construction of school buildings, and the need to hire foreign teachers due to the small number of local teachers.

But problems in Saudi education may be intractable due to its roots lying in an essentially political compromise that sacrificed attention to practical, mundane subjects such as mathematics and science for the sake of placating the Wahhabi establishment, which has insisted on maintaining a heavy dose of religious subject matter at all school levels. Moreover, the dismissive, even hostile, attitude toward modern science exhibited by some leading religious figures can only hamper the incentive for achievement in technical subjects. For example, one of the most influential sheikhs in the later decades of the twentieth century, Abdulaziz ibn Baz, adhered to a pre-Copernican cosmology.[16] Furthermore, the emphasis in Saudi schools on the religious formation of young people compresses the amount of time they spend on other subjects, including science and mathematics. These subjects' relative neglect is probably responsible for the kingdom's low ranking in a 2007 survey of math and science education in 47 countries.[17] Reliance on rote learning and the primacy assigned to respect for authority have a deadening effect on creative thought and analysis.[18]

Elementary education lays a heavy emphasis on the Quran, Islamic law and theology, and Arabic handwriting and spelling. Only about one-third of classroom hours are devoted to arithmetic, science, history, and geography. The priority of religious lessons is such that pupils may advance to the next level in school even if they fail in all subjects, as long as they pass the course on religion. The religious impact on education goes beyond the dedication of classes to theology because Islamic themes permeate history, civics, and literature classes as well.[19] Moreover, pupils learn that only the Wahhabi interpretation of Islam is correct. The legacy of other theological groups and Muslim philosophers are treated as deviations that brought disastrous schism to Muslims.

Western and Saudi critics of the education system pinpoint the intolerant spirit in the curriculum, frequently blaming it on Wahhabi doctrine, but the history of curriculum in the kingdom is not so simple. Because of the shortage of qualified personnel in the first decades of expansion in education, the government welcomed teachers from Egypt, Syria, and Jordan. Most of the newcomers came not only for professional opportunities but to escape political persecution since they were members of the Muslim Brotherhood, which fell foul of the secular Arab nationalist regimes that came to power in the period after World War II. With positions in the Ministry of Education as textbook consultants, they inscribed their ideology in schoolbooks. Members of the Muslim Brotherhood also had a major role in writing official policy for the national education system.[20] As teachers and principals, they ensured that a conspicuous strain of Muslim Brotherhood ideology permeated classrooms. Studies of Saudi schoolbooks reveal a blend of that ideology with Wahhabi principles, particularly in religious lessons.

The Wahhabi imprint is evident in high-school texts on religious doctrine that include a biographical sketch of Muhammad ibn Abd al-Wahhab and his role in the establishment of Saudi Arabia. The texts review tenets regarding the evils of ritual innovations that constitute forms of polytheism such as magic, Shiite customs such as visiting the shrines of the Prophet's family, and Sufi practices such as seeking a saint's intercession. The concept of allegiance to believers and enmity toward infidels that filled many nineteenth-century treatises figures prominently. Hence, pupils learn to exhibit enmity toward infidels in various ways, such as refusing to greet them on one of their holidays or to offer them condolences on the death of a loved one. They are warned against living among them because doing so will diminish their own belief by inclining them to adopt infidel ways and to take up prohibited customs like going to movies, playing sports, listening to music, and dancing. The eleventh-grade text on Islamic law discusses the death penalty for apostasy and enumerates what constitutes apostasy: any expression of polytheism, mocking religion, and doubting a religious obligation.

The Muslim Brotherhood's ideology shows up in texts on the Prophetic Tradition that discuss threats to Islam, starting with the medieval Crusades and resuming in modern times with Christian missionaries seeking to wipe out Islam, and later in assaults by cultural imperialism. Classic Wahhabi texts do not mention any of these manifestations of peril from Western civilization; rather they focus on what they call the polytheistic practices of lapsed Muslims in Arabia and the Ottoman Empire. Schoolbooks also highlight the assault mounted by Jews against Muslims, teaching that Zionism is an expression of religious hostility and that it aspires to dominate the territory between the Nile and Euphrates rivers.[21] Finally, the Muslim Brotherhood's political adversaries find a place in Saudi textbooks, where they list threats to Islam from alien ideologies such as Arab nationalism, socialism, and secularism.

The xenophobic tenor of Saudi textbooks drew close scrutiny after 9/11, with critics asserting that they bred the sort of hatred that resulted in the terrorist attacks. Under heavy pressure to scrub messages of hate from textbooks, the Ministry of Education undertook curriculum revisions in 2003. A new edition of the textbook on religious doctrine for tenth graders was supposed to represent the first step in a multiyear effort to rewrite the curriculum, and it did impart a spirit of tolerance toward other faiths. For example, it drew attention to the common heritage of Judaism, Christianity, and Islam. Sections about bearing enmity to infidels were removed altogether. Other textbooks also reflect the new agenda by explaining that Muslims may have friendly relationships and engage in trade with non-Muslims. The tone of tolerance might have placated critics of Saudi education, but religious conservatives angrily attacked the changes as nothing but surrender to American interference.[22] Such charges suggest that reformers have a steep hill to climb. As education reformers elsewhere would acknowledge, there is more to changing what pupils learn in school than making textbook revisions.

Thousands of teachers and school staff, fully convinced that they have faithfully carried out their duties by teaching the customary curriculum, are skeptical of top-down directives to change their ways, much like their counterparts in other countries. Told that they must discard or suppress their convictions, they resist by continuing to give lessons as they have for years and gloss over new wording on the pages in the hands of schoolchildren. High-ranking officials in the Ministry of Education have a vision of improvements to curriculum and periodic reviews of teacher performance, but the ministry is similar to most others in the kingdom that have a lackluster record of implementing new policies and procedures. Moreover, conservatives dominate the ministry's intermediary levels. They view reform as a liberal agenda that threatens belief and they are determined to stifle change.[23]

University Education

Ever since the birth of higher education in Saudi Arabia with the establishment of Riyadh University (presently King Saud University) in 1957, it has been divided between secular and religious institutions. At present, secular universities offer degrees in engineering, medicine, natural sciences, and social sciences, while students in religious universities study for degrees in Islamic law, Quranic studies, and theology. Students at secular universities in Riyadh, Dammam, and Jeddah prepare for careers in the petroleum sector, public administration, and business, whereas the religious universities in Mecca, Medina, and Riyadh generally turn out religious court judges, muftis, preachers, and teachers for religious subjects. How many of the latter the modern Saudi economy could absorb was not an issue that engaged the attention of religious leaders eager to dilute the political and social influence of graduates with Westernized outlooks.[24]

The impetus to establish religious universities came from the unease in religious quarters at the prospect of a secular monopoly in higher education. To allay the concerns of the ulama, the rulers turned recently created institutes for advanced sharia studies into religious universities. In 1961, Medina University was established as a center for Islamic studies that also served large numbers of non-Saudi Muslims. As antidotes to the prospective increase in the weight of secularism, the religious universities fulfilled two roles. First, by training thousands of students, they ensured the broad dissemination of Wahhabi doctrine inside Saudi Arabia through graduates employed in mosques, religious institutes, and schools. Second, by enrolling thousands of foreign Muslims, they broadcast Wahhabi doctrine to the rest of the Muslim world through alumni returning home.

It is worth noting that the government formulated a common policy to encompass both secular and religious universities according to which the purpose of higher education is to advance and defend Islam. Therefore, neither secular nor religious universities offer classes in music, art, and philosophy, due to their incompatibility with Wahhabi doctrine. Courses in Islamic studies are graduation requirements for students at secular universities. The instructor of a course on Islamic political systems at King Saud University might teach students that secular concepts such as democracy and human rights are contrary to Islamic principles because they do not have a divine origin. Furthermore, the holdings of university libraries are scrutinized for prohibited images of women to be blacked out and heretical books to be removed. Students have been denied degrees on the grounds of showing improper religious character, and candidates for professorships are interviewed to ascertain their religious views. Faculty have lost their jobs for expressing nonconformist ideas and beliefs. At religious universities, the centrality of Islam influences the way secular subjects such as economics, psychology, literature, and the natural sciences are taught, primarily by excluding ideas that are contrary to Islamic teachings. In literature courses, for example, modern literary theory is overlooked. The aspirations of religious university administrators to compete with secular counterparts have led to the establishment of faculties of medicine, sciences, and engineering.[25]

Women's access to higher education trailed the establishment of universities, not only because conservatives felt women did not need to further their learning after high school, but also because the prohibition on gender mixing meant separate campuses for women had to be constructed. While Saudi women had a late start in university studies, the attraction of a diploma for work, status, and personal satisfaction proved so strong that they now surpass men as a percentage of students, comprising nearly 60 percent of the total. By the early 2000s, there were campuses for women at secular and religious universities in Jeddah, Mecca, Riyadh, Medina, Abha, and Dammam.[26]

Conservative religious views affect the university experience for women in different ways. Students report that to enter the campus, they must undergo a search to enforce a code for what they wear under their *abaya*s (cloaks) – jeans are not allowed. Once on campus, they face restrictions on laptops and internet use. To prevent interaction between male professors and female students, lectures are delivered via closed-circuit television.[27] To address complaints about the inferior quality of women's higher education, the government invested $5 billion in a new Riyadh campus, Princess Nora Bint Abdulrahman University, which opened in 2011 with a capacity for 50,000 students.[28]

Two years earlier, the kingdom opened its first coeducational institution, King Abdullah University of Science and Technology (KAUST). A pet project of its namesake, it is designed to attract top graduate students and is supposed to represent a commitment to make the kingdom a center for advanced scientific research. Skeptics consider it extravagant window dressing that conceals deep flaws in the national education system. They point to its remote location and the tight controls over access to the campus that bar ordinary Saudis. In their eyes, the key to raising the standard of education is to improve pre-university schools by introducing rigor to science and mathematics classes and scaling back the place of religious subjects in the curriculum. Without such changes, critics maintain, KAUST will remain the equivalent of a foreign residential compound, located within Saudi territory but detached from society. The debate over KAUST reflects the dilemmas of a political system dedicated to upholding Wahhabi doctrine at the same time as it strives to prepare citizens for productive roles in a modern technical economy.

The Pilgrimage

The supreme embodiment of Muslim unity is the annual pilgrimage that takes place during the second week of the last month in the lunar Muslim calendar. First instituted by the Prophet Muhammad upon his conquest of Mecca, the hajj is an obligation for every able-bodied believer possessing the financial means for the journey. The feeling of unity is underscored the moment pilgrims enter the sacred precinct, where men shed their everyday clothing to don the *ihram*, a simple garment of two white strips of cloth to cover the upper and lower parts of their bodies (women do not wear the ihram). The rituals, which take several days to perform, symbolically re-enact episodes in the life of the Prophet Abraham, regarded by Muslims as the founder of the world's first monotheistic shrine at Mecca. Women have the same obligation as men to perform the pilgrimage, during which the usual Wahhabi ban on gender mixing does not apply.

When pilgrims arrive at the Grand Mosque, they perform a counter-clockwise circumambulation of the Kaaba, making seven circuits. The next stage of the ritual is rushing the roughly 400 yards between two low elevations called Marwa and Safa. Pilgrims then make their way out of Mecca to a nearby town called Mina and stay there overnight. The next day they head for the Plain of Arafat. There they spend the day gathered on a vast plain from which rises the Mount of Mercy, where prayers for forgiveness are believed to have special potency. At sunset, pilgrims move on to a site called Muzdalifa to spend the night. On the next day, they go to the Plain of Mina, where they hurl seven stones at each of three pillars representing Satan. The rite concludes with the sacrifice of an animal, marking the Feast of the Sacrifice, one of two legal holidays in Saudi Arabia (the other is the Ramadan Feast). Believers are expected to eat a portion of the sacrificial meal and share the rest with the poor.[29]

The pilgrimage is a major component in Al Saud's repertoire of religious responsibilities. Saudi television broadcasts scenes from the pilgrimage to emphasize the government's effectiveness at ensuring hygiene and safety, as Muslims from around the globe gather to celebrate what for many is a once-in-a-lifetime experience. Around seven thousand security forces patrol Mecca and surrounding precincts to

2. Pilgrims at the Mount of Mercy

keep order in the huge crowds that throng to Mecca, between 1.5 and 2 million pilgrims in recent years. The Saudis have spent billions of dollars on air conditioning, escalators, and electric lighting to make the pilgrimage easier and more comfortable. At the vast outdoor venues of Mina and Arafat outside Mecca, the government maintains air-conditioned tents, medical clinics, and sprinklers to cool pilgrims when the hajj falls during the hot season.[30]

Due to the ritual's significance for Muslims around the world, it is more than a religious ceremony. It also provides a backdrop for political rivalries to play out. During the 1980s, Saudi oversight of the pilgrimage became a sore point in its relations with Iran's revolutionary Islamic Republic. Tensions erupted during the hajj of 1987, when Saudi security forces clashed with Iranian pilgrims demonstrating against United States policies, and by association against Riyadh's close relationship with Washington. The fighting and panic it caused resulted in 402 deaths and hundreds more serious injuries. Riyadh and Tehran blamed each other for inciting the violence, and for the next three years Iran took the extraordinary step of boycotting the pilgrimage, offering the spectacle of an Islamic government suspending a fundamental religious duty. Saudi Arabia responded to the failure of security forces to maintain crowd control by seeking approval from the Organization of the Islamic Conference (OIC) for a limit on the number of pilgrims equal to 1 percent of the world Muslim population. Even with the OIC's blessing for a quota, the 1990s were punctuated by stampedes and fires that killed hundreds in three different years.[31]

The pilgrimage is a high-profile annual test of how well the Saudi government handles its responsibility as custodian of the holy places, but it is not the only one. Ever since the seventh century, Muslim rulers from Umayyad caliphs to Ottoman sultans have bolstered their claims to religious legitimacy by improving and enlarging the Grand Mosque. When the Saudis took over, the sanctuary could hold nearly fifty thousand worshipers. A series of projects in the past 50 years has increased capacity to around one million. Controversy trails the remaking of the Grand Mosque and its environs, in part because of its scope, in part because it has erased physical vestiges of the city's history by encroaching on adjacent neighborhoods to clear the way for their absorption into the gargantuan holy site of today. What Saudis consider improvement, other Muslims regard as wanton destruction of revered historical sites associated with Companions of the Prophet and members of the Prophet's family. The house where the Prophet was born was removed for the construction of a library; his first wife Khadija's house was turned into a public restroom; the mosque of his father-in-law and the first caliph, Abu Bakr, was demolished and a hotel erected in its stead. Paving over ancient cemeteries to make way for royal palaces, luxury hotels, and apartment buildings has opened the Saudi government to charges of erasing a heritage that belongs to all Muslims and trampling the equality and unity of believers by elevating the interests of the wealthy and the powerful. The Wahhabi religious authorities maintain that, apart from the Grand Mosque and Medina's Mosque of the Prophet, historic places have no special status to warrant protection, so the government may do with them as it wishes without compromising the duty to maintain the holy places.[32]

Projects to modernize Mecca have proceeded at a hectic pace. Proponents see them as urban renewal essential to making the holy city more beautiful and hospitable to pilgrims, but critics condemn the obliteration of cultural heritage by erasing traces of old quarters and streets. In 2002, an international controversy erupted when Saudi authorities announced plans to raze an eighteenth-century Ottoman fort to make way for a massive new luxury complex called Abraj al-Bait Towers to include hotels, residences, restaurants, a mall, and a clock tower resembling a giant version of London's Big Ben. To construct the complex, the contractor, Saudi bin Laden Group, leveled the mountain spur that the old fort dominated. Coming on the heels of construction projects that obliterated other traces of the Ottoman heritage in Arabia, the demolition of the fort sparked outrage in the Turkish press and protest from the Turkish government. The episode could be read as historical payback since the fort's original purpose was to defend Mecca against the first Saudi state.[33]

Religious Police

Some Saudi schoolgirls became fed up with a young man who was hanging around their school, hoping to pass along his phone number, so they contacted the Commission for the Promotion of Virtue and Prevention of Vice, requesting it to send a unit to make the guy leave them alone. According to a spokesman for the Commission, its officers warned the man three times to stop but he continued his behavior. When a Commission patrol arrived to arrest him, he skittered under his car to call for help. The officers were able to detain him, but only after a struggle that left everyone with injuries. That is one version of the incident. According to a different version, the man was taking photographs of the street as part of his work as a surveyor when the religious police spotted him and suspected he was taking photos of girls at a nearby school. They started roughing him up, so he resisted and got away long enough to call his father for help. When the father arrived at the scene, he too fought with the religious police and drove off with his bleeding son to get him to hospital, but the religious police cut him off and arrested them both, releasing the father after a short detention. The suspect wound up in hospital because of injuries he claims he suffered at the police station, where he was thrown down a stairwell. His family got in touch with the Saudi human rights organization to seek its help in dealing with the religious police, who presumably want to know how they can possibly prevent vice without using a little force.[34]

One of Saudi Arabia's distinctive institutions is the Commission for the Promotion of Virtue and Prevention of Vice, often referred to in English as the religious police. The Commission is an independent agency that acts as the enforcer of public morality, ensuring that shops close during prayer time and that Saudis comply with the rules against mingling among unrelated men and women. The roots of the institution go back to the principle in Islamic law that each believer has the duty to command right and forbid wrong, either by hand, word, or thought. The duty has a long history of interpretation regarding how believers should best fulfill it. The first record of an official responsible for carrying out the duty dates back to eighth-century Baghdad under the Abbasid caliphate. The title of the official was *muhtasib*. His mandate to ensure public morality included fair commerce, so he was also a market inspector of weights and measures. The medieval theologian most respected in Wahhabi circles, Ibn Taymiyya, considered enforcing the duty to be a complex matter that could backfire when undertaken with zeal untempered by discretion and could result in more harm than good.[35]

In the nineteenth century, Saudi emirs instructed local governors to ensure that all men attend mosque by taking attendance and punishing absentees unless they had a valid excuse such as illness. There was no formal institution dedicated to implementing the duty of commanding right and forbidding wrong, but there apparently were men responsible for punishing vices such as alcohol, tobacco, and music.[36] Exactly when Saudi rulers first employed religious police is not clear. The Commission for the Promotion of Virtue and Prevention of Vice was first mentioned in 1926, when the official Saudi newspaper announced its establishment in Mecca. By the late 1930s, branches of the Commission had spread throughout the kingdom.[37]

Today, the Commission has branches in each province. In terms of government organization, it does not come under a ministry but reports to the Council of Ministers. About five thousand religious police patrol cities in Range Rover-like vehicles bearing the Commission's insignia. They do not wear a uniform, but they have a distinctive badge. They do not have powers of arrest, interrogation, or detention; only when accompanied by regular police may they carry out an arrest. The Commission's personnel look for violations of the ban on unrelated men and women meeting in public and private, the prohibition on illegal religious (non-Muslim) expression, and possession of alcohol and pornography. They also ensure that shops and offices close during prayer time, and they monitor women's adherence to their definition of proper dress.[38]

The influence of the religious police has waxed and waned over the years. To stem a conservative backlash in the late 1970s, the government increased their funding, numbers, and the scope of activity. In the past decade, however, their influence shows signs of diminishing.[39] The Commission's supporters regard them as performing the essential function of preserving public morality, but many Saudis hold them in contempt as rude busybodies.[40] A properly veiled woman could incur the wrath of the religious police for the sin of raising her mask to browse a book in a store.[41] Not all Saudis are intimidated by the religious police. A Saudi woman blogger described in a post her encounter with them in Riyadh when she took a taxi to meet a foreign man to purchase an item she had bought over the internet. She managed to prove that she had legitimate business and then made them back off by threatening to charge them with slander, a crime punishable by 80 lashes under Islamic law.[42]

Censorship

One of the earliest accusations against Muhammad ibn Abd al-Wahhab was that he burned a famous collection of prayers for the Prophet Muhammad because it included expressions that amount to worshiping the Prophet instead of God alone.[43] The urge to censor did not diminish in the second Saudi state. The foremost Wahhabi sheikh ordered the confiscation of books and manuscripts belonging to a fellow sheikh who had deserted the Wahhabi camp over the issue of takfir.[44] The imperative to erase idolatry meant preventing the spread of writings bearing its traces. Before the twentieth century, geographical isolation made the task of suppressing religious subversion manageable. Censorship became more difficult when printing became widespread in the early twentieth century. It was one thing to keep on the alert for the occasional manuscript that might bear suspicious doctrine, but it was something else to develop a way to bar thousands of copies of mass-produced printed publications. In addition to filtering what might arrive from abroad, the introduction and spread of print inside the kingdom presented new challenges to the task of preventing believers from getting their hands on books, magazines, and newspapers that might express false religious beliefs or contain immoral images and stories.

Abdulaziz ibn Saud found that printing offered an effective medium to disseminate official political and religious positions for home and foreign consumption. When his forces conquered Mecca in 1924, he took over Sharif Husain's newspaper and made it into his official government newspaper, called *Umm al-Qura*. In the past 80 years, newspapers have come and gone; some focused on local issues such as sanitation and economic development, others exhibited a literary bent. Today, the Ministry of Culture and Information has responsibility for ensuring compliance with Wahhabi standards of religious and moral rectitude. To publish a newspaper requires a license from the ministry and the one news agency, the Saudi Press Agency, is part of the ministry. The kingdom has about 15 daily newspapers, in addition to two Saudi-owned papers published in London. While the newspapers are nominally independent and privately owned, they are in fact associated with various members of the royal family. For instance, *al-Riyadh*, the capital's daily paper, is under the sway of Crown Prince Salman. In general, censorship is self-imposed, on the basis of tacit understandings (no criticism of the royal family) rather than explicit rules, yet reporters and editors sometimes provoke royal ire and then must endure suspension of publication.[45] Foreign newspapers and magazines allowed into the kingdom are also subject to censorship. News stories about sensitive political issues are torn out of publications. Censors used to black out women's arms and legs in photographs; technological advances make it possible to use computer programs such as Photoshop to block immoral images.

Even though there is no press freedom, the scope and content of newspaper stories has fluctuated over the years. In the 1960s and 1970s, admiring stories about the royal family and religious affairs predominated but there was also space for some muckraking to move authorities to address problems such as sanitary water and sewage as well as lively debate on cultural issues.[46] After the 1979 Mecca Uprising (see Chapter 6), the government imposed stricter control over press coverage and curtailed discussion of controversial matters such as loosening restrictions on women. In the wake of 9/11, the government saw fit to permit vigorous debate in the press on a variety of domestic issues as long as articles did not target the royal family. Women's rights, drug addiction, AIDS, and corruption became common topics for stories and editorials. Even the religious establishment came under questioning for fostering an intolerant outlook that some thought responsible for nurturing terrorism.

In the kingdom today, censors keep an eye out for deviant religious writings and immoral images of women. Customs officers at airports have special rooms to inspect videotapes and DVDs to guard against the smuggling of pornography and subversive political materials. Self-censorship by businesses is common. The owners of stores selling bed linens attach black stickers to boxes to cover up the picture of a woman in a nightgown. For a Western company to practice self-censorship, however, is less common: when the Swedish furniture giant Ikea removed women from photos in catalogues it shipped to Saudi Arabia, it had to apologize to critics at home. In any case, figuring out what to censor is not obvious as there are no hard-and-fast guidelines. In 2005, a Saudi writer published a piece of 'chick lit' called *Girls of Riyadh*, an account of young women's romantic dreams, adventures, and frustrations. It came out with a Lebanese publisher and was banned at home. Saudi readers were able to get around the censors by circulating electronic copies on the internet and the authorities decided to allow the English translation that appeared a few years later. The widening spectrum of modern electronic media poses formidable challenges to censorship, with consequences we examine in the next chapter.

3. *A censored fashion billboard in downtown Riyadh*

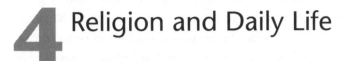

4 Religion and Daily Life

Daily life in Saudi Arabia has a rhythm marked by the call to prayer, dividing the day into five intervals. The work day commences well after the dawn prayer, pauses for the noon and afternoon prayers, and ends for most office workers shortly before or after the sunset prayer. Social life commonly gets underway following the evening prayer, when cell phones ring and streets become crowded with cars heading to the malls, restaurants, and the homes of family members. Other Muslim societies keep a similar beat to ritual time, but Saudi Arabia is unusual if not unique in putting a Wahhabi imprint on individual behavior, demanding an outward show of conformity, be it from eager compliance or grudging acquiescence. What is not always clear to visitors, or even to Saudis, is whether deeply ingrained social habits have roots in custom or divine guidance.

Religious Observance

Religious duties permeate the days, weeks, and months of the Saudi calendar and impart unity to a society that is pulled in different directions by a sense of obligation to fulfill the kingdom's established doctrine on one side and the idea that one can step outside the lines drawn by Wahhabi clerics while remaining a good Muslim. One of the fundamental religious duties for all Muslims is to pray five times a day: at dawn, noon, mid-afternoon, sunset, and evening. The believer performs a ritual ablution before prayer that may be carried out alone or, preferably, with a group. When traveling through the country by car, Saudis pull to the side of the road at prayer time, much as Bedouin formerly stopped their camels to dismount, use a stick to draw a line in the sand with a half-moon indentation in the direction of Mecca, and perform the rite before continuing their journey.

Where Saudi Arabia differs from other Muslim countries is the requirement that all stores and offices close during prayer time to ensure that men gather at a nearby mosque for communal prayer. On the typical work day, business stops for the noon and mid-afternoon prayers. Therefore, for offices that observe an eight- or nine-hour work day, prayer does not take more time than a lunch hour and a couple of coffee breaks. Stores tend to stay open past the evening prayer, so they must shut down for the two last prayers. In the shopping malls, women – whom the religious police do not oblige to pray – sit and mill about, checking cell phones for messages and quietly conversing while they wait for stores to reopen. Diners at restaurants are not expected to leave during prayer, but shutters and blinds are drawn to shield them from street view, and new customers may not enter until prayer time ends.

Fasting during the month of Ramadan is a second religious duty. Believers do not eat, drink, smoke tobacco, or have sexual intercourse during daylight hours. In Saudi Arabia, as in other Muslim countries, daily routines adjust to the rigors of fasting and a heightened mood of piety. Ramadan is a time of more intensive socializing among relatives and friends, invitations to meals, late-night gatherings, and a tardy start for the work day. The end of the month is marked by the Feast of Breaking the Fast, Id al-Fitr, one of only two holidays celebrated throughout the Muslim world that Wahhabi clerics also recognize as sacred. Over three days, family members exchange gifts and hold large banquets. As on Thanksgiving holiday in the United States, transplants to the major cities will return to their hometowns and villages to celebrate with relatives.

Religion and Family Life

The emergence of a modern urban economy transformed all facets of life. Today, half the population live in three primary urban zones: Jeddah, Riyadh, and Khobar–Dhahran–Dammam. The shift from rural to urban setting was remarkably rapid, creating a country where people over 50 vividly remember life in closely nestled mud-brick homes in villages and towns where members of extended families lived near one another. For women residing in cities and towns today, modern amenities make life easier and more comfortable, but restrictions on movement outside the home leave many of them with little to do but watch television and wait for male relatives to come home from work to take them on errands. Family often defines the physical and social boundaries of their lives.

Indeed, the family has long been and remains the core of Saudi society. The deeply ingrained sense of responsibility toward one's kin buffers the unfortunate from the worst life can dish out. Driving is dangerous due to the reckless habits of young men (and to lax enforcement of traffic laws) and fatal accidents leave families devastated by the loss of loved ones. Survivors of serious wrecks may suffer permanent debilitating injuries, but thanks to family ties, they enjoy strong support from an extensive kinship network. On the other hand, family obligations limit individual choice in ways that Westerners would find suffocating. Decisions about education, marriage, and work are hammered out in consultation with parents and elders. The upside is that one has broad support when the going gets tough, be it in work or marriage. The downside is that collective decisions may feel like meddling in one's life.

Until recent times, Wahhabi clerics and Saudi custom viewed men as responsible for the welfare of women, a role that not only gave men the duty to provide basic needs such as shelter and food, but also the authority to decide when women could leave the home, and whether they could attend university, and work outside the home. Young married couples today lead lives very different from their parents' and grandparents', in part because attitudes about gender roles have changed. While women still need a guardian's permission to travel abroad, education is now regarded as a right for all Saudis. A university degree bestows status in both liberal and conservative families, which helps explain why the rate of female attendance and graduation surpasses that of males and why young women increasingly enter professional careers. There do remain ultra-conservative families that limit schooling for daughters and arrange marriage for them at a young age with little regard for their wishes. An extreme expression of male authority occurs when fathers withhold permission for daughters to marry, even though doing so violates Islamic law. Few women seek the only legal remedy – suing in court to strip the father of guardianship – because of pressure from family members. Moreover, religious courts have confounded some women by ordering them to be punished for disobeying their fathers.[1]

Not all women consider male guardianship oppressive. In response to calls for expanding women's rights, conservative women launched a counter-movement affirming the authority of male guardians. They argue that very few Saudi men abuse their authority, and that when properly exercised, it is a sign of affection and respect for the well-being of daughters and wives. Defenders of male guardianship face a multipronged reform movement that seeks to ban child marriage and to grant women the right to set up businesses without their guardian's permission.[2]

Marriage marks the passage from one's birth home to the conjugal unit; it establishes a legal relationship between husband and wife; it creates a bond between the families of the spouses; and it opens the way for a new generation of sons and daughters. In traditional culture, marriage established a relationship between two families, not just the two spouses. Consequently, the compatibility of the families was as important as how well husbands and wives got along. Men discussed potential matches and consulted with female relatives. If the families agreed on the suitability of a match and on the dowry, the groom and one of the bride's male relatives would get the approval of a religious figure, primarily as a formality, before proceeding to the wedding. Even with the care taken to determine the compatibility of the families, divorce was common, reportedly most often due to strife between a wife and her mother-in-law. A divorced woman might return to her parents; among the nomadic Bedouin, she might set up her own tent if she had children.

In urban Saudi society, the interests of families continue to weigh heavily in the selection of a mate, but the pressures of a capitalist economy on families and the new scope for interaction between genders have made arranged marriages based on reputation less common. Gender segregation makes it difficult, but not impossible, for young Saudi men and women to become acquainted with the opposite sex. As such opportunities increase, young people normally try to keep their love interest secret until they decide to seek family approval for their marriage.[3] Since there is no consensus on rules for courtship outside of family supervision, how a love match gets to marriage varies quite a bit, but may take a route to the male guardian through sympathetic female relations. It remains more common for parents, uncles, aunts, and sisters to take the lead in finding a mate, enquiring about eligible singles, and about their families' reputations, but also their character, education, income, military rank, and professional prospects. Ordinarily, someone from the groom's family contacts a girl's parents to see if they would approve of the match. The girl's family then discusses the matter and if all are agreed, including the girl, they let the groom's family know. According to Islamic law, the groom and the bride must give their consent in order to proceed with a marriage. Families sometimes lean hard on daughters and sons to comply with their wishes, putting them in a position of entering a forced arranged marriage. A woman may not marry a man without the approval of her male guardian, so if she does somehow find a man she wants to marry, the outcome depends on her guardian's goodwill.

When two families agree on a match, they negotiate the dowry, a payment from the groom's family to the bride that is often divided into two installments, one paid up front and one deferred until the husband either dies or divorces the wife. Until recently, the dowry consisted of jewelry and gold; now it is commonly a cash payment. The cost of a dowry has gone up considerably, making it unaffordable for many young men. It has become common to postpone marriage until one has saved enough for a dowry and wedding celebration; the government sometimes holds collective weddings for over a hundred couples in order to overcome the financial obstacles.[4] Once the families give their blessing to a couple, the period for getting better acquainted may last from a few months to a year, depending on the couple's readiness for setting up a new household. During that interval, the prospective couple may speak on the phone or exchange e-mail and text messages. Conservative families prefer to limit contact to supervised visits. The final step is to draw up the terms of a marriage contract that is signed by the fathers before male witnesses and a religious official.[5]

Marriage age depends on factors such as whether a family lives in a major city (where marriage age tends to be older) or a small town (where marriage age is younger), and whether a girl attends university (older) or not (younger). Men tend to wait longer to get married in order to become established. There is no legal minimum age for marriage, and some families arrange for very young girls to get married. In 2009, the Saudi press covered the case of an eight-year-old bride and her 40-something husband. Apparently, the girl's father owed the groom money and they agreed to the match in exchange for dismissing the debt. When the mother learned of the deal, she objected and requested that a court declare the marriage contract void on grounds that the girl was too young to give her consent, but the judge upheld the contract, stipulating that the girl could petition for divorce when she turned 18. In similar cases, such young brides are not expected to have sexual relations with their husbands before puberty.[6]

Saudi reformers have had modest success in a campaign to eliminate child marriage. The kingdom's Human Rights Commission has turned the practice into a matter of public debate by directing the attention of the media to cases, and in one instance it managed to get the families of an 11-year-old girl and her 40-year-old groom to void the marriage contract. Wahhabi clerics are divided on the issue, with some favoring a minimum age while others maintain that the practice plays a positive role in shielding girls from premarital sex. Some clerics point to the example of the Prophet Muhammad, who wed an eight-year-old, but others argue that circumstances have changed so much that the practice is no longer justified. Whether the Saudi government will set a minimum age for marriage is an open question because it does not want to provoke a conservative backlash.[7]

Ordinarily, courtship culminates with a wedding party. Actually, there are two wedding parties, because rules of gender segregation apply. Weddings are a facet of life where regional customs persist. Thus, in Riyadh, the groom's party is a polite and sober affair held at a reception hall. As the guests arrive, they congratulate the groom and his male relatives, and then seat themselves on chairs lining the hall, engage in conversation, and sip coffee. After a while, the guests are invited to supper in the next room, where platters of lamb, rice, and vegetables await them on mats spread on the carpet. Once the meal is over, the guests wash up and return to the sitting room for more conversation and cups of tea. At no point is there music or dance. After a decent interval, the guests take their leave. The only hint a Westerner would get that this was a wedding celebration would be the echoes of music blaring through the walls from the bride's party. In Jeddah, on the other hand, men perform a traditional dance, twirling swords and canes, and chanting verse.

In 2011, a group of women in Jeddah created a Facebook page to call on the government to encourage polygamy as a way to alleviate financial pressures on divorcees and widows. The story may seem odd to the Western reader, but it makes sense when viewed in a context where polygamy is legal, even if it is not the typical arrangement; divorce is an easy option for husbands, and widows frequently endure poverty and loneliness. At the same time, the prospect of sharing one's husband with one to three additional wives is seldom an occasion for the first wife to celebrate. According to anecdotal accounts, husbands are quite aware that their wives do not welcome an additional wife and try to placate first wives with gifts.[8] Few women would choose to become a second wife, but often do so under family pressure or to alleviate financial distress.

Under Islamic law, a man may have up to four wives and he is obliged to divide his time and means equally between them, but the habits of polygamous husbands often diverge from that ideal. Even when a man meets it, the wives and their children see their husbands and fathers less frequently than in a monogamous household. Husbands may treat their wives differently for various reasons. Sometimes, the first wife belongs to the same extended family, so the husband prefers her and spends most of his time with her children in order to placate his relatives. In the meantime, the second wife and her children endure neglect as well as enmity from the first wife and her children.

The prospect of a woman's husband taking another wife adds to men's already considerable power over women and constitutes a source of worry for many women.[9] If a woman finds the situation intolerable, she may not cite polygamy as a cause for divorce unless her marriage contract stipulated it. If a woman has children and gets a divorce, the husband gains custody of the children once they are above a very young age. The usual advice to such unhappy women is to pray, try to win their husbands' affections, and if that does not work, then learn to live with it.[10]

Some Muslim countries have passed legislation stipulating that a man may take an additional wife only with the consent of his current wife. Reformers are seeking a similar provision in Saudi Arabia, but defenders of polygamy justify it on several grounds. First, in religious terms, it is allowed in the Quran and the Prophet Muhammad had multiple wives after the death of his first wife Khadija. Critics reply that polygamy in the early Muslim community provided a way to cope with the hardships borne by widows of men slain in war. A second defense is that, as a practical matter, divorced women may see becoming a second wife as the only way to remarry. Third, becoming a second wife may be the only marriage prospect for older single women who want children. Most Saudis admit, however, that jealousy usually mars relationships between wives and their children. Fourth, defenders point out that in Western societies, husbands frequently cheat on their wives, making a travesty of monogamy, so legal polygamy has the virtue of dispensing with hypocrisy.[11]

Whether Saudis are in monogamous or polygamous marriages, the primary purpose of marriage is to have children. A large family is considered a blessing; nevertheless, fertility rates in Saudi Arabia roughly track with trends in other countries that have undergone rapid urbanization, with a gap opening between smaller urban families and larger rural ones. Limiting family size through birth control, however, is frowned upon by the Wahhabi establishment. In 1994, the United Nations convened the International Conference on Population and Development in Cairo to discuss ways to slow the rate of global population growth. Conference planners were prepared to recommend the adoption of a program that endorsed family planning, reproductive rights for women, and broader steps to empower women. On the eve of the conference, the Council of Senior Ulama called for a boycott, leading both Saudi Arabia and Sudan to pull out at the last minute while the prime ministers of Turkey and Bangladesh, both of them women, decided not to attend and sent lower-level officials in their stead. The kingdom's religious authorities had previously pronounced birth control to be contrary to God's purpose in creating humans, except when a woman's health is in jeopardy or when both spouses agree to delay having children if it is in the interest of the family's general welfare. In such instances, contraception is permitted to prevent pregnancy, and abortion is allowed during the first seven weeks of pregnancy.[12]

While some Saudi couples wrestle with the question of limiting offspring, others seek ways to cope with infertility. The matter is especially compelling for wives since religious and cultural norms place so much emphasis on motherhood as the highest calling for women. Before recent advances in fertility treatment, the husband in a barren couple would often seek to satisfy his desire for children by taking a new wife, supposing that he was not the infertile partner. At times, a man would divorce his first wife, depending on his capacity to provide for multiple wives. Because modern treatments such as in vitro fertilization promise to fulfill what religious authorities consider a woman's natural role, they allow such treatments, which are available at major hospitals and specialized clinics. King Saud University in Riyadh has a special section in its medical school for the study of infertility.

The public face of many urban residential neighborhoods is a long stretch of blank high walls pierced by metal gates and doors that open to driveways and courtyards. Long, blazing summers make it impossible to add much green to soften the appearance of side streets. The effect is to highlight the anonymity of streets and the privacy of the homes behind their walls. Behind the street door is a courtyard, the first layer of privacy between public and family space. The main entrance often opens to a high-ceilinged foyer, with a large sitting room to one side for male visitors. Such rooms are furnished with chairs, sofas, side tables, and a large serving table. The rest of the house is the family's private living area (roughly, the meaning of 'harem'): kitchen, dining room, living room, bedrooms, and bathrooms. Naturally, the size of homes varies according to a family's means, but the division between a public reception area and a private area is maintained to balance the values of hospitality and honor. Since there are few places outside the home where families can go together, they spend most of their time at home. Household members typically consist of the nuclear family. As in other Arab countries, the custom is for children to live with parents until they marry and set up their own households.

Men come and go as they wish, but the movement of women and girls in and out of the home depends on the individual family. Most girls attend school, and many young women go to university, but only a very small percentage of adult women, around 15 percent, work outside the home, in spite of government steps to promote female employment in recent years.[13] This means that the prospect of spending time outside the home shrinks when a woman marries and has children. In the traditional view, it is by devoting herself to her husband and children that a woman fulfills her role, sanctified by religion and in accord with her nature. In conservative families, women seeking to earn money or to find ways to occupy their time should learn to embroider or weave, crafts long practiced by Arabian women and entirely feasible to pursue at home. In the past, women sold crafts in special women's sections of city markets. Nowadays, they can set up businesses online through the internet, as virtual interaction with men is not a violation of the gender-mixing taboo. In the absence of children or work, though, sitting around at home all day can feel more like confinement than enjoyment of the honor afforded by male protection. Evenings and weekends provide occasions for social interaction, normally with members of one's extended family, often gathered around the television set in the living room.

Religion, Custom, and Gender Rules

Saudi Arabia is notable for its rigorous enforcement of gender segregation. Boys and girls are not to mix in schools and universities; men and women are not to mix at the workplace. Anything that might result in gender mixing is suspect, if not prohibited, according to the principle in Islamic law that Wahhabis frequently invoke which calls for 'blocking means to a prohibited end'. The religious police are responsible for upholding gender segregation, appreciated by some for ensuring the safety of female relatives from unwanted male attention and despised by others for meddling. A number of exceptions to segregation are made, notably in hospital clinics and medical schools.

There are different explanations, not entirely related to religion, for the kingdom's distinctive regime of gender segregation. One view suggests that strict segregation was a response to forces of economic and social modernization. When royal pressure for girls' education met religious objections, the compromise was to set up separate schools. The spread of modern workplaces (businesses, hospitals, media companies, banks) resulted in the creation of multiple gender-segregated spaces.[14] Another explanation maintains that it was customary among Najdi villagers, townsmen, and nomads for centuries. It is true that the Bedouin normally shielded women from male strangers, but the context and the effects were quite different in the desert milieu. In the predatory desert world of nomadic tribes, there was no authority or power superior to the household, a more or less extensive family unit often designated as a 'tent'. If a household came under attack, it could not go to the police because there were no police. The Bedouin man was expected to protect female relatives. Women did not owe men obedience or submission in return for protection, but they were expected to keep to their side of the tent in order to maintain the symbolic separation between the perilous public world of men where violence might erupt and the secure private world of women that was safe under the Bedouin honor code. In practical terms, the separation between male and female sides of the tent consisted of a woven partition, a marker more than a barrier and certainly not a wall shutting women inside.

Moreover, Bedouin women did their share of the work outside the home, or the tent. The tents themselves were woven by women from goat hair and were considered women's property. They were responsible for setting up and taking down the tent when the household migrated. Bedouin women restricted direct interactions with men to relatives, but the set of permitted relatives was more extensive than under Wahhabi doctrine. By comparison to women in villages and towns, Bedouin women had more freedom to move about to do daily chores and to accompany men to urban markets. It was acceptable for widowed and divorced women with children to maintain a household without a man.[15]

The cultural explanation for today's gender segregation sees it as the persistence of custom in circumstances where the underlying rationale no longer applies. The majority of Saudis live in large cities in either flats or houses; tribes are no longer responsible for the security of their members. In arguments over gender segregation today, its defenders reaffirm the traditional idea that the public world is dangerous and that male strangers are a threat to female family members. From a Western perspective, the implication is that men do not feel bound to respect women outside their own family, and that women who venture into the public, presumably male, world, are 'asking for it'. A problem with the cultural explanation is that the effects of gender segregation are very different between the world of small oasis settlements or Bedouin tents in the desert compared to the world of a crowded city. In the desert, women's daily life included plenty of time 'outside the tent' because the neighbors were part of the same extended family. The definition of a woman's kin was also different then. It was normal for a woman to interact with a more extensive set of male relatives than Wahhabi doctrine permits. Even today, Bedouin women abide by a set of norms that their urban sisters do not share: they tend sheep, they drive vehicles, and they interact with a wider range of men.[16] The longing expressed by some women for the greater freedom of the Bedouin is not just a nostalgic ideal. On the other hand, few urban women would return to the hard work and austere material conditions of the desert.

A third explanation for gender segregation relates to the Wahhabi interpretation of Quranic verses that have bearing on modesty and interaction between genders according to degree of kinship.[17]

And say to the believing women, that they cast down their eyes and guard their private parts, and reveal not their adornment save such as is outward; and let them cast their veils over their bosoms, and not reveal their adornment save to their husbands, or their fathers, or their husbands' fathers, or their sons, or their husbands' sons, or their brothers, or their brothers' sons, or their sisters' sons, or their women, or what their right hands own [slaves], or such men as attend them, not having sexual desire, or children who have not yet attained knowledge of women's private parts; nor let them stamp their feet, so that their hidden ornaments may be known. And turn all together to God, O you believers; haply so you will prosper.[18]

In addition to close male relatives, women may freely mingle with elderly men, young children, and slaves. The relationships allowed in this verse are referred to as *mahram*. It may help to think of a woman's mahram as close family members with whom she may freely interact and before whom she is not required to veil. Another Quranic verse (4:23) enumerates the degrees of kinship within which marriage is not allowed: father, son, brother, uncles, father-in-law, step-son, and nephew. In Muslim societies where gender mixing is a matter of custom, the pious may scrupulously observe mahram rules, but most Muslims consider it a matter of individual preference rather than government enforcement.

While there is no disagreement on the definition of mahram, Wahhabi jurists depart from other Muslim opinion when they specify where unrelated men and women may meet. Essentially, they expand the scope of what is understood as *khalwa*, or a private meeting with a stranger, beyond enclosed spaces. As an official fatwa proclaimed: 'Khalwa [. . .] can be manifested as chatting between the sexes with no one hearing their conversation, even when they are seen in public [. . .] Khalwa is forbidden because it constitutes a means to fornication, thus, any such contact is liable to lead to this forbidden end.'[19]

In practice, defining and maintaining strict gender segregation in a consistent way turns out to be a complicated matter.[20] Take the commonplace pastime of going out to eat. Restaurants are divided into sections for men and families. Diners in the men's section are visible to one another and may be seen from the street. Families, however, gather at tables shrouded from view, either by a curtain, partition, or wall. The waiter (there are no waitresses) announces to family diners that he is about to enter their space with a knock, a cough, or a word to give women time to cover their faces. Although family sections are not intended for women unaccompanied by a male guardian, groups of friends sometimes meet in restaurants.[21] Many Saudis like to dine in food courts at shopping malls and here the rules for gender mixing are routinely breached. Like a restaurant, a food court is divided into men-only and family sections. The family section, however, is not partitioned. Rather, it is an open space where tables are arranged as they would be in other countries. And, as in other countries, the food court is a lively, noisy space. Some women are careful to keep their faces covered as their children gobble down pizza slices and hamburgers, others face the wall to eat inconspicuously, and some eat unveiled, dispensing with the rules for modesty.

One of the most visible signs of Wahhabi influence is the universal dress code, observed by women garbed in black from head to toe and wearing a face veil. The rules for modest dress are embedded in two Quranic verses, the first one already cited in defining mahram relations: 'And say to the believing women, that they cast down their eyes and guard their private parts, and reveal not their adornment, save such as is outward; and let them cast their veils over their bosoms, and not reveal their adornment.' The second: 'O Prophet, say to thy wives and daughters and the believing women, that they draw their veils close to them; so it is likelier they will be known, and not hurt. God is All-forgiving, All-compassionate.'[22]

In the Wahhabi view, the verses mean that women must cover their entire bodies and allow only their eyes to show, even though Muslim scholars interpret them in different ways and argue that covering hair, arms, and legs suffices to comply with the Quran. Wahhabi clerics maintain that the Arabic word translated as veil, *jilbab*, means a cloak that is thick, loose, and plain.[23] In recent decades, the official dress code for women, a black abaya and *niqab* (face veil), became a sort of national uniform that displaced regional diversity in women's clothing. When women enter an all-female space, such as the women's university campus, they may shed the abaya, beneath which they wear long skirts and long-sleeved blouses. Within the confines of the dress code, women manage

4. Caution sign at a mall in Riyadh

to express individual taste and flair by donning abayas and niqabs with beaded trim, designer initials (YSL), or satin piping. Young women sometimes wear a large hair piece under their niqabs for a bit of flair. Fashionable sunglasses and handbags offer additional ways to break the monotony of basic black. In upscale malls of large cities and the relatively liberal social climate of Jeddah, young Saudi women have begun to go without their face veils, but still cover their hair and wear the abaya.

Leisure

Watching television is such a common pastime in Saudi homes that few young people can imagine that it was ever a point of controversy, but when television was introduced in 1965, it sparked violent protest because conservatives believed that it would undermine religion and corrupt morality. When the Riyadh television station began broadcasting, a crowd of protestors tried to storm it. Police fire on the demonstrators killed a nephew of King Faisal. (Ten years later the nephew's brother avenged his death by assassinating King Faisal.) To placate Wahhabi religious leaders, the king promised them a role in determining television content, which is primarily religious and news programs. Years later, Grand Mufti Abdulaziz ibn Baz issued a detailed fatwa on the permissibility of watching television.[24] The fatwa had to find a way around the Prophetic Tradition that bans the creation of human likenesses, the same ban that was formerly applied to photography. Ibn Baz argued that if television were used to support a religious purpose, such as spreading Islam, then it would be permitted. Until the arrival of satellite television in the 1990s, the Ministry of Culture and Information determined what Saudis could watch, ensuring a bland diet of news and religious programs.

Today a government television company, Saudi TV, has about a dozen channels that offer news, sports, and religious programs. With satellite television, Saudis have access to entertainment programs, movies, and alternate news sources such as Qatar's al-Jazeera network, which began broadcasting in 1996. At first, the religious authorities condemned the satellite dish because it could beam forbidden images of romance and sex into Saudi living rooms, but they could not block access to multiple television stations. For a while, the religious police did their best to implement the ban and harassed families whose dishes were visible from the street. But Saudis quickly figured that all they had to do to elude detection was place the dish at ground level behind the high walls surrounding their homes. When religious police clambered up a wall for a peek inside a courtyard to see if there was a dish, they were guilty of illegal search according to a well-established principle of Islamic law. A verse in the Quran forbids snooping.[25] Nowadays satellite television is commonplace in Saudi homes and even the religious camp uses satellite to broadcast news programs, recitation of the Quran, and children's shows that adhere to Wahhabi rules, including the prohibition on music. Saudi parents can block access to satellite stations that they find objectionable, just as American parents can set up controls on their televisions to limit their children's access to shows with sexual content or violence.

Some of the major Arabic satellite television stations based in London are owned by Saudis, such as Middle East Broadcasting Corporation (MBC), owned by King Fahd's brother-in-law; Rotana, owned by Prince al-Waleed bin Talal; and al-Arabiyya. While their location outside the kingdom frees them from government restrictions, they have not escaped the censure of Wahhabi authorities for broadcasting popular Arab and American movies. In 2008, the head of the judiciary, Sheikh Salih Luhaidan, proclaimed on a radio call-in show that owners of television stations that broadcast immoral movies should be killed for spreading sedition and corrupting morals. When fellow clerics admonished him, he qualified his remarks by saying that punishment would depend on the outcome of a judicial process.[26]

The internet arrived in the kingdom in 1999. The government prepared for its introduction in two ways. First, it fostered a debate in the Saudi press over the advantages and disadvantages of the internet, with conservatives warning against the threat it could pose by spreading Western ideas and values that would undermine Islamic ones, while liberals asserted that the country could not afford to be left behind. Second, the government set up a special bureau, the Internet Services Unit, to monitor internet traffic, tasking it with blocking access to pornography and gambling sites as well as sites associated with political dissidents living in exile.[27] The government filters and monitors the internet and has adopted regulations that prohibit attacks on the royal family and Islam as well as incitement to violence. In March 2007, a special commission appointed to protect Saudis from harmful websites identified 400,000 such sites to block.[28] After bending to accommodate television, it was not a stretch for the Wahhabi jurists to find the internet acceptable under similar conditions. If the government could censor the internet and promote the dissemination of religious messages, then the benefit it would bring would outweigh the harm.[29] Thus, Saudi religious institutions and personalities overcame their usual initial resistance to new things and seized on the internet as a platform for publishing classic and contemporary Islamic treatises, advice columns, and fatwas. While many people added the internet to the ways they find religious guidance, others turned to it for amusement. The number of users grew rapidly, from a few hundred thousand at the beginning of the decade to ten million in 2010. Young people in particular embraced it to expand the scope of leisure and entertainment, so that in the early years of the internet, online games and chat rooms became popular ways to pass the time, and when Facebook and Twitter emerged they rapidly drew Saudi users.[30]

Public musical entertainment is absent in Saudi Arabia but the internet harbors a world of popular music and music videos that Saudi youth avidly download in spite of the official Wahhabi prohibition on music. Clerics find warrant for banning it in a Quranic verse that condemns 'idle tales' and a Prophetic Tradition that places musical performance alongside adultery in a list of sins. A fatwa issued by the Council of Senior Ulama justified the ban by arguing that songs stimulate sexual passions and therefore threaten to undermine morality. From that fundamental position, other fatwas prohibit trading in musical instruments and giving music lessons. The only exception is the chanting of the Quran, a highly developed art that is popular throughout the Muslim world. Pious Saudis play recordings of renowned chanters on tapes and compact discs in their cars. Quran recitation is a staple of state radio and television stations, which frequently broadcast competitions among 'star' chanters, both Saudi and foreign.

Were Saudis to rigidly obey the Wahhabi religious authorities and order their lives according to fatwas, they would not listen to music. But they do. Notwithstanding edicts condemning music – including ring tones on cell phones – the kingdom has had a national anthem since 1950. Saudi families enjoy satellite television broadcasts of entertainment programs featuring famous Arab singers and game shows staging musical talent contests. Recordings of Arab and Western pop artists are widely available. Even small shops attached to petrol stations in remote parts of the kingdom stock compact discs by Madonna and Snoop Dogg. Like their Western counterparts, young Saudis download their favorite songs to iPods. In recent years, a Saudi music scene has emerged, at times out of the public ear through private performances, at other times through the internet's YouTube channel. In 2009, a young prince stirred a minor royal scandal with a music video, 'Never Too Late', even though the song's lyrics affirm the Islamic taboo on suicide and urge listeners to turn to God for strength and forgiveness.

Recent electronic inventions have opened new windows on the world for Saudi homebodies, while options for diversion outside the home remain limited. For a Saudi who grew up in Jeddah, Riyadh, or Dhahran during the 1960s, the cities they inhabit today are unrecognizable as they have transformed from compact towns into sprawling cities covering dozens of square miles of formerly empty desert lands. The extensive character of Saudi cities stems from the absence of planning and lack of oversight of real estate development. In a single generation Saudis have gone from roaming the desert or residing in small towns and villages, where everything was accessible on foot or by donkey, to large cities where you cannot get anywhere without a car. Since only men may drive, unless the family can afford a full-time driver, wives and daughters wait for husbands to get home from work to get out of the house.

When Saudis go out, their destinations are limited. Back in the 1970s, Saudi Arabia had some movie theaters but that ended after the 1979 Mecca Uprising. As part of the government's measures to appease conservative opinion, Jeddah's four movie houses were shut down. To this day, there are no public cinemas, satisfying the Wahhabi prohibition that condemns them as sources of temptation because films frequently contain what clerics regard as obscene images. The clerics do approve of educational films on television. In the last few years, there has emerged an underground cinematic culture with occasional clandestine showings of Saudi-produced films on sensitive topics such as migrant workers and the roles of women.[31] In 2008, the governor of the Jeddah region, a prominent Saudi prince, gave his backing to a one-week run of a comedy (produced by a company owned by a different Saudi prince) that drew crowds to gender-segregated venues in Ta'if and Jeddah.[32] Unlike satellite television and the internet, cinemas are public spaces and therefore resistance to their opening may have greater staying power than resistance to loosening restrictions on what Saudis do behind the tall walls of their homes.

For everyday diversion the most popular destinations are shopping malls and restaurants. Shopping malls are emblems of material consumption and the one public space where men and women can meander for hours from shop to shop in the comfort of air-conditioning. Riyadh's landmark Kingdom Tower has a women-only floor where shoppers can doff their face veils. In other malls, the presence of unrelated men means that women remain completely covered, although adventurous young women test the limits by showing their faces at upscale malls that draw an affluent crowd. For families with children, some malls have playgrounds with rides, swings, and plastic climbing apparatus. If the home can sometimes feel claustrophobic, the high ceilings of multistory shopping centers, roomy food courts, and play areas offer a safe place for Saudis to repair.

Visitors often comment on the shopping malls, perhaps because they are something familiar in a country where so much seems strange, but there are also outdoor urban spaces where families pass the time. Jeddah has a seaside corniche dotted with cafés, playgrounds, and stores. A gigantic Ferris wheel similar to the London Eye will soon be the main attraction. In Riyadh, a large courtyard known as Deera Square stretches behind the Ministry of

Justice to the old Mismak Palace, now a museum. To foreigners, the place is known as Chop Chop Square because beheadings were carried out there until recent years. In mild weather, on Thursday evenings (the beginning of the Saudi weekend), the square is a busy place where families eat snacks and chat while children play football (soccer). On weekends during the cool months, families drive to the desert for picnics and go to city parks such as Riyadh's al-Yamama Park, which has children's playgrounds, paths shaded by large palm trees, and patches of grass for picnicking.[33]

A foreign visitor in his hotel room flipping through the television channels will often find two or three stations broadcasting football matches. Saudi stations dedicated to sports show Saudi, Arab, and European football matches. The prevalence of football on television is natural because it is highly popular in the kingdom. The national team is the three-time Asia Cup champion and has qualified for the World Cup four times. The Saudi Professional League has 12 teams that compete in two tournaments, the spring Champions' Cup and the fall Crown Prince Cup. Stadiums in Riyadh, Jeddah, Mecca, and other towns hold from 7,000 to nearly 70,000 spectators. Saudi

5. A family out for a stroll in Deera Square in Riyadh

Arabia also fields national teams in tennis, basketball, cricket, and handball. The attitude of the religious authorities toward sports has been spelled out in an official fatwa that endorses activities such as archery and horse racing because they complement the obligation to prepare young men for jihad by honing fighting skills. When it comes to modern sports, they do not come under the ban on innovations or imitating infidels as long as there is no element of gambling such as monetary prizes, and as long as they do not result in the players neglecting religious duties.

Sports for girls and women are another matter because Wahhabi clerics object to them. Public schools for girls do not have physical education classes. Girls and women may not use hotel swimming pools or swim at beaches.[34] All-women fitness clubs were banned in the 1990s, but have reappeared and may operate if they can demonstrate affiliation with a hospital.[35] When conservatives succeeded in getting some women's gyms closed down in 2009, women countered with the slogan, 'Let her get fat.' The clerics insist that participating in sports would detract from a woman's duties in the home and they object to the notion of women appearing in athletic wear. They have also asserted that running and jumping may cause a girl's hymen to tear, thereby hurting her marriage prospects since she would not be deemed a virgin. On the other side of the argument, liberals point to the harmful effects of inactivity on women's health evident in rising rates of obesity, diabetes, and osteoporosis. As in other realms of daily life, some Saudis just ignore the clerics. In Jeddah, women play basketball on a dozen or so teams, eschewing shorts for long pants when they take the court.[36] Volleyball and football teams for girls have sprouted up, part of the cultural struggle to loosen the grip of Wahhabi edicts. In 2010, a Saudi teen broke a gender barrier by going to the Youth Olympic Games in Singapore, where she won the bronze medal at an equestrian event.[37] Notably, she was not part of the official Saudi team but entered as an unaffiliated athlete.

As in other spheres of tension between conservatives and liberals, gaining royal allies for female participation in sports is essential. In 2009, the governor of Mecca, a son of former King Faisal, endorsed physical education in girls' schools as long as it upheld gender segregation. And one of King Abdullah's daughters has spoken out about the need for women and girls to exercise in order to reduce obesity.[38] The controversy is not solely a domestic issue. Until 2012, Saudi Arabia was one of three countries (along with Brunei and Qatar) that barred women from the Olympic Games. International women's rights groups urged the International Olympics Committee to lean on the Saudis to allow women athletes to join the national team for the 2012 Olympic Games, wielding the threat of banning the men's team if the kingdom continued to bar women. As a result, the Saudi delegation to London included two women, in judo and track and field (Qatar and Brunei also sent female athletes to the Olympics).

Travel outside the kingdom is a common option for Saudis seeking greater latitude for diversion. The 1970s oil boom provided large numbers with the means to visit other Arab countries (Egypt, Lebanon, and Syria were the most popular destinations), Europe, and the United States. After the construction of the causeway connecting the Eastern Province to Bahrain in 1986, the island neighbor became a popular weekend destination for its more permissive climate that allows cinemas and night clubs, but since the violent crackdown on pro-democracy demonstrations in Bahrain in March 2011, Dubai has become a more attractive nearby destination. As much as three-quarters of the Saudi population travel outside the kingdom each year. Egypt, Jordan, Lebanon, and Syria (before the anti-government revolt) have been the most common destinations.[39] In recent years, Malaysia and Indonesia have emerged as popular tourist spots for their lush, green landscapes, medical facilities, and Muslim culture.[40]

5 Islam in Contemporary Saudi Society

On the morning of 11 March 2002, a girl waiting for classes to begin at Intermediate School No. 31 in Mecca was smoking a cigarette in the hallway. When she noticed a school employee looking at her, she carelessly threw the cigarette on a pile of papers and made for class. Less than half an hour later, a fire had ignited, putting the lives of the school's 835 pupils in jeopardy.[1] The walls along the street designed to screen the girls from public view trapped them on school grounds. When they rushed to one of the gates, the religious police blocked their exit because, in their haste to escape the deadly blaze, they had not donned their abayas and niqabs. Civil defense personnel at the scene argued with religious police to allow the girls out, but they staunchly refused. Instead, they forced the 'undressed' girls back into the school, fought with civil defense workers, and blocked frantic parents trying to help the girls. By the time the regular police dispersed the religious police, 15 girls had perished in the panicky crush to escape. The tragedy triggered outrage in the Saudi press, which targeted not only the religious police but also the General Presidency for Girls' Education for failure to practice basic fire safety measures such as having fire extinguishers at hand.[2] A government investigation resulted in the abolition of the General Presidency and the transfer of responsibility for girls' education to the Ministry of Education. The investigation absolved the religious police of blame, probably at the insistence of its royal sponsor, the powerful Interior Minister Prince Nayef. Instead, the investigation found the General Presidency guilty of neglecting warnings from the principal that the school's crowded conditions posed a danger.[3]

Fifty years from now, the first decade of the twenty-first century may look like a turning point for Saudi Arabia. In 2011, it seemed as if Saudi society was moving step by step in a liberal (by Saudi standards) direction: women were pushing the limits on gender mixing and access to employment; Shiites were making headway in their struggle for religious freedom and social equality; and Sufis were coming out of hiding. Such broad changes meant a shift away from the country's heritage of Wahhabi domination, unless the religious establishment could find a way to exhibit flexibility while remaining true to its core doctrine. The 9/11 attacks on the United States had sparked a mood of introspection, even though many Saudis rejected the idea that Wahhabi schools and mosques sowed the seeds of terrorism. Interior Minister Prince Nayif declared it part of a Zionist conspiracy designed to make Muslims look bad. The Mecca girls' school fire six months later reinforced the growing feeling that the country was too beholden to Wahhabi clerics. Al-Qaeda in the Arabian Peninsula's (QAP) bloody four-year jihad against infidels – Western expatriates in the kingdom – and Saudi security forces strengthened the hand of men and women advocating liberal reforms.

Royal Support for Reform

King Abdullah favors reform at a gradual pace that stretches the patience of liberal activists. Starting in the mid 1990s when he was crown prince, Abdullah fostered a lively public conversation on social and religious issues to pave the way for incremental reform. The appearance of a new newspaper, *al-Watan* (the Nation), in May 1998 was a harbinger of robust exploration of taboo subjects. Like other Saudi newspapers, *al-Watan* had royal sponsorship, in this instance, from Prince Khalid al-Faisal. Unlike other newspapers, *al-Watan* broached sensitive social and religious issues. The arrival of the internet the next year heralded a proliferation of platforms for presenting and debating different opinions in chat rooms and forums.[4] Intellectuals and activists began to hold salons that were incubators for ideas that showed up in newspaper columns. At the same time, Crown Prince Abdullah's quiet support for freer expression had tacit limits recognized by journalists and intellectuals: social criticism was fine but the royal family was off limits.

The reform cause got a new push in January 2003, when a group of about one hundred intellectuals, writers, and businessmen sent the crown prince a petition called 'Vision for the Present and the Future of the Homeland'. The document framed its recommendations in religious terms, principally the concept of consultation (*shura*) as the foundation for relations between the people and the government. Its agenda included changing the Consultative Council from an appointed to an elected body, ensuring free speech and association, reforming the judiciary, and establishing a national committee for human rights.[5] Crown Prince Abdullah signaled his support for the spirit of reform by meeting some of the men behind the petition, but did not indicate that he would implement measures that would move the kingdom down the road to constitutional government with checks on royal power. Rather than institute changes in the kingdom's political system, he called for 'national dialogue' to foster a more tolerant and moderate social climate.

National Dialogue

The first national dialogue on the theme of 'Reinforcing National Unity' brought together leaders of the kingdom's different Muslim tendencies: Wahhabis, Twelver and Ismaili Shiites, Sufis, and non-Wahhabi Sunnis (Malikis from the Eastern Province and Shafiis from Hijaz). While plans for the experiment in intra-faith dialogue were moving forward, the United States' invasion of Iraq exacerbated sectarian tensions in the Gulf, and al-Qaeda terrorists struck the Saudi capital. The need for religious toleration was more compelling than ever. In June 2003, the first national dialogue session convened for three days in Riyadh. Public recognition of Shiites and Sufis as fellow Muslims alongside Wahhabis was an important step. In fact, it was too big a step for the prominent Sahwa Sheikh Safar al-Hawali, who could not bring himself to accept the invitation to mingle with men he considered infidels.[6] On the other hand, Sheikh Salman al-Awda, another Sahwa leader, not only attended but engaged directly with Shiite leader Sheikh Hasan al-Saffar. In symbolic terms, the session ruptured the two-hundred-year-old Wahhabi monopoly on religious representation. In concrete terms, the main impact was to break the ice for subsequent intra-faith encounters. Two months after the session, Crown Prince Abdullah established the King Abdulaziz Center for National Dialogue to plan future meetings.

At the end of 2003, the second national dialogue session was held in Mecca to discuss extremism and moderation. Participation was expanded to include members of the business community as well as ten women, who gathered in a separate room and followed the proceedings via closed-circuit television. The third session, in June 2004 in Medina, concentrated on women's issues. The organizers invited 70 participants, half of them women, but reformers were outnumbered by conservatives. Nevertheless, the session had the effect of allowing liberal activists and religious conservatives to get acquainted for the first time. Discussion skirted the sensitive issues of women driving and the authority of male guardians but did address employment and domestic violence.[7]

Since the fourth session on youth at the end of 2004, meetings have become an annual event organized by the King Abdulaziz Center for National Dialogue. Saudis differ on whether the national dialogues are substantial contributions to fostering a new social climate or window dressing. Critics view them as diversions designed to divert calls for curbs on royal authority. They note that the agenda is set by the authorities, attendance is by invitation only, proceedings are not released, participants have to observe implicit red lines during sessions, and recommendations for action are ignored. Detractors also deplore the turn away from dialogue among different social and religious groups to sessions dedicated to particular issues such as education, employment, and health. Defenders assert that such sessions give the rulers a sense of how different segments of the population feel about pressing issues and that they offer a venue for Saudis with different perspectives to become better acquainted. When sessions focus on matters such as health and education, participants – Sunnis and Shiites, women and men – see that they confront common problems that demand a national solution rather than one for a particular group. Furthermore, proponents note that a 2009 spinoff for cultural dialogue promotes further discussion of delicate matters such as tribalism, regionalism, and religion. Another recent innovation is the development of training programs to spread expertise in conducting dialogues. The King Abdulaziz Center employs more than 1,500 trainers to amplify its impact throughout the kingdom.[8] As far as religion is concerned, the challenge for the national dialogue process is to find a way to accommodate the Wahhabi establishment to the country's other Muslim sectors that have endured decades of discrimination.

Twelver Shiites

About 1.5 million Saudis belong to the Shiite branch of Islam, which itself consists of several sub-sects. The largest Shiite group in the kingdom, and in the Muslim world, is the Twelver Shiites (also known as Imami Shiites), most of whom live in the Eastern Province, with a small community of a few thousand in Medina, followed by the Ismailis, concentrated in the southwest Najran region, and the Zaydis, who live along the border of Yemen. Because Wahhabi doctrine brands all Shiites as polytheists who must convert to Islam, they suffer various forms of discrimination, not only in religious expression but also in education, employment, and access to public services. For example, history textbooks focus on the story of Al Saud as champion of Islam and celebrate the deeds of King Abdulaziz in unifying and pacifying the kingdom's territories. Such patriotic narratives glorifying founding fathers are standard schoolbook fare in many countries, but they pass over in silence the histories of the kingdom's Shiite citizens. For many years religious textbooks condemned Sufism and Shiism as illegitimate innovations and taught that Muslims have a duty to wage jihad against Shiites. Derogatory references to Shiites were only dropped in the 1990s and it was not until 2005 that history schoolbooks stopped listing Ismailis as a deviant sect. Shiites are still banned from teaching religion courses.[9] Saudi Shiite responses to their plight have included passive resignation, underground revolutionary action, and lobbying for reform. A few Wahhabi clerics have exhibited flexibility in their view of Shiites as infidels, and in recent decades the ruling family has taken steps to improve their lot for the sake of political stability.

For centuries before al-Hasa's annexation to Saudi Arabia in 1913, its Twelver Shiites belonged to a Shiite cultural zone encompassing Iran, Iraq, Bahrain, and Kuwait. Clerics and religious pupils circulated through those lands to teach and study while laymen performed pilgrimages to imams' shrines in Iraq and Iran. Al-Hasa's absorption into Saudi Arabia made life difficult for the Shiite population but did not cut them off from fellow Shiites. Moreover, they had come under Saudi rule before. The first Saudi state conquered al-Hasa in 1795 and ruled it until 1818. The second Saudi state ruled it intermittently for four decades before the Ottomans seized it in 1871. In spite of Wahhabi hostility, the Shiites had made practical adjustments to Saudi rule, and while its return was not welcome, it was not an existential threat.

Indeed, Abdulaziz ibn Saud initially exhibited his usual prag-matism, purging Ottoman loyalists to consolidate his power and levying a special tax on Shiites in lieu of their participation in jihad. When it came to religion, Ibn Saud left alone Shiite teachers and prayer leaders. After a few years, however, the Ikhwan showed up in al-Hasa and demanded the Saudi governor prohibit Shiite festi-vals. The status of Shiites soon became a point of friction between Ibn Saud and the Ikhwan, who insisted on applying Wahhabi doc-trine, which meant either converting the infidel Shiites or expelling or killing them. At a conference held in Riyadh in 1927 to deal with Ikhwan complaints, Ibn Saud agreed to their demands for measures to wipe out Shiism. Al-Hasa's governor convened the Shiite clergy and extracted a pledge to abandon their festivals and pilgrimages to imams' tombs. He then appointed Wahhabi clergy to take over mosques. They destroyed some and preached Wahhabi doctrine to Shiite congregations in others. Some Shiite clergy responded by emigrating to Bahrain and Iraq. The phase of religious suppression ended when Ibn Saud put down the Ikhwan revolt in 1929. After-ward, the governor allowed the Shiite population to expel Wahhabi clerics, and Shiite clergy were permitted to serve their communities as long as they were discreet about their religious festivals.

In the early decades of the modern Saudi kingdom, the best the Shiites of al-Hasa could hope for was royal sufferance and protection from the full force of Wahhabi clerics seeking to wipe out Shiism. But even the partial weight of Wahhabi authority meant that Shiites faced disadvantages. In general, Shiites are not allowed to recite their call to prayer because it includes a phrase proclaiming Imam Ali's special relationship to God. Whereas in other Muslim countries, Twelver Shiite communities hold Ashura ceremonies in special buildings called *husainiyyas* to commemorate Imam Husain's martyrdom, in Saudi Arabia it is often difficult to get permission to construct them. Saudi Shiites have circumvented the ban by obtaining permission to construct community centers and banquet halls for weddings that are really intended to observe Ashura. For decades Shiite religious books were banned and Shiites were not allowed to set up their own schools, so their children attended public schools where they were taught that they belonged to a heretical sect established by hypocrites for the sake of sabotaging Islam from the inside by importing Jewish and Christian beliefs. In religious courts, Shiites' testimony is not admissible because in the eyes of Wahhabi judges they are polytheists. Until the 1970s, Shiites could follow their legal tradition only by going to the home of a Shiite judge for private adjudication. King Khalid, however, introduced a reform that allowed Shiite courts to handle family issues such as marriage, divorce, and inheritance, subject to the oversight of a Wahhabi judge.

Wahhabi hostility toward Shiism has affected access to certain occupations. Shiites may not work as butchers because their meat does not qualify as *halal* (permissible under Islamic dietary rules), because Wahhabi clerics regard them as polytheists. However, the strict Wahhabi ban on usury means that Shiites enjoy opportunities in the banking sector. Their exclusion from the armed forces and the National Guard rests on the notion that they may not be completely loyal to the dynasty. In terms of social interaction, intermarriage between Sunnis and Shiites is rare, but some mixing does occur at the workplace, especially at Saudi Aramco, where Shiites make up a large portion of the labor force.[10]

During the oil boom, few Shiites shared the bounty pumped out of their region. Largely Sunni cities in the Eastern Province – Dhahran, Dammam, and Khobar – underwent physical transformations into modern urban centers while Shiite towns and villages were essentially forgotten. In the late 1970s, they lacked basic services such as regular garbage collection, clean water, and sewage disposal. When planners in Riyadh drew up budgets to erect schools, clinics, and hospitals, they overlooked Shiite areas. Not only were Shiite areas not included in the new prosperity of the oil boom, the living conditions there deteriorated, thanks to a falling water table that caused shortages and high salinity in the shrinking supply of water. It took the Shiite uprising of November 1979 to get Riyadh's attention.[11]

The main religious Shiite opposition tendency was embedded in a larger movement of Gulf Shiites in Iraq, Kuwait, and Bahrain loyal to the Iraqi cleric Muhammad al-Mahdi al-Shirazi. The leading Saudi figure in the Shirazi network was Sheikh Hasan al-Saffar. After undertaking religious studies in Iraq and Iran, he met Shirazi in Kuwait in 1974. Back in Saudi Arabia, Saffar set up a branch of the Shirazi movement and encouraged religious students to head for a Shiite seminary in Kuwait. The 1979 uprising prompted him to establish the Organization for Islamic Revolution (OIR). Because Saudi security forces arrested and imprisoned Shiite activists in putting down the uprising, the OIR was primarily a movement of exiles scattered between Iran, Syria, and the United Kingdom. In the early 1980s, the OIR broadcast anti-government sermons and smuggled into the kingdom pamphlets condemning royal corruption and the squandering of billions of riyals on arms. From Riyadh's perspective, the OIR was an arm of Iran's hostile foreign policy, so the authorities concentrated on finding and arresting members, who reported that security officials subjected them to torture.

In 1984, a new provincial governor, Emir Muhammad, a son of King Fahd, tried a lenient and constructive approach to the

Shiite population that combined amnesty to political prisoners with funds for economic development. His policy brought improvements to sewage and road systems in addition to new schools and hospitals. King Fahd issued a second amnesty three years later, signaling his desire for reconciliation with his Shiite subjects. Soon after, the OIR leadership moved from Iran to Syria to clear itself of the implication that it was an Iranian puppet. Debate within the OIR led to a moderation of its position. In 1991 it jettisoned revolution and adopted a new name, the Reform Movement, and a new platform emphasizing human rights and democracy. The Saudi rulers had already duly noted how the Shiite population had supported the government during the 1990–1 crisis over Kuwait, as opposed to the harsh condemnation that issued from the Sahwa movement. Emissaries from Riyadh met with the Reform Movement to discuss terms for allowing Sheikh Saffar and his colleagues to come home. They agreed in October 1993 that if the dissidents stopped publishing criticism of the government abroad, then all members would be allowed to return.

Back in Saudi Arabia, the Reform Movement espoused religious tolerance and pluralism in order to improve the lot of Shiites. It sought the right to build Shiite mosques and husainiyyas to celebrate religious festivals, and to publish religious works. It also wanted the government to end denunciations of Shiites by Wahhabi preachers. In addition to religious issues, the Reform Movement called for equal access to universities, employment, and public services. Stiff opposition to easing restrictions came from the Sahwa leaders Safar al-Hawali and Salman al-Awda but the religious establishment's hostility toward Shiites inched toward accommodation when Grand Mufti Abdulaziz ibn Baz invited Hasan al-Saffar to his home in October 1995. The gesture was enough for lenient Wahhabi clergy to accept invitations from Saffar and his colleagues to attend his weekly salon and religious celebrations. The authorities took steps to improve public services and Saudi newspapers allowed Shiite writers to discuss their aims. The decision to promote tolerance after 9/11 and the rise of al-Qaeda in the Arabian Peninsula also boosted the Shiite cause: applications to build mosques and requests to observe Ashura were approved; more Shiite students were admitted to universities and received scholarships to study abroad.

The strength and weakness of Hasan al-Saffar's moderate approach is its dependence on the goodwill of Al Saud. He was among the invitees to the national dialogue session on religious tolerance. He concluded that arranging frequent contact between different religious sects could change Sunni attitudes and improve conditions for Shiites. For example, a young Sunni woman invited to visit the mostly Shiite city of Qatif ignored friends who warned against mixing with people they suspected of owing allegiance to Iran. The gulf between the sects is evident from her assumption that the Shiites spoke Persian instead of Arabic and her surprise at learning that the Quran is their holy book too. In 2008, one of Saffar's associates, Jafar al-Shayeb, took inspiration from the national dialogue to form the National Exchange Program dedicated to promoting Sunni–Shiite understanding. The exchanges include women as well as men, primarily journalists, artists, and professors, in the hope that they might shape broader opinion.

After the 1993 accord between the government and the Reform Movement, the Shiite population witnessed progress in both religious and material conditions, but the gradual pace of change frustrated the young. On one hand, they saw that Shiites participated in the 2005 nationwide municipal elections where members of the Reform Movement won most of the seats in Qatif. On the other hand, there was practically no Shiite representation in national institutions: none in the Council of Ministers; no ambassadors; and only five out of 150 members of the Shura Council. And, in spite of the king's calls for a more tolerant public discourse, hard-line Wahhabi clerics continued to issue harsh condemnations of Shiites. In 2009, one of the prayer leaders at the Grand Mosque of Mecca called them infidels; a prominent Wahhabi sheikh posted a fatwa to his website prohibiting the sale of real estate to Shiites; another Wahhabi sheikh declared that Sunnis should not pay visits to Shiites or return their greeting. Part of the problem is that moderate Wahhabis tell Shiite leaders they disagree with such statements but are too timid to say so in public.

In February 2009, underlying sectarian tensions burst in clashes between Shiite pilgrims to Medina and security forces. The pilgrims had come from the Eastern Province to observe the anniversary of the Prophet's death on 24 February. It is their custom to visit the Mosque of Prophet, which contains his tomb, and the adjacent al-Baqi` cemetery, where several Companions, wives, and members of the Prophet's family are buried. Wahhabi clerics consider parts of the Shiite observance the sort of illegal innovations in ritual that constitute polytheism: their prayer invokes blessing on the Prophet's family; they visit the graves of Companions; and they take a handful of soil from graves for blessing. In several incidents over the course of three days, the Mosque of the Prophet was the scene of scuffles and fights as pilgrims tangled with religious police, security personnel, and Wahhabi zealots, such as a man who stabbed a Shiite cleric entering the mosque. Furthermore, the pilgrims reported harassment by the religious police, while the government asserted that it was the Shiites' cursing of righteous Companions and the Shiite 'Zoroastrian' customs that triggered the disturbances. When word of the disturbances reached the Eastern Province, protesters took to the streets in several towns and villages. A hard-line Shiite preacher gave a sermon declaring that if the government did not treat Shiites with dignity, they would secede. This was exactly the sort of comment that confirmed common Sunni suspicion of Shiite disloyalty and undermined moderates such as Hasan al-Saffar. It did not help his cause when the interior minister declared that Shiites should conform to Wahhabi doctrine when visiting the holy places.

Twelver Shiites' long uphill struggle for equality is hampered by factors beyond their control, such as the sharpening of sectarianism in the Gulf. Perennial mistrust and intermittent hostility between Saudi Arabia and Iran makes it even harder for Shiites to prove they are loyal citizens. The American overthrow of Saddam Husain in 2003 exacerbated Sunni–Shiite relations throughout the Gulf. When viewed through a sectarian prism, the dominant position of Shiites in post-Baathist Iraq reflects a shift in the balance of power to the disadvantage of Sunnis. Calculation of the regional sectarian balance of power also colored Riyadh's perception of and response to the February–March 2011 democracy movement in Bahrain, where the majority Shiite population regards Al Saud as the patron of an oppressive Sunni dynasty. Saudi Shiites feel pulled between the need to affirm loyalty to the kingdom and sympathy for the political fortunes of fellow Shiites. Expressions of Shiite solidarity, however, incur suspicion of harboring secret affection for Iran, which by playing the sectarian card undermines the standing of Shiite minorities in Sunni-ruled countries and thereby makes some Shiites look to Tehran for leadership and support.

Domestic politics also hinder the Shiite cause. The government's silence in the face of Wahhabi clerics branding Shiites as infidels in mosques and on television shows and websites diminishes the effects of the national dialogue. Habits of suspicion color popular Sunni and Shiite attitudes toward each other, fed not only by Wahhabi clerics but also by Shiite hard-liners broadcasting harsh anti-Sunni views on websites and satellite television. The conciliators on both sides of Saudi Arabia's sectarian divide have royal goodwill on their side, but that is not guaranteed over the long term.[12]

Ismaili Shiites

Saudi Arabia's Ismaili community of about half a million has endured the same pattern of discrimination as their Twelver Shiite cousins. Their homeland is the Najran valley in the southwest corner of the kingdom along the border with Yemen. Since the early 1600s, Najran has been the center of the Sulaimaniyya branch of Ismailis, with fellow adherents in Yemen, Pakistan, and India. The story of Najran's absorption into Saudi Arabia is more complicated than the conquests of al-Hasa because it took place against the backdrop of a power struggle involving Yemen, Saudi Arabia, and an independent principality in Asir, a mountainous region tucked between Hijaz and Yemen. Briefly, in the 1920s, both Asir and Najran looked to Ibn Saud for protection from Yemen's maneuvers to annex them. Asir became a Saudi dependency in 1927, but its ruler soon grew restless with having to take orders from Ibn Saud's deputy. With Yemeni encouragement, a revolt broke out in 1932, but Saudi forces were able to stamp it out, forcing Asir's ruler to flee. Najran's final annexation took place two years later in the course of a short border war between Saudi Arabia and Yemen. The Bani Yam tribe (which is Ismaili) took the Saudi side to repulse Yemen's bid to occupy Najran.[13]

The early decades of Saudi rule in Najran were uneventful except for occasional friction arising from Wahhabi restrictions on Ismaili religious expression. Like the Twelver Shiites, Ismailis face various forms of discrimination: Wahhabi preachers call them infidels in fatwas and sermons; their prayer books are banned because they contain prayers to Shiite imams that Wahhabis consider polytheistic; obtaining permission to repair and build mosques is frequently denied; Ismaili religious leaders have been sentenced to jail and lashings on sorcery charges; marriages performed by Ismaili religious leaders do not have legal standing; Wahhabi schoolteachers sometimes try to force students to renounce their beliefs and profess Wahhabi doctrine. In addition to sectarian discrimination, Ismailis suspect the authorities of tampering with Najran's demographic balance by granting citizenship to Sunnis from Yemen, and by providing the newcomers land grants and funds to develop new urban districts. The provincial governor favored Sunnis when it came to allocating resources for mosques and offering jobs in the civil administration while access to government jobs for Ismailis in their home district is constricted.

One of the minor religious differences between Sunnis and Ismailis has to do with determining when to celebrate the end of Ramadan. According to Sunni law, witnesses must see the new moon, therefore the exact day is not known in advance. Ismailis have a fixed date for observing the Ramadan Feast. In some years, the different methods have resulted in Ismailis holding their feast a day before Sunnis. Wahhabi clerics demonstrate characteristic rigidity when it comes to the religious calendar. In January 2000, the Ministry of Interior ordered Ismaili mosques in Najran to be shut down and declared a prohibition on attending mosque on the 'wrong day'. This was not the first time Ismailis had to delay their religious celebration to conform to Wahhabi practice and most people just stayed home rather than risk arrest.

A few months after the mosque closure, the authorities arrested an Ismaili cleric on sorcery charges. A delegation of Ismaili leaders went to the Holiday Inn, where the Saudi governor kept his residence, and called on him to release the cleric, but the governor refused to meet with them. Meanwhile, townsmen gathered at the hotel to protest the cleric's arrest. A standoff ensued and lasted several hours before shots were fired, killing two or three men. Army troops then entered the city and formed a cordon around the neighborhood where the Ismaili religious leader had his headquarters. They withdrew the same day without incident. In subsequent days, weeks, and months, the security forces arrested around five hundred men for alleged roles in the demonstration. Investigators for Human Rights

Watch obtained multiple accounts of beatings, electric shocks, sleep deprivation, and other forms of torture to extract false confessions that resulted in 17 death sentences and 65 life sentences, later reduced by a series of royal pardons. In the months after the Holiday Inn demonstration, more than four hundred Ismaili civil servants and government employees were dismissed and transferred to remote parts of the country. The Ismaili religious leader was prohibited from giving religious lessons.[14]

Sunni Hijaz

The Saudi takeover of Hijaz in the 1920s meant much more than the replacement of one ruler for another. The Hashemite Kingdom's religious and moral climate bore the imprint of Ottoman pluralism and leniency. Sufi brotherhoods, saints' tombs, and a wide assortment of popular religious practices abhorrent to Wahhabi doctrine flourished in Jeddah, the holy cities, and small towns. When Najdi clerics and Ikhwan religious police arrived, they sought to impose a new order. In matters of ritual, the Wahhabis made attendance at prayer compulsory for men and shortened the formula for the call to prayer to conform to their doctrine. The Wahhabi view of domes over tombs as invitations to worship the dead resulted in the destruction of structures associated with famous early Muslim heroes in Mecca and Medina. In Mecca alone, the new rulers razed shrines erected at the Prophet's birthplace and the house of his first wife Khadija.[15] The censorious eyes of Ikhwan vigilantes enforced a host of prohibitions against alcohol, tobacco, gambling, fortune-telling, and dancing. Men had to grow their beards and give up wearing any gold or silver. While enforcement of these rules was loose enough for the determined to get away with vices in secret, over time sustained pressure reshaped everyday life to fit the Wahhabi mold.[16]

The Saudi rulers looked the other way as long as the people of Hijaz outwardly conformed to the demands of Wahhabi doctrine and kept a low profile when holding Sufi ceremonies and observing the Prophet's Birthday. Consequently, stamping out religious festivals that are popular in Hijaz and in much of the Muslim world has eluded the Wahhabi establishment. For centuries, believers have celebrated holidays associated with major events in the lives of the Prophet and his Companions. The Prophet's Birthday, *mawlid al-nabi*, is observed throughout the Muslim world as a public holiday. It is an occasion for banquets, donating food to the poor and public recitation of poetry praising Muhammad for his exemplary character and miraculous deeds. It is customary to recite *al-Burda* (*The Prophet's Mantle*), a long poem composed nine hundred years ago by the Moroccan Sufi al-Busiri. In the 1800s, the legitimacy of reciting the poem became a point of controversy between Wahhabis and other Muslims because of verses that, in the Wahhabi view, express excessive veneration for the Prophet, ascribing to him powers possessed by God alone. So not only is the festival an innovation, first recorded in the twelfth century but it is the occasion for additional innovations. That is the standard view of Wahhabi clerics toward all but two holidays, the Feast of Breaking the Fast at the end of Ramadan and the Feast of the Sacrifice at the conclusion of the pilgrimage. All other religious festivals fall into the category of forbidden innovations. Consequently, Saudi Arabia is one of the few Muslim countries that do not observe the Prophet's Birthday. In the view of Wahhabi clerics, it resembles the customs of Christians and Jews, so it violates the taboo against imitating nonbelievers, and its observance frequently entails additional forbidden behavior such as gender mixing and playing music.[17]

Implicit toleration of popular Hijazi religious observances dissipated after the 1979 Mecca Uprising, when the government felt it had to placate Wahhabi clerics determined to suppress Sufism. A prominent Sufi, scion of a leading Meccan family of scholars,

Muhammad al-Maliki, was banished from teaching at the Grand Mosque due to pressure from Wahhabi clerics. Possession of Sufi religious texts became a crime. For twenty years, celebrating the Prophet's Birthday became a clandestine affair. A more tolerant atmosphere returned after 9/11. The national dialogue's recognition of religious pluralism included Sufis, and Muhammad al-Maliki was invited to the inaugural 2003 session. When he died the next year, Crown Prince Abdullah attended his funeral. While some Wahhabi clerics have continued to denounce Sufis as infidels, Sufis no longer conceal their gatherings by meeting in basements and remote rural areas. And as with the Shiites, a dialogue has begun between Sufis and moderate Wahhabis, such as the Sahwa Sheikh Salman al-Awda, who attended a mawlid in 2006.[18]

The Status of Women

King Abdullah's calls for toleration and dialogue emboldened Saudis to question standard Wahhabi positions on matters other than religious diversity. The roles of women and the rules for gender relations are at the forefront of issues discussed at conferences, in the media, and on the internet. A variety of political, economic, and cultural forces are reshaping the status of women. Royal support for coeducation at King Abdullah University of Science and Technology was taken as a gesture to chip away at gender segregation. Economic strains on household budgets incline families to think of women working outside the home as a necessity that is hindered by the prohibition on gender mixing. Satellite television and the internet provide Saudis regular access to images of less restrictive Arab Muslim societies. A quick flight to Dubai or the 15-mile drive from Khobar to Bahrain across the King Fahd Causeway, which opened in 1986, reveals a less restrictive lifestyle in Gulf societies where women observe modest standards without compulsion. Conservatives strive to hold the line against change, but pressures emanating from so many directions seem irresistible.

Classical Wahhabism did not dwell on the question of women working outside the home. This is not because women did not work, but because they worked in desert encampments and villages, where custom governed interactions between men and women, without clerical supervision since Wahhabi clerics had little contact with villagers and Bedouin. In fact, they lamented the Bedouin's wayward beliefs and practices until they managed to settle them as Ikhwan in agricultural colonies. The Bedouin division of labor allocated certain chores to women, but, given their living conditions, the notion of keeping them from working outside the home never arose. Among the settled population, there was again a division of labor defined by custom, not the idea that a woman's duties prevented her from working. At the same time, it was normal for women to avoid contact with unrelated men.

In the 1940s, tending livestock became easier as shepherds roamed the desert in trucks and watered animals at permanent, government-excavated wells. As herding chores became less onerous, women took on a larger role. At the same time, former Bedouin, cultivators, and townsmen invested in agriculture to feed growing urban populations and hired expatriate men to undertake arduous work in the fields. Diminishing engagement in cultivation eventually curtailed women's participation in the rural labor force (some studies indicate three-quarters of rural women still worked in the early 1970s). While young men moved into new occupations in the oil sector, construction, government offices, and banks, opportunities for women were restricted to jobs as teachers and staff at girls' schools, tellers at the women's branches of banks, and nurses at clinics and hospitals. But those occupations required formal education and only a small proportion of girls were completing secondary school in the early decades of national education.[19]

6. Separate section for women at a bank in Riyadh

The question of women and work assumed significance in the 1970s when the number of educated women seeking modern careers pushed against restrictions on their roles in public life. Newspapers carried debates over whether women should gain the right to drive and access to professional careers in education, health, and business. Women appeared on television programs with their faces uncovered. Then the Mecca Uprising prompted the government to reverse women's gains, banning their photographs in newspapers and appearances on television, and enforcing the Wahhabi rule that they have a male relative's permission to operate a business.

As Wahhabi clerics see it, if women commonly worked outside the home, there would be several negative effects. First, they consider the home the natural, divinely ordained place for women to spend most of their time, attending to the duties of wife and mother. If a woman took on a 'second shift', she would have less time for her husband and children. Second, work would jeopardize a woman's morality because she would have to mix with men. Third, if women worked, there would be fewer jobs for men, and their ability to fulfill their duties as breadwinners would be undermined. But many Saudi families struggle to make ends meet on one salary and question the point of a girl getting an education if she will never put it to use. The clerics do not prohibit women from working altogether; rather they seek to limit women to occupations that match their roles as homemakers, and they insist that women fill positions where they will not come into contact with unrelated men.[20]

Many young Saudis have different reference points when they think about women in the workplace. Apart from financial pressures, many see examples of women at work not just in the West but in the Arab world, even in nearby Gulf countries that have much in common with the kingdom. Finally, there is a political dimension to the debate. Defenders of morality and tradition not only object to women's employment as a matter of principle, but also from apprehension that giving way on that issue would breach the dike holding back a flood of liberal changes. Women cite a number of reasons for working outside the home. For some, like women whose husbands are too ill to work or who earn small incomes, the paycheck is the primary reason. Educated professional women might enjoy the feelings of self-respect and independence that come from working in a field they studied hard to get into. Many women just want to escape the monotony of staying home all day.[21]

The debate over women working outside the home is symptomatic of the tensions generated by collisions between dogma and traditional values on one side and social transformation and economic development on the other. The rate of female participation in the labor force is around 15 percent and is one reason for the kingdom's continued reliance on six million expatriate workers. Twenty years ago, development planners wanted to see more women fill jobs occupied by expatriates, but only modest headway has been achieved due to resistance from conservative quarters. From a purely instrumental point of view, preventing women from working is a case where culture clashes with the logic of economic development, in which it is a waste of their potential contributions. Due to the authority of male guardians, women need permission to work outside the home, so individual cases depend on the disposition of fathers and husbands. A determined woman may overcome opposition when financial pressures are at play or with support from a sympathetic mother. Even with her family's full support, a woman's opportunities are limited by the ban on driving. Public transport facilities for women are few, so they either depend on male relatives to take them to and from work, or on a driver if their family can afford one.

What is peculiar about the debate over female employment is how the clerics are so vocal about modern occupations while at the same time they ignore women plying traditional ones. For centuries it was common for women to share the chores of cultivation and tending livestock, and for marketplaces to include a separate section for women vendors selling food and household items.[22] When cities expanded in the 1950s and 1960s, new market areas sprang up and continued to allocate a section for women vendors. In the Batha Suq in central Riyadh, for instance, women sell clothing, toys, and costume jewelry stacked on wagons or on blankets spread on the ground, and they interact with male customers.[23] Likewise, on the eastern outskirts of Riyadh stretches a vast outdoor market for second-hand goods called Suq Haraj bin Qassim. While most of the vendors are men, some are women, usually enveloped in black robes and facemasks, seated on bits of carpet or matting, conducting business, haggling with customers, men and women.

7. Women street vendors in Jeddah

Some Saudis wonder why if women vendors work outdoors in the blazing heat, the clerics get agitated about women working in the comfort of malls and food marts. For instance, in 2010, a food chain announced plans to hire women cashiers if they met certain criteria: they had to be either a widow or a divorcee, presumably to establish the necessity for working outside the home; they had to meet a minimum age requirement of 28; and they had to adhere to a dress code. Nevertheless, opponents raised the usual objections: women would be taking jobs from men, and women cashiers could be subject to harassment by men (opening the question of why Saudi men are not held to higher standards). Yet another argument was that it could result in women taking low-status jobs, like maids, that are humiliating, and, implicitly, reserved for Asian guest workers.

A middle ground emerged that allows women to join the workforce on condition they respect three conditions: they may not interact with men as co-workers or clients; their jobs may not cause them to neglect family obligations; and their jobs must be compatible with their feminine nature, allowing work in education, health, and social welfare. In line with those conditions, in the mid 1990s about half of working women were teachers and staff at girls' schools with others holding jobs at women's universities and welfare societies. When banks set up women's sections, they created positions for women, often university graduates with degrees in business and economics. While the government backed the establishment of nursing institutes, few Saudi women entered that profession because it could entail interaction with men and work on night shifts. Government offices in some ministries (Health, Higher Education, and Planning) have women's sections that hire university graduates. Opportunities exist in the private sector because, according to Islamic law, women control their own wealth; consequently, Saudi women operate businesses that cater to female customers, primarily women's beauty salons, nurseries, and tailoring and clothing stores.

Pressure for opening new occupations to women arises in part from the large number of university graduates. Young women accustomed to getting out of their homes to attend classes suddenly find themselves bored with nothing to look forward to but marriage, which often promises a monotonous life of sitting around the home. Middle-class families under financial stress could use the second income. And if more Saudi women participated in the workforce, the country could reduce its dependence on expatriate labor. Conservatives, however, show little inclination to give way. Consequently, departures from the norm remain rare and dependent on the patronage of powerful figures. For example, the Rotana Company can maintain gender-mixed offices because its owner is Prince al-Waleed bin Talal, one of the wealthiest men in the world and a voice for gradual opening of society. Some hospitals have broken the barrier against gender mixing in their workforces. Opportunities seem to be increasing inch by inch. In

2011, an innovative entrepreneur launched a website dedicated to posting job ads for women offered by Saudi and foreign firms.[24] A small number of university graduates in history and archaeology work as tour guides at museums and archaeological sites, but a newspaper poll found that three-quarters of respondents opposed the idea completely and those who considered it acceptable made it clear that they approved on condition that female guides work exclusively with women tourists.[25]

Government-sponsored initiatives such as the national dialogue and the expansion of the scope for media outlets to cover social issues altered the climate of public discourse, but they left ordinary Saudis as spectators rather than participants in debates. The spread of internet social media gave Saudis new platforms to push for social change. In 2008, Reem Asaad, a female instructor at a Jeddah women's college, launched a campaign to change labor regulations for employment at lingerie shops. At the time, most shops employed expatriate men. Many Saudi women felt awkward dealing with men when shopping for underwear and could not try on merchandise because the religious police prohibited changing rooms. The only way to check the fit was to purchase an item and then go to a public restroom. Two years before Asaad mounted her campaign, the Ministry of Labor proposed replacing foreign shop-keepers with Saudi women, but religious conservatives mounted stiff opposition because it would have resulted in a slight degree of gender mixing as many lingerie shops are located in malls, so the ministry shelved the idea.[26] Asaad's slogan, 'Enough Embarrassment', was a logical choice for the Facebook page set up to back the campaign. She called for a two-week boycott of shops that employed men. In June 2011, her efforts paid off when King Abdullah announced that lingerie shops had to hire women. The Ministry of Labor gave shop owners a year to change their staff.[27]

One of the powerful forces keeping women out of the workplace is the doctrine of keeping unrelated men and women from mixing. Debate over gender mixing is part of a broader discussion of women's roles in the kingdom, initiated under the auspices of the national dialogue's third round in 2004. The published recommendations were bland statements reiterating the primacy of family in women's lives, and their right to work as long as their jobs did not infringe on Islamic law. While no concrete measures were proposed and some of the participant women expressed disappointment, the session did pave the way for more candid coverage of women's issues in the media. The liberal camp favoring some relaxation of restrictions on allowing men and women to mingle has found tacit support from King Abdullah. The octogenarian ruler gave his blessing to making the new King Abdullah University of Science and Technology coeducational. He also named the kingdom's first female deputy minister and gave conservatives a jolt when he allowed a newspaper to publish a photograph of him in the company of bare-faced women. The royal intervention rattled nerves in clerical ranks. When one sheikh denounced the violation of gender segregation at KAUST on television, the king responded by dismissing him. Then a rift opened among the clerics when the head of the religious police in Mecca opined that gender mixing was allowable. A senior cleric issued a fatwa reiterating the prohibition and asserting that anyone who supported gender mixing deserved the death penalty.[28]

Liberal Saudi newspapers predictably lauded the new university as a token of the kingdom's commitment to joining the modern world by advancing the cause of science education. Conservative clerics were already engaged in verbal warfare against liberals, frequently referring to them as 'hypocrites', a term loaded with negative connotations. (In the time of the Prophet, the hypocrites were people who pretended to embrace Islam but worked in secret with its enemies to destroy it.) Conservatives also accused liberals of seeking to impose an American version of Islam in the name of moderation, implying they were unwitting agents of an infidel power. King Abdullah took the unusual step of intervening in the debate when a member of the Council of Senior Ulama mixed praise for KAUST's contribution to science education with mildly critical remarks about the negative effects of gender mixing for putting students in the way of temptation. Even though the sheikh claimed he did not mean to criticize the king, he was removed from the Council.

Two months later, Saudis were astonished to read a newspaper column penned by the director of the religious police in Mecca stating that gender segregation is a matter of social custom, not a religious requirement. Anyway, he noted, to suppose that the official prohibition was effective any longer required one to pretend that men and women did not interact in private via webcams. The writer, Sheikh Ahmad al-Ghamdi, apparently had a more ambitious agenda in mind, namely, to challenge other Wahhabi positions as matters of ijtihad, the individual conclusion of a jurist that lacks the binding force of a ruling based on an explicit text in the Quran or Prophetic Tradition. He used the same logic to challenge closing offices and stores during prayer time. Not surprisingly, conservative clerics reacted with a wave of furious condemnations of al-Ghamdi's reasoning and his character. In February 2010, a champion of the ultra-conservative camp, Sheikh Abdulrahman al-Barrak, came out with a declaration that rehearsed the standard argument based on the legal principle of blocking means to the prohibited: that which leads to something prohibited is itself prohibited. Gender mixing leads to mutual attraction, flirting, and private meetings, which is code for fornication. The sheikh added that whoever permits gender mixing is an apostate who must repent or be killed.[29]

Women Driving

Saudi Arabia's sprawling cities are built for automobiles. Supermarkets and shops are concentrated along broad boulevards some distance from most residential neighborhoods, making it impractical to do errands on foot. Even if one wished to walk, pedestrian sidewalks are usually in such disrepair that it is easy to stumble, particularly for women covered from head to toe in abaya and with the niqab reducing peripheral vision. For months on end, the heat is so fierce that a woman spending much time outdoors would develop face blisters under her niqab. In short, driving is necessary to get around cities, but only the male half of the population drives in the kingdom. While there is no official legislation that bars a woman from driving, a de facto ban suffices to prevent them from doing so. Whether there is a sound religious basis for that ban is a matter of debate. To provide women access to motor transport, many families have the means to hire a driver, always an expatriate worker; there are around 800,000 such drivers. A hired driver, however, creates a problem from the Wahhabi point of view because for a woman to be alone in a car with a non-mahram male violates the prohibition on khalwa, a private meeting with a stranger. Nevertheless, this is an instance where practical need prevails over religious law.[30] In families that cannot afford the roughly $600 a month for a driver, women have to wait for husbands to come home from work to go on errands. If a woman chooses to get a taxi, she must walk a few blocks to a commercial street and wait in the scorching sun until one comes along.

Saudi society is divided on whether it is time to abandon the prohibition on women driving. Conservatives consider it necessary to uphold morality and they condemn proponents of women driving as agents of blind Westernization. Advocates argue that the religious rationale against women driving is a screen for perpetuating the subjection of women to male authority. The issue burst on the scene on 6 November 1990, when about fifty women mounted a demonstration by driving around downtown Riyadh. The Iraqi invasion of Kuwait three months before and the arrival of tens of thousands of Western military forces, including women soldiers who drove military vehicles down Saudi boulevards, brought to the surface tensions over political and social issues, including women's rights in general and the matter of driving in particular. The authorities were not inclined to excuse the demonstrating women, even though the sight of a woman driving would draw no attention in any other Muslim country. Traffic and religious police rounded up the women and placed them under arrest, releasing them to the custody of their male guardians only after they agreed to sign a pledge to refrain from driving. That was not the end of the matter. Religious conservatives delivered sermons and recorded lectures denouncing the women as prostitutes; the offending drivers who held government jobs as teachers were suspended for nearly three years.

The issue did not resurface until the political opening that followed the 9/11 attacks on the United States. It was among the topics previously deemed too sensitive for public discussion that newspapers could now broach with stories about women's discomfort with foreign drivers and interviews with liberal sheikhs opining no rule in Islamic law bars women from driving. In 2005, leading members of the royal family aired opposing views on the matter, with King Abdullah telling an American television journalist that he believed Saudi women would drive one day. Two years later, activists turned to the internet to solicit more than one thousand signatures for a petition to the king seeking a royal decree to lift the ban.[31]

In spring 2011, Saudis watched the historic events unfolding in the Arab world from North Africa to the Gulf. In Tunisia, Egypt, Bahrain, and Yemen, Arab women participated in demonstrations and marches demanding democracy. Inspired by the boldness of their Arab sisters, a group of Saudi women used the same social media that fueled protest movements elsewhere to launch a movement for the right to drive. Then on 21 May 2011, Manal al-Sharif, a Saudi technician, decided that she would take her car for a drive in Khobar. After all, if she could drive on the Aramco compound where she worked, why not on city streets? Her joyride was brought to a halt when the religious police stopped her. She spent one day in detention before she was released in return for signing a statement that she agreed to abide by Saudi laws. The very next day, however, she was again behind the wheel and arrested once more. This time her detention lasted more than a week.

Sharif's defiance of the ban on women driving drew both national and international attention, thanks in large measure to the YouTube video she uploaded of herself at the wheel and her creation of a Facebook page called 'I will drive my car myself' and a Twitter account, Women2Drive, that called on other Saudi women to protest the ban by driving cars on 17 June. Twitter and Facebook buzzed with anticipation as the date neared. Conservatives railed against the movement and threatened to beat women caught driving. On the appointed day, several dozen women drove in a number of cities. Police stopped some of them and took them to their homes rather than placing them under detention. One woman reported that at first traffic policemen did nothing when she drove past them, but eventually half a dozen patrol cars pulled her over and gave her a ticket for driving without a license. Given Saudi Arabia's pattern of resistance to and then acceptance of change on matters such as girls' education and television, it is reasonable for reformers to believe that if they continue to press for women's right to drive they will eventually get their way.[32]

Christian Expatriates

Among the profound changes brought about by the 1970s oil boom is the rapid rise in the number of foreigners residing in the kingdom. Jeddah and the holy cities had long been accustomed to the annual arrival of pilgrims, some of whom settled permanently, lending the cities of Hijaz an air of Muslim cosmopolitanism. To a lesser extent, the small ports along the Gulf coast too were exposed to perennial population movements of Arab, Persian, and Indian traders, pearlers, and fishermen. Central Arabia, however, saw few strangers apart from caravaneers making haste from one desert station to another.

It is normal for societies to go through painful adjustment during periods of high immigration. For a hermetic region like Central Arabia, guided by Wahhabi mistrust of outsiders, Muslims and non-Muslims alike, the sudden influx of foreigners in the mid twentieth century must have been a sharp jolt. When the first Americans came in the 1940s to explore for oil, they and their hosts had no desire to mingle: Americans did not wish to conform to local custom and the Saudi religious leaders did not want Americans' infidel ways to infect local society. Isolating the Westerners by constructing special residential compounds for them was a mutually satisfactory solution. The King Faisal Specialist Hospital, for example, attracted expatriate talent by setting it up as an enclave in the middle of Riyadh. Its residential complex included furnished housing, swimming pools, and gyms as well as its own cafeteria and post office.[33]

The arrival of millions of Arab and Asian workers since the mid 1970s posed different challenges, even if the vast majority of them were fellow Muslims. Wahhabi clerics doubted their religious standing as true believers, but saw them as ripe for conversion to true monotheism (for their part, some Arab and south Asian Muslim workers fault Wahhabi doctrine for concentrating on matters of external conformity rather than faith and moral character). The wave of foreigners included thousands of Christians, not only Americans and Europeans but also Filipinos and Indians. Expatriate workers, be they Muslim or Christian, are generally subject to the same rules of public behavior as Saudis, with the exception that Christian women – Western and Asian – need not cover their faces, although they must wear modest dress, covering them from shoulders to feet.

Foreign Muslims from less puritanical countries may find it more or less troubling to conform to Wahhabi norms. Christians, on the other hand, confront a blanket prohibition against public religious services due to the Wahhabi interpretation of a Prophetic Tradition that proclaims, 'Let there be no two religions in Arabia.' Not only are churches not allowed, but Christians may not wear crosses, and Christian websites are blocked. The government says that non-Muslims may possess religious materials for personal use, but if Bibles are discovered by customs inspectors at border posts or by the religious police searching a home, they are confiscated. Saudi authorities, however, tend to turn a blind eye to discreet activity and many Christians hold clandestine services. The government maintains that non-Muslims may worship in their homes, although religious police do sometimes carry out raids and arrest Christians. On expatriate residential compounds, Christians put up lights and Christmas trees and enjoy singing carols outside neighbors' homes without inhibition.[34]

In the eyes of the religious police, Christian worship is a form of blasphemy. Punishments include prison, summary dismissal from work, and deportation.[35] Recent incidents include the jailing of 14 Indian Christians for several days and eventual deportation when their employers were pressured to cancel their work contracts. A raid by religious police on a private home found a few Indian Christians holding a religious service. They were held at a police station for several days.[36] An Eritrean pastor who served a few hundred foreign Christians escaped from the kingdom after receiving threats from the religious police. The religious police made a big bust in October 2010 with the arrest of a dozen Filipino Christians and a French priest who was leading a Roman Catholic Mass in a hotel conference room attended by 150 Filipino Christians.[37] Such incidents are too sporadic to deter faithful Christians but frequent enough to foster a climate of anxiety.

By no means do all Saudis share the enmity of the religious police toward Christian religious expression. In some workplaces, during the Christmas season, Saudi employers permit Christian workers to put up holiday decorations, purchased at local shops, and mark the occasion with gifts to Christian employees.[38] Such accommodation to Christian customs is unacceptable to Wahhabi clerics, who insist on the need to prevent the spread of foreign customs in general. Thus, they view celebrating a birthday as a form of imitating the infidels; likewise, Mother's Day and Labor Day. St. Valentine's Day, with its Christian roots and celebration of romantic love – temptation to sin, in Wahhabi eyes – also comes under the general ban. It seems, however, that not all Saudis respect the sweeping prohibition of infidel holidays. Otherwise, it would not be necessary for the religious authorities to remind believers not to mark St. Valentine's Day or for the religious police to order shop owners to remove flowers and red gift wrap from window displays in the days leading to 14 February.[39] The stubborn persistence of this celebration of romantic love is a bit furtive. Shops do not advertise their chocolates and teddy bears under Valentine's Day banners; and couples are careful to keep their doings out of the public eye. It is one of the small hypocrisies that elicit newspaper columns lamenting the decline of morality and the infiltration of infidel ways.

Given the strong proselytizing impulse in Islam, it is not surprising that some Christians convert. Approximately 1.3 million Filipinos work in Saudi Arabia, of whom a large number are Christians. While some who convert to Islam cite pressure from Muslim colleagues and employers, others say they converted out of conviction not coercion or because they noticed that Muslims made better wages and had an easier time getting new jobs when their contracts expired. Some of the new Muslims revert to Christianity when they get back to the Philippines, but others keep their new religion.[40]

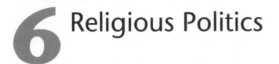

6 Religious Politics

At dawn on 20 November 1979, as Saudi worshipers joined with the remnants of the year's pilgrims for prayer at Mecca's Grand Mosque, a band of zealots roughly pushed aside the prayer leader and announced the advent of the Muslim messiah. The leader of the mosque takeover, Juhaiman al-Utaibi, accused Al Saud of betraying Islam by selling the land of the holy places to infidels and tolerating the spread of immorality (in other words, by allowing Western commercial and cultural influence). Likewise, he denounced the religious establishment for defending such unworthy rulers. In the weeks before seizing the mosque, Juhaiman and about three hundred followers had smuggled weapons and food into the sanctuary to prepare for a siege they expected to end in divinely sanctioned triumph over the unholy government.

King Khalid and the senior princes were stunned to find themselves facing an adversary using their dynasty's claim to rule on behalf of Islam against them. To deal with the challenge, they needed the backing of the religious leadership, especially if they were to retake the mosque by force. The king turned to the Council of Senior Ulama for authorization and it obliged with a fatwa stating that if the renegades did not surrender, then the government could resort to force. The battle for the Grand Mosque raged for two weeks. After Juhaiman's fighters repelled government efforts to regain control, the royals obtained assistance from French special forces, who reportedly undertook a nominal religious conversion that allowed them to enter the Muslim sanctuary. Even with their training and guidance, the fighting took more than two hundred lives before security forces overwhelmed the rebels and captured Juhaiman and 60 of his men. The rebels were tried and found guilty of capital crimes, including killing Muslims and violating the Grand Mosque's sanctity. The government sentenced 63 men to death. The condemned men were divided up and sent to seven cities for public execution by beheading on 9 January 1980.

This event, the Mecca Uprising, was the second of three violent rebellions against the Saudi dynasty rooted in the feeling that the rulers were betraying Islam. In the first, the Ikhwan challenged Abdulaziz ibn Saud; in the most recent, from 2003 to 2006, al-Qaeda in the Arabian Peninsula waged a terrorist campaign to expel Westerners. All three episodes revealed weak points in the Saudi monarchy's claim to rule in the name of Islam. By wrapping themselves in its mantle, Al Saud is able to tap a reservoir of symbolic power as the custodian of the holy places, protector of the pilgrimage, and enforcer of sharia. As sponsor of the country's dense network of religious institutions, it controls the salaries of thousands of employees. Nevertheless, it is not immune to charges of faint-hearted commitment to divine principles. Surveying the trail of religious dissent in the last half-century reveals that Wahhabi officialdom seldom departs from the habit of supporting Al Saud. Since the 1950s, the springs of dissent lay outside the kingdom and seeped in through channels cut by royal decisions to integrate the country with the outside world. Doing so dented the dynasty's religious armor by dropping the original Wahhabi insistence on blocking interaction with the outside world of infidels, including Muslims who had lapsed into idolatry as well as non-Muslims.

The Muslim Brotherhood

Starting in the 1920s, King Abdulaziz deemed it essential to admit both sorts of infidel for the sake of stabilizing his reign. Wahhabi doctrine has not easily digested the presence of non-Muslims due to the threat of infidel ideas and habits. Foreign Muslims represent a different kind of danger because they outwardly share with Saudis the same beliefs, rituals, and morals. Moreover, during the 1950s and 1960s, Muslim immigrants tended to see world politics the same way as Saudis, regarding communism, socialism, and secularism as the most serious dangers confronting believers. Over time, however, it became clear that foreign Muslims, particularly those coming from Arab countries, did not see eye to eye with the Wahhabi establishment, and as their outlook took hold with younger Saudis, they offered a platform for dissident religious politics based on the activism and ideology of the Muslim Brotherhood.

Founded in 1928 by a young Egyptian schoolteacher named Hasan al-Banna, the Muslim Brotherhood quickly evolved into the first modern Islamic revivalist movement. Banna was convinced that the only way Egyptians could overcome European domination of politics, economy, and culture was by returning to religious observance and morality in personal life and applying Islamic principles in public life. In the span of a decade, his knack for organization and his personal magnetism enabled him to turn what began as an association of a few men in a town on the Suez Canal into a national, social, and political force. In the early 1940s, the Brotherhood had a network of branches and cells that stretched across the country. Much of its attraction derived from its claim that Islam is not just a matter of belief and worship but also a source of principles that apply to every kind of mundane problem. In essence, it offered a reading of Islam for the era of resistance to Western imperialism and the ideological competition between communism and capitalism.

One ingredient in the Brotherhood's popularity was Banna's refusal to get embroiled in disputes over what he regarded as religious minutiae. As a student at the teachers' college in Cairo, he became disillusioned with Egypt's traditional religious leadership ensconced at the Azhar seminary. Their feuds over the details of prayer, Sufi practices, and the like struck him as distractions from more urgent matters, particularly the inroads made by Western customs at the expense of morality and piety. Upper- and middle-class women were trading their veils for European dress, while men squandered money at dance cabarets and nightclubs serving alcohol. It seemed to Banna that the Azhar's clerics should have been more worried about dealing with the general climate of moral decay than fussing about the fine points of theology and congregational prayer. In Banna's eyes, moral corruption was only one dimension of Egypt's subjugation to European domination. While Egypt attained formal independence in 1923, its treaty with Great Britain surrendered to London control over defense, the Suez Canal zone, and the property of foreigners and minorities. Banna believed Egypt had fallen under foreign domination because its people were deeply divided, so the way to recover independence and dignity was through unity on the basis of allegiance to Islam. Clerical feuds, therefore, were not only futile but harmful. His ecumenical position on religious doctrine and practice was intended to avoid self-defeating schisms.

In the Egyptian context of confrontation with European domination, the formula made sense, and it made Brotherhood ideology suitable for export to Arab countries striving to escape colonialism. By the early 1950s, the Muslim Brotherhood had branches in Sudan, Syria, Jordan, and Yemen, but not in Saudi

Arabia. Hasan al-Banna made several visits to the kingdom to perform the pilgrimage, and on one occasion he reportedly asked King Abdulaziz for permission to set up a branch, only to be told that since all Saudis are brethren in Islam, there was no need. Behind the glib response was the fact that the king did not allow political parties or organizations. And even had he been open to the suggestion, the Wahhabi establishment would have opposed admitting a Muslim organization that did not share its doctrines. For instance, Wahhabi ulama considered Sufi ceremonies forms of polytheism and prohibited them, whereas the Muslim Brotherhood took a lenient view of them as perhaps misguided but certainly not grounds for excommunication. Similarly, the Wahhabi definition of monotheistic belief was the central pillar of their doctrine but the Muslim Brotherhood considered theological questions the sort of secondary issues that kept Muslims divided.

Hasan al-Banna also diverged from Wahhabi doctrine over the correct relationship between rulers and subjects. Wahhabi clerics followed the line that sincere believers may offer a ruler discreet counsel and advice, a tenet that played into the sort of disengagement from public affairs that Banna thought made Egypt's renowned Azhar seminary irrelevant. He did not embrace the political theory of Ibn Taymiyya, if he was even aware of it, so the Wahhabi tenet requiring obedience as long as the ruler upheld sharia did not have a place in the Muslim Brotherhood. Banna was a natural activist and he felt perfectly at ease in the rough-and-tumble world of political debate, delivering speeches, and publishing his views in the Muslim Brotherhood's newspaper and magazine.

The Muslim Brotherhood's ideology took a radical turn after Hasan al-Banna's assassination by the Egyptian police in 1949. In the next two decades, the most influential thinker to emerge was a onetime literary critic named Sayyid Qutb. His writings reflected the mood of anger and despair that gripped the organization in the 1950s and 1960s when Egypt came under the rule of Gamal Abdul Nasser, whose regime banned, imprisoned, and tortured many Muslim Brothers, including Qutb. As he sat in prison, he pondered how Muslims could torment fellow believers, and he concluded that it was impossible. The only explanation was that Nasser was not a believer and that the society which tolerated his rule was not Muslim either. Qutb defined the contemporary world as a reversion to pre-Islamic ignorance of God's word, *jahiliyya*, a bit like the way Muhammad ibn Abd al-Wahhab regarded his time as steeped in idolatry. The few remaining believers, in Qutb's view, must form a vanguard on the model of the Prophet Muhammad's initial band of disciples and wage jihad against their 'jahili' oppressors. In 1966, he paid for his ideas with his life as the Egyptian government had him executed for his alleged role in a revolutionary plot. He became a martyr whose life and writings inspired a generation of 'Qutbist' militants who felt that Hasan al-Banna's emphasis on preaching and education was admirable but insufficient in the face of pervasive forces of infidelity, polytheism, and jahiliyya.

In the decades following World War II, disagreement between Wahhabi clerics and Muslim Brothers over religious doctrine and political activism seemed minor compared to their agreement that Islam was being threatened by a rising tide of godless forces such as communism, socialism, Arab nationalism, and Western materialism. Moreover, prominent Muslim Brothers residing in the kingdom took to explaining away differences with Wahhabism. One of the central figures in that effort was Sayyid Qutb's younger brother Muhammad. After spending some years in Egyptian prisons, Muhammad Qutb was released in 1971 and moved to Mecca, where he became an instructor at the sharia college, which later became Umm al-Qura University. He published several books reinterpreting his brother's ideas and arguing that there was no difference between them and Wahhabism. It was not an easy argument to make, but it helped that new editions of Sayyid Qutb's books omitted sections that hinted at the virtues of socialism, which would surely annoy the Saudis. In addition to reinterpreting, if not distorting, his brother's ideas, Muhammad Qutb gave moderate readings of Wahhabi doctrine. While not everybody was convinced by his synthesis, it was effective as part of a broader trend taken up by Saudi writers that produced a hybrid religious discourse coupling Wahhabi theology with Muslim Brotherhood politics and social activism, a hybrid that characterized the vibrant religious awakening – the *Sahwa* – that surfaced in the 1970s.[1]

In the 1950s and 1960s, hundreds of Muslim Brothers sought refuge in Saudi Arabia from persecution by Arab nationalist regimes in Egypt and Syria. They found a home congenial to their religious bent and the kingdom benefited from their training as educators at a time when the kingdom was developing a national school system in which they played an essential role as teachers and curriculum designers. When the Saudi government created the Islamic University of Medina in 1961, Muslim Brothers filled many faculty and administrative posts. The university's emphasis on educating foreign Muslims made it an effective vehicle for spreading Brotherhood ideology through graduates returning to their home countries. Members of the Brotherhood also assumed influential positions in international Islamic organizations that the Saudis were instrumental in establishing to counter secular and radical forces abroad. The Muslim World League was formed in 1962 to strengthen Islam and proselytize through support for religious education and advocating implementation of sharia. Ten years later, the Saudi government took the lead in founding the World Assembly of Muslim Youth. Muslim Brothers in the kingdom played prominent roles in both organizations. The World Assembly of Muslim Youth in particular became a preserve of the Brothers that they used to spread their views throughout the Muslim world and the Muslim diaspora in Europe and North America.[2]

While the Muslim Brothers found footholds to propagate their views, the one area off limits to them was the traditional religious establishment, especially the sharia courts and the Council of Senior Ulama. These remained the exclusive preserve of Saudi-born Wahhabi clerics. From the 1980s onward, a political fault line became visible, with the Wahhabi strongholds proving stalwart backers for Al Saud on one side, and on the other the institutions under the sway of the Muslim Brotherhood, incubating dissidents ready to take the rulers to task for their policies.

The Saudi government's ban on independent organizations prevented the establishment of a formal branch of the Muslim Brotherhood. Nonetheless, young Saudis enthused by its activist ideology developed close-knit networks, known as *jama`at*, the Arabic word for groups. By the early 1970s, five such groups were building up a broad following among young Saudis through contacts in classrooms, summer camps, sports clubs, and associations for the memorization of the Quran. The groups shared the agenda of the Muslim Brotherhood, but developed separate identities due to their origins in one part of the country or another. One of the groups stood apart because it adhered to the views of a Syrian named Muhammad Surur, who broke with the Muslim Brotherhood over the issue of using violence against Arab nationalist governments. In an illustration of how the most heated political disputes can occur among former comrades, Saudi Muslim Brothers condemned Surur's followers and coined the nickname 'Sururi' to mock them.[3]

At the same time that the Muslim Brotherhood was taking root in the kingdom, the number of Western-educated Saudis was growing as the government sent young men to American universities for training to fill administrative, professional, and technical positions. Their exposure to Western manners, culture, and political ideologies spurred the emergence of an intellectual tendency that advocated the fusion of religion and modernity.

Similar cultural trends had surfaced in other Muslim lands that had close encounters with Western powers in the nineteenth and early twentieth centuries, and these trends had triggered a cultural backlash expressed in terms of Islamic revival. The Muslim Brotherhood had its roots as a response to Egyptian admirers of the West, so its Saudi networks naturally took up the cause of challenging Westernizers in the name of the Sahwa religious awakening.

The kingdom's culture conflict of the 1970s took place against the backdrop of the first oil boom, which ran its course between 1973 and 1981. Those were years of stupendous wealth that transformed Saudi Arabia. The nation entered a frenzy of construction, laying down highways, enlarging airports and seaports, building hospitals and schools, and constructing new houses with modern amenities. So many construction cranes cluttered the skyline that expatriate wags would refer to them as the national bird. Cities rapidly spread as pavement and concrete covered desert lands with new shopping and residential districts. The planning and execution of the multibillion-dollar projects demanded more labor and technical skill than the country could provide, so millions of expatriate workers arrived to design, build, and maintain the national infrastructure.

The leap in expatriate numbers and the flood of cash reshaped everyday life. Previously, Arab, Asian, and Western workers were visible but not very conspicuous, as they resided in special neighborhoods separate from Saudis and worked in the oil sector, hospitals, and finance. During the oil boom, however, foreign workers toiled at construction sites and staffed the hundreds of new shops that opened to sell imported goods to Saudis flush with cash. Furthermore, newly affluent families began to vacation in Europe and North America. It turned out that the Wahhabi clerics of the nineteenth century were correct in their apprehension that rubbing shoulders with infidels would weaken the resolve of some to avoid adopting their ways. A handful of cinemas appeared in Jeddah. Saudi television stations hired women news broadcasters. Stores selling Western clothing styles fared well. Hip young Saudis shaved their beards and let their hair grow long. In the eyes of the pious, it seemed that the kingdom would soon drown in infidel ways because of the blessing of oil abundance. The Muslim Brotherhood groups viewed the tide of Western influence with concern, perhaps recalling the Egyptian and Syrian experiences that resulted in the establishment of secular nationalist regimes. They waged a war of words against defenders of Western ways, but did not make much of a dent in their influence until the November 1979 Mecca Uprising, an event that took everybody by surprise and revealed that while the Muslim Brotherhood may have been the most pervasive foreign Islamic element in the kingdom, it was not the only one.

Salafis and the Sahwa

When the Islamic University of Medina opened in 1961, its faculty included an Albanian-born, Syrian-raised specialist in the Prophetic Tradition, Sheikh Nasir al-Din al-Albani. Eschewing the lessons given by sheikhs in the mosques of Damascus according to time-honored custom, Albani took a solitary path to religious expertise. By the early 1950s he had a reputation as one of his generation's masters of the Prophetic Tradition. His firm theological convictions and disdain for the spread of secularism made him seem a perfect candidate to teach his specialty at the new university near the Prophet's Mosque. The trouble was that he did not have the Muslim Brotherhood's sensitive political antennae. While they were content to respect the Wahhabi establishment's authority on ritual and doctrine, he bowed only to the texts of the Quran and the Prophetic Tradition. If he detected any departure from them, he said so, and this created friction with his hosts on matters of general principle and detail.[4]

For instance, Albani maintained that the Wahhabis were correct when it came to theology but wrong when it came to Islamic law because they adhered to the Hanbali School; he asserted that the law schools were late innovations and that believers should refer only to the Quran and the Prophetic Tradition. On particular matters, he believed that there was no basis in either source for obliging women to cover their faces. Students in awe of his command of the Prophetic Tradition began to follow him on details of prayer that diverged from Wahhabi practice. This was precisely the sort of nitpicking that Hasan al-Banna considered a distraction, but Albani made no secret of his disdain for what he considered the Muslim Brotherhood's excessive involvement in politics at the expense of religious rectitude, in particular their toleration of Sufi beliefs.

Albani's formidable knowledge drew a modest following of young men who revived a name from early Islam to describe themselves: the Folk of Prophetic Tradition (Ahli Hadith), setting them apart from the official establishment's Hanbali affiliation and the Muslim Brotherhood's activist leanings. When the Saudi government allowed his teaching contract to lapse after a few years, he returned to Syria, but his disciples remained a distinct faction known for their zeal even compared to other pious circles. Some of them felt a duty to look beyond questions of how to pray to the public realm, where they witnessed the influx of devilish foreign influences. One night in 1965, a few of them attacked a store in Medina for displaying female mannequins in its windows. Other members decided to seek endorsement from the official religious establishment. They met with Sheikh Abdulaziz ibn Baz and he approved their initiative to organize themselves as the 'Salafi Group', the name indicating that their purpose was to preserve the ways of the Pious Ancestors. Ibn Baz assigned one of his lieutenants to act as a liaison, and perhaps as a monitor to keep an eye out for vigilante excess.[5]

In the next decade, the Salafi Group attracted new members, thanks to its headquarters in Medina where pilgrims visited the Prophet's Mosque and students came to attend the religious university. New recruits carried its message to their hometowns, giving it broad reach across the kingdom even though its failure to attract large numbers meant it had shallower social penetration than the Muslim Brotherhood groups. Over time, the Salafi Group's conspicuously different way of performing prayer caused friction with the religious establishment. One steamy evening in 1977, Sheikh Ibn Baz sent a deputy to meet with the Salafi Group and its leader, Juhaiman al-Utaibi, on the roof of their communal residence on the edge of Medina. The deputy's mission was to persuade them to conform to the common way of group prayer, but the meeting ended in acrimony and a rift opened between Ibn Baz and the Salafi Group.

At that point, Juhaiman began to make subversive criticisms of the Saudi dynasty for allowing jihad to lapse in the 1920s and for permitting banks to charge interest, violating the sharia ban on usury. He also accused members of the royal family of squandering the country's oil wealth and scandalously immoral conduct. When rumors that the Salafi Group was gathering weapons reached the authorities, they made some arrests but Juhaiman eluded them and fled to the desert, where he spent the next two years as a fugitive. While on the run, he became convinced that one of his followers was the Muslim messiah, the Mahdi (the rightly guided one), sent by God to overthrow corrupt rulers and wipe out oppression. His reading of the Prophetic Tradition told him that the Mahdi's advent would coincide with the start of the fifteenth century in the Muslim lunar calendar, 20 November 1979 in the Western calendar.

The Mecca Uprising was not the only shock to Saudi politics that year, or even that month. As security forces puzzled over how to regain control of the Grand Mosque, anti-government demonstrations erupted in the Eastern Province, where local and regional currents stoked Shiite discontent. The Wahhabi religious establishment scorned and persecuted them for decades; the oil boom passed them by, leaving their towns and villages awash in sewage. Saudi Shiites were emboldened in early 1979 when Iranians overthrew their unpopular secular monarchy and installed a populist Islamic government led by Ayatollah Khomeini. The new Islamic Republic summoned Shiites throughout the Gulf to rid themselves of tyrants. Protests roiled through Saudi Arabia's Shiite towns for two weeks until a combination of repression and government promises to improve conditions settled things down.

The revolutionary government in Iran, which dubbed itself the Islamic Republic, turned into a long-term problem for the Saudi government for a number of reasons. First, Iran is a Shiite majority country, and consequently Wahhabi–Shiite sectarian animosity is never far from the surface. Iran's Shiites are mindful of the horrible Karbala massacre carried out by Saudi-Wahhabi forces in 1802, they are aware that the Wahhabis consider them to be unbelievers, and they sympathize with the plight of Shiite populations under Sunni rule. Second, the Iranian Revolution drew much of its energy from anger at the United States for its support for the Iranian monarchy. The revolutionaries painted Washington as the 'Great Satan', conniving with 'Little Satan', namely Israel, to extinguish Islam by working through puppet rulers such as the former Iranian shah. Saudi Arabia's close relations with the United States made it a natural target for the revolutionaries seeking to uproot American influence from the region. Third, as two of the three largest Gulf countries, along with Iraq, Saudi Arabia and Iran are geopolitical rivals. Muhammad Reza Shah had thought of Iran as a rising world power and the natural leader of the Gulf. Even though the Islamic Republic rejected the shah's policies, it shared his sense of Iran's right to regional leadership, which the Saudis have always opposed.

Fourth, there is an ethnic layer to Saudi–Iranian tensions, arising from the history of enmity between Arabs and Persians, sometimes expressed in terms of deeply rooted stereotypes.

All these factors came into play during the Iran–Iraq War that began when Iraq's Saddam Husain ordered an invasion, seeking to bring down the Islamic Republic. His gambit failed as Iraq's first burst of military momentum petered out after a year. Iran then seized the initiative with a counterattack that expelled enemy forces. Saudi Arabia openly sided with Arab Iraq against Persian Iran, and wound up lending billions of dollars to help Baghdad. The Iranians intensified their verbal attacks on the Saudis and turned the annual pilgrimage into an occasion to needle Riyadh by fomenting demonstrations against the United States for supporting Israel, an indirect jibe at the Saudis.

A less direct threat to Saudi Arabia loomed in December 1979, when the Soviet Union invaded Afghanistan to prop up a shaky Marxist regime. Saudi authorities had barely begun to recover their poise after quelling uprisings at opposite ends of the country and now Soviet troops were moving closer to the Gulf than ever before. The Saudis were able to turn the Afghan cause to their advantage by making solidarity with the Afghan resistance to the Soviet occupation a central plank in domestic and foreign policy. In the 1980s, the Afghan jihad galvanized religious solidarity and a feeling that the royal family was aligned with popular sentiment.[6]

The Saudi rulers interpreted Juhaiman's uprising as a sign that it was time to roll back Western influence and to bolster the monarchy's religious credentials. Women disappeared from television and newspapers stopped publishing photographs showing them; gender segregation was more strictly enforced; cinemas and video stores were shut down; censorship of university textbooks was tightened. In 1986, King Fahd adopted a new title, Custodian of the Two Holy Cities. More broadly, the rulers augmented the budgets of religious universities and the Commission for the

Promotion of Virtue and Prevention of Vice. Gone were the days when expatriates and Saudis, men and women, could attend chamber music concerts at Riyadh's Intercontinental Hotel.[7]

The religious turn in domestic policy dovetailed with the emphasis on solidarity with the Afghan jihad. The government opened ways of assisting the Afghan jihad, primarily through fundraising, but also paving the way for volunteers to join. Sahwa partisans responded with strong support for the kingdom against Iran in their Muslim cold war – not that they needed much more than permission to publish, given their fervent animosity toward Shiism. In terms of the culture war between modernists and their religious critics, the latter gained the upper hand in the late 1980s, as newspapers and magazines under royal patronage began to shun liberal writers and opened their pages to Sahwa supporters instead. As the decade ended, economic problems arising from low oil prices stirred grumbling over inflation and unemployment, but overall it looked as if the new blend of Islam in domestic and foreign policies had succeeded at capturing the Sahwa's political energies and retaining the Wahhabi establishment's firm backing.

A new crisis erupted on the morning of 2 August 1990 when 100,000 Iraqi troops rolled into Kuwait. Saddam Husain was irritated by his neighbor's refusal to forgive billions of dollars in loans dating to the Iran–Iraq War. Furthermore, Kuwait was exceeding the oil quota set by the oil cartel, OPEC. By doing so, it kept oil prices low, cutting Baghdad's revenues and damaging its efforts at postwar economic reconstruction. Rather than tolerate what he regarded as economic warfare, Saddam decided to seize Kuwait. By the evening of 2 August, nobody knew whether Saddam's forces would hunker down in Kuwait or advance into Saudi Arabia to occupy its oil fields a few hundred miles away. As the Saudi rulers digested the sudden blow to regional stability, the United States government decided to offer military protection against a possible Iraqi invasion. A delegation of American politicians and generals tried to persuade King Fahd and the senior princes to accept United States military intervention.

The stakes for the ruling family could not have been higher. Saudi military forces would not be able to withstand an Iraqi offensive but Al Saud was mindful of the political sensitivity of admitting non-Muslim military forces into the kingdom. For one thing, Riyadh's relationship with Washington was a delicate matter because of American support for Israel, viewed by many in Saudi Arabia as an assault on fellow Muslims in Palestine. Furthermore, seeking the assistance of infidels would violate a sharia principle that Wahhabi clerics had long upheld. In 1871, they had condemned a Saudi emir for soliciting Ottoman help to defeat dynastic rivals. If King Fahd was to open the country to American troops, he needed the endorsement of the Council of Senior Ulama. Yielding to intense political pressure, the Council supplied a carefully worded fatwa permitting the rulers to bring in forces qualified to stave off external aggression. Having covered his religious flank, King Fahd informed the United States that its military support was welcome. Washington then rounded up support at the United Nations for resolutions demanding that Iraq withdraw from Kuwait at the same time that it gathered an international military coalition to protect the kingdom.

In the next few months, more than 500,000 foreign troops assembled in Saudi Arabia. Notwithstanding the Council of Senior Ulama's fatwa, religious dissidents regarded the arrival of infidel troops as a blatant violation of the ban on seeking their assistance. A few days after the fatwa's pronouncement, a leading figure in the Sahwa movement, Sheikh Safar al-Hawali, denounced it as an erroneous reading of the Americans' motivation, which in his view came down to controlling oil supplies. A few months later, the debate over admitting non-Muslims gave way to a new concern. American forces included female soldiers operating military vehicles in Saudi cities, immune from the ban on women driving.

Liberal Saudi women decided the time was ripe to challenge that ban. On 8 November 1990, about fifty of them took a drive around Riyadh. Even though the authorities had them arrested, Sahwa dissidents suspected that the government was opening the way to complete liberal domination that would overturn conformity to strict religious morality. The fear of a secular cultural revolution brought the Sahwa into the open as an opposition movement for the next four years.

Starting with a Letter of Demands in January 1991, the Sahwa movement called on the government to reaffirm its commitment to Islamic principles through concrete measures such as vetting the piety of all government employees. The rulers took umbrage at the suggestion that they fell short in meeting their duty to govern according to Islam and summoned the Wahhabi leadership to denounce Sahwa sheikhs as misguided upstarts. This put the religious establishment in the middle of a struggle between royal power and religious idealism. The few clerics who supported the Sahwa were sacked from their posts. Most senior clerics stood by Al Saud and condemned the signatories to the Letter of Demands, not for what they demanded but how: they violated the Wahhabi tenet of offering rulers private counsel rather than public criticism. The political picture was complicated by the liberal camp's circulation of its own petitions calling for broad reforms to strengthen the country's economic and political foundations.

The royal response to religious and liberal demands came in the form of the Basic Law of Governance, issued in March 1992. The first of the Basic Law's 83 articles states that the constitution of the kingdom is the Quran and the Prophetic Tradition. Articles pertaining to the kingdom's legal framework stipulate that all fatwas refer to the Quran and the Prophetic Tradition (Article 45), that in applying the sharia, the judiciary possesses independence (Article 46), although judges are appointed and dismissed by royal decree (Article 52), that the courts apply the sharia to all cases

(Article 48), and that the king or his deputies implement judicial rulings (Article 50).[8]

King Fahd may have supposed that the Basic Law would satisfy religious and liberal demands, but the document merely affirmed the supremacy of dynastic authority and its commitment to ruling according to Islam without committing to new initiatives sought by activists. Sahwa activists issued a follow up to the Letter of Demands known as the Memorandum of Advice, repeating most of the points set forth in the first document. Confrontation between the authorities and dissidents escalated when Sahwa activists announced the formation of the Committee for the Defense of Legitimate Rights (CDLR) in response to the arrest of a colleague. It was one thing to circulate cassette tapes of dissident preachers and petitions, but the kingdom did not tolerate independent organizations. The government started harassing, arresting, detaining, and jailing Sahwa leaders. In September 1994, the two leading Sahwa spokesmen, Sheikh Safar al-Hawali and Sheikh Salman al-Awda, were sent to prison. The movement's leadership then shifted to men who had fled the country to lead the religious opposition from exile in London. Muhammad al-Mas`ari and Sa`d al-Faqih kept the CDLR alive as the voice of the Sahwa outside the kingdom, but their communiqués and faxes to news agencies made no visible impact on the inside.

In addition to using sheer repression, Saudi authorities sought to erode public support for the Sahwa by encouraging loyal sheikhs to attack the dissidents on religious grounds. The lead was taken by two specialists in the Prophetic Tradition from the Islamic University in Medina, the Saudi cleric Sheikh Rabi al-Madkhali and the Ethiopia-born Sheikh Muhammad Aman al-Jami. Madkhali's intellectual pedigree went back to Nasir al-Din al-Albani. Madkhali, Jami, and their associates denounced the Sahwa as a local version of the Muslim Brotherhood, sharing its defects in matters of theology, exhibiting a superficial grasp of religious learning, and dividing believers with partisan political bickering. Given their propensity for doctrinal nitpicking, schisms soon divided the loyalists and they became immersed in their own disputes.[9] Meanwhile, the rulers took steps to shore up control over the religious establishment. A royal decree in 1993 created the Ministry of Islamic Affairs, *Waqfs* (Religious Endowments), Preaching and Guidance. The new ministry gave loyalist clergy control over the appointment of preachers, proselytizing activities, and the substantial funds invested in religious endowments known as waqfs.[10] Furthermore, university appointments were placed directly under royal authority. In short order, the government dismissed Sahwa sympathizers and replaced them with loyalists.

Osama bin Laden and al-Qaeda

The suppression of the Sahwa did not spell the end of religious dissent. On 13 November 1995, a massive car bomb detonated in Riyadh in front of a building for an American military training mission, killing five Americans and two Indians. Investigators identified the perpetrators as a band of four Saudis, three of whom were veterans of the Afghan jihad.[11] The bombers targeted Americans because they considered the United States the real force behind the Saudi government's suppression of religious dissenters. Even though they were never tied to an organization, their terrorist strike foreshadowed the emergence of al-Qaeda. Saudi Arabia's volatile brew of religion and politics certainly played a role in the rise of al-Qaeda, but the organization's founder, Osama bin Laden, played for larger stakes than the kingdom. Nevertheless, his family roots and the support he found among Saudi veterans of the Afghan jihad made his homeland part of the story.

Osama bin Laden's father Muhammad migrated from Hadhramaut (the eastern region in Yemen) to Saudi Arabia in the

1930s. He arrived at the dawn of the kingdom's petroleum era, gained the confidence of King Abdulaziz, and amassed a fortune as a contractor on road-building and construction projects, including the expansion of Mecca's Grand Mosque. His son Osama grew up in Jeddah, where he came under the influence of Muslim Brotherhood ideology at the hands of schoolteachers and university instructors. In the early years of the Afghan war, he joined the stream of young Saudis flocking to the Pakistani city of Peshawar, headquarters for the jihad. He first served the Afghan cause as a fundraiser in the kingdom before settling in Peshawar in 1986 to coordinate the delivery of equipment and supplies to Afghan mujahedin. During his sojourn, he participated in one battle against Soviet-backed Afghan forces, enhancing his stature as a champion of the cause. As the war wound down, Bin Laden created a register of volunteers that became the kernel of al-Qaeda, an Arabic word meaning 'the base'.[12]

With the evacuation of Soviet troops, Bin Laden returned to Saudi Arabia, like so many other heroic volunteers for the jihad. At the time of Iraq's invasion of Kuwait, he tried to dissuade the rulers from depending on the Americans and vowed that he could recruit a volunteer force to defend the kingdom against Saddam Husain's army. His offer was not accepted and he soon joined the ranks of religious dissidents opposing the arrival of infidel troops. He supported the Sahwa protest movement but was more interested in finding new Muslim causes, so he moved to Sudan, where an Islamic military junta had seized power.

From the safety of Khartoum, Bin Laden entered the Saudi political fray by forming the Advice and Reform Committee to espouse the Sahwa cause. His strident attacks on the monarchy and the Wahhabi religious leadership, including Sheikh Ibn Baz, led the Saudi government to strip him of citizenship in 1994. By that time, however, politics in his native land was just a small piece in what he considered a grander global struggle between Islam and the West. Suspicion in Washington and Riyadh of his involvement in a number of militant attacks on Western targets in Somalia and Egypt led to pressure on the Sudanese authorities to expel him. In 1996, he left for a new home in Afghanistan. Not long after settling there, he issued a fatwa declaring jihad against the United States, citing a litany of its crimes against Muslims, including what he called its military occupation of the land of the two holy places, Saudi Arabia.

It was a clever rhetorical stroke. Even though American troops had come at the invitation of the rulers and with the blessings of the religious leadership, many Saudis had the feeling that the Americans were more interested in protecting oil fields than shielding a friendly Arab country. Furthermore, after the liberation of Kuwait, thousands of American troops stayed in the kingdom, again with the concurrence of the rulers, who felt US forces supplied an effective deterrent to Saddam Husain's aggressive impulses. But much of the Saudi public suspected that Washington's true intention was to use their country as a base for dominating the Muslim world. Over time, the American military presence fueled discontent and eroded the monarchy's credibility, proving a strategic asset in regard to Iraq but a liability in domestic politics.

In August 1998, al-Qaeda carried out its first major terrorist operation, dispatching suicide truck bombs to attack the American embassies in Nairobi in Kenya and Dar es-Salaam in Tanzania. Africans made up most of the over two hundred casualties, although 12 Americans were killed. Washington retaliated with cruise missile attacks on suspected al-Qaeda targets in Afghanistan and Sudan, but Bin Laden was not deterred from continuing his terrorist jihad. Two years later, al-Qaeda struck again, this time in Aden harbor, where suicide bombers detonated an explosives-laden launch as it approached the USS *Cole*, killing 17 sailors. The first two operations in al-Qaeda's anti-American jihad were but a prelude to the grand terrorist attack of 9/11 that killed nearly three thousand Americans.

In Saudi Arabia, responses to 9/11 reflected the spectrum of religious opinion, from enthusiastic applause for striking a blow in the holy war against the United States in circles sympathetic to Bin Laden to stern condemnation of mass murder by Wahhabi officials. Many Saudis flatly refused to believe that al-Qaeda was responsible for the suicide hijackings and speculated that the American CIA or the Israeli Mossad agency was behind them. Meanwhile, American officials, media, and public opinion suspected that the Saudi connection to the attacks went beyond the nationality of 15 of the 19 hijackers. Fingers pointed to Wahhabi influence as the inspiration for hatred toward the West and the root cause of al-Qaeda terrorism. Public denunciation of the suicide attacks as violations of Islam by leading figures in the Saudi religious establishment were ignored or deemed disingenuous.

By September 2001, the Saudi authorities had released the Sahwa sheikhs Safar al-Hawali and Salman al-Awda. They emerged from prison in 1999, chastened and ready to reframe the Sahwa movement as a contender for religious leadership rather than challenger to the ruling family. Their rehabilitation proved useful to the dynasty's efforts to strengthen the foundations of religious legitimacy that had weakened under the impact of Sahwa protests and Osama bin Laden's fatwas. The return of Hawali and Awda coincided with the deaths of the two dominant Wahhabi clerics of the 1980s and 1990s. Sheikh Abdulaziz ibn Baz and Sheikh Muhammad al-Uthaimin had had impeccable reputations for learning, piety, and integrity, making them powerful resources for the monarchy's religious legitimacy. When Ibn Baz died in 1999, and Uthaimin in 2001, the ranks of Wahhabi ulama included no one of comparable stature to replace them. True, a member of Al al-Sheikh was appointed Grand Mufti in Ibn Baz's stead, but he did not command the same degree of respect. The chastened

Sahwa sheikhs were in one sense rivals with the now-diminished clerical leadership, but they served a similar political function for the monarchy, namely, furnishing religious cover, especially by condemning al-Qaeda's suicide terrorism.

The United States' response to 9/11 was framed in terms of a policy known as the Global War on Terror. It included the October 2001 invasion of Afghanistan to overthrow the Taliban and destroy al-Qaeda, support for Israel's suppression of the second Palestinian uprising – the al-Aqsa Intifada – that erupted in late September 2001, and the March 2003 invasion of Iraq to overthrow Saddam Husain. In Saudi Arabia and much of the Muslim world, the Global War on Terror looked like a Global War on Islam. Saudi religious dissidents sympathetic to Bin Laden and the Taliban condemned the Saudi government for allowing the Americans to use military bases in the kingdom as a violation of the Islamic prohibition on lending assistance to infidels attacking fellow believers. In the eyes of Saudi dissidents, the Americans were following in the footsteps of the Soviets, and some took off for Afghanistan to wage jihad against what they labeled a Christian crusade against Islam, ignoring the fact that the Americans coordinated their military campaign with the Afghan Northern Alliance, a coalition of Muslim rivals of the Taliban.

It took two months for the American–Afghan coalition to oust the Taliban and force Bin Laden to flee the country, but the political fallout was lasting, in large part due to the establishment of a concentration camp on the American base at Guantánamo Bay, Cuba, to hold prisoners captured in the Afghan conflict. The US government refused to grant them prisoner-of-war status because they were not part of a regular army and therefore not entitled to protection under the Geneva Conventions. Instead, Washington coined the term 'enemy combatant' and justified indefinite detention of the prisoners on the grounds that they were terrorists. The inmates at Guantánamo came from several

Muslim countries, including over one hundred from Saudi Arabia. Because the Americans suspected the detainees of ties to al-Qaeda, they subjected some of them to harsh interrogation techniques tantamount to torture. Reports of mistreatment of Saudi prisoners reached the kingdom, fueling anti-American feeling and resentment at the ruling family's tacit support for Washington.

The United States' invasion of Iraq in March 2003 further inflamed Saudi public opinion against Washington. Yet again, the question of Americans using Saudi bases to attack a Muslim country came up. Riyadh refused to allow the Americans to use them for combat missions, only for supplies and logistics. Saddam's fall in early April 2003 meant the US did not need the bases to deter Iraqi aggression any longer and Washington announced it would redeploy to nearby Gulf countries. By that time, however, Saudi supporters of Bin Laden were in the final stages of planning a terrorist campaign to expel Americans and other Westerners from the kingdom.

A few months after being chased from Afghanistan by US forces, Bin Laden had decided to turn Saudi Arabia into a new front for his anti-Western jihad. Veterans of the Afghan jihad gathered around Yusuf al-Uyairi, a former bodyguard for the al-Qaeda leader. Uyairi took his time to raise funds, store weapons, construct a network of cells, and devise a propaganda strategy.[13] On 12 May 2003, Uyairi's men executed a coordinated string of suicide bombings and attacks against three residential compounds for foreigners in Saudi Arabia, killing nine Americans and 17 others. The Saudi public was shocked by the carnage in the middle of Riyadh. The government was ill-prepared to uproot al-Qaeda in the Arabian Peninsula (QAP), as Bin Laden's disciples called themselves.

For the next three years, QAP executed Bin Laden's 1998 fatwa calling on Muslims to kill Americans everywhere, with suicide attacks on foreign residential compounds and business offices, in addition to gunning down Westerners working in the kingdom.

Saudi security forces and QAP militants waged fierce gun battles, some lasting for days, in different parts of the country. Wahhabi clerics and Sahwa sheikhs closed ranks with the government against the men who brought al-Qaeda's jihad against the United States to Saudi soil. As it turned out, few Saudis apart from the several hundred men who had trained in al-Qaeda camps in Afghanistan felt any enthusiasm for a jihad in their own country. Deadly shootouts from Mecca to Riyadh to remote farms took their toll on both sides, as dozens of Saudi policemen and security forces were killed rooting out the militants. A fundamental problem for QAP was its failure to attract new recruits to replace the men it lost to gun battles and arrests. Its propaganda accused Sahwa leaders Hawali and Awda of selling out, but they had found a better outlet for jihad: fighting the US military invasion in Iraq.

Debating the Role of Religion

By the end of 2006, the Saudi government had decapitated the QAP, forcing sympathizers deep underground or out of the country, often to Yemen, where militants were able to exploit the shaky grip of central government authority to recuperate and recommence anti-American operations. The trail of blood, fire, and smoke blazed by QAP had a sobering effect on the kingdom's religious politics. The government's description of the militants as misguided deviants resonated with the country's silent majority. It seems that just about all quarters wanted to lower the political temperature. Debates over social and moral issues certainly did not end, nor were they always models of civility, but jihad inside the kingdom was off the agenda.

When QAP's brief and bloody rampage broke out, the kingdom's religious politics were well into a new phase of public debate on a wide range of subjects that had long been taboo, such as gender mixing and the standing of non-Wahhabi Muslims. The arrival of the internet broadened channels for discussion of divisive issues. Royal leadership also played a part in promoting introspection and discussion. In 1995, King Fahd suffered a massive stroke that rendered him incapable of exercising his duties any longer but he was not deposed; rather, Crown Prince Abdullah became the acting head of state. He was considered a proponent of incremental social reform, a leaning he demonstrated in early 2003 with his call for national dialogue on extremism, women, and religious pluralism. When King Fahd died in August 2005, in the middle of the QAP's terror campaign, Abdullah ascended the throne. The first task was to eradicate QAP, but not long after that was accomplished, the newly crowned king took initiatives to curb religious extremism and to coax Wahhabi clerics to bend on some of their long-established positions. Many were alarmed at the specter of young Saudi men killing fellow Saudis in the name of jihad; some felt that Wahhabi doctrine's xenophobic streak had something to do with violent extremism.

Royal support for moderation through National Dialogue and revising school textbooks may not be enough to uproot the spirit of intolerance firmly entrenched with much of the population. To illustrate the obstacles hindering the advance of moderation, Saudis refer to the story of a chemistry teacher in Buraida named Muhammad al-Harbi. Days after the May 2003 terrorist attacks in Riyadh, the Ministry of Education instructed schools to warn students against fanaticism. Mr. Harbi took it as a signal to do something at his school, where he pinned up a copy of a newspaper article that condemned al-Qaeda for twisting the minds of young people. He soon felt the wrath of conservative colleagues who went to the authorities to accuse him of drinking alcohol, shutting his classroom windows during the call to prayer, and 'mocking religion'. His trial ended with a guilty verdict and he was sentenced to a three-year prison term and public whipping. Mr. Harbi was spared only when Prince Nayef responded to a campaign in the media and revoked the sentence.[14] The episode is but one example of what liberal Saudis describe as intense pressure on teachers who challenge long-held positions on takfir and jihad.

By 2010, the Saudi government had weathered two political challenges – from the Sahwa movement and al-Qaeda – in a long crisis spawned by the Iraqi invasion of Kuwait. The Arab Spring of 2011 represented an entirely unprecedented force in regional politics. Starting with the overthrow of Tunisian President Zine El Din Ben Ali and his flight to Saudi Arabia, a wave of protests swept Egyptian President Hosni Mubarak from power and triggered demands for democracy, from Bahrain and Yemen to Syria and Libya. Chronic dissatisfaction with unresponsive autocratic regimes and economic malaise throughout the Arab world motivated crowds, whose efforts to mobilize and coordinate were facilitated by social media such as Twitter and Facebook. Saudis and Saudi-watchers wondered whether and how the Arab Spring would affect the kingdom. Liberal and Islamist reformers circulated petitions online calling for elections to a national legislature, freedom of expression, and other measures to bring transparency to governance.[15] But apart from cyberspace activism, the regional spirit of protest made little headway in the kingdom. Nevertheless, the rulers were on the alert for signs that unrest could spread to their realm. They considered the escalation of Bahrain's protests particularly alarming given its proximity, its sectarian aspect, pitting a Sunni monarchy and favored Sunni minority against a Shiite majority, the prospect it could generate unrest among Saudi Shiites, and the fear that any gain for Arabian Shiites would give Iran a foothold on the southern shore of the Gulf.

While Riyadh kept a close watch on Bahrain, Saudi opposition websites called for national protests on 11 March 2011. To preempt mass demonstrations, the rulers resorted to religion, force, and reward. Beginning in February, Wahhabi ulama issued fatwas proclaiming anti-government protests unjustified and harmful to believers because they sow division and strife. On the appointed day, the Ministry of Interior blanketed cities with security forces. Apart from the heavily Shiite Eastern Province, where demonstrations for ending discrimination and the release of political prisoners had begun in mid February, just a handful of protesters came onto the streets. A week later, King Abdullah, recently returned from medical treatment in the United States, announced a generous package of subsidies and benefits amounting to $130 billion.[16] One issue did rise to the surface that spring, namely, the right for women to drive, otherwise the kingdom proved immune to the infectious wave of popular protest that swept the region. The absence of protest does not mean the Saudi public is complacent. Young people produce YouTube videos that address social issues such as poverty and the shortage of affordable housing. Twitter has become the preferred platform for airing dissent and criticism of corruption and wasteful spending by the royal family.[17]

While the grand mufti condemned the use of Twitter for spreading malicious lies, clerics have taken to tweeting just as they overcame their instinctive mistrust of the new to sign on to the internet and Facebook.[18] Such flexibility is one reason religion will continue to matter in the kingdom's ongoing political debates, but how religious tendencies evolve is an open question. The Wahhabi establishment commands the resources of multiple government offices and the loyalty of a large if indeterminate segment of the population. But Wahhabi ulama are a less coherent bloc than before. Some are faithful to customary views and mightily resist change on matters such as gender mixing, while others exhibit a pragmatic tendency to bend with shifts in mainstream culture. Meanwhile, the rebellious Sahwa sheikhs of the 1990s have softened their tone and now form a kind of loyal opposition more attuned to social and economic strains on ordinary Saudis. Signs that a spirit of religious pluralism is taking hold with the young generation could bolster the marginal position of a liberal trend.[19] Political events such as the Arab Spring and the coming generational change in royal leadership, along with pressure on living standards and the multiple channels for global cultural opening will affect the respective influence of each religious trend and may spur the emergence of new ones.

7 The International Reach of Wahhabism

Islam, like Christianity, is a proselytizing religion. Striving to spread God's guidance revealed to the Prophet Muhammad is a good deed for one's own sake and for the sake of converts. In Arabic, calling others to Islam is *da`wa*. It reaches back to Muhammad's first public recitation of Quranic verses to the people of Mecca. For centuries, Muslim traders, mystics, scholars, and preachers have called nonbelievers to Islam. Saudi Arabia's activities to spread Islam stem not only from the general Muslim inclination to proselytize, but also Wahhabism's own roots in a preaching mission that targeted people it regarded as lapsed believers. What critics refer to as the export of Wahhabi doctrine, through financial support for building mosques, operating schools, and distributing religious literature, is the continuation of Al Saud's backing for Sheikh Muhammad ibn Abd al-Wahhab's mission.

Societies on the receiving end of Saudi proselytizing today are similar to Arabia on the eve of Sheikh Muhammad's call. They possess diverse traditions of Muslim religious expression, or, from the Wahhabi perspective, they lack comprehension of the duty to expunge their lives of all innovations and polytheistic customs.

Just as many in Najd harshly condemned and rejected Sheikh Muhammad's teachings, so do many Muslims reject them today. But not everything is the same. For one thing, at present the Arabian provenance of Wahhabism can be an asset or a liability, depending on whether it is seen as the way Islam is practiced in the land of the Prophet or as a foreign import. Wahhabi missionaries say they are merely spreading Islam in its pristine Salafi form as practiced by the Pious Ancestors before it was corrupted by converts and foreign influence. However it is perceived, be it vilified or justified, Wahhabism has a long record as a controversial claim to know God's will. Consequently, wherever we find Wahhabi proselytizing, we find converts and opponents duplicating polemical skirmishes fought long ago.

Engaging the Muslim World

In the 1700s, Wahhabi doctrine gained little traction beyond the canopy of Saudi power. As the first Saudi state reached its height in the early 1800s, Wahhabi religious leaders dispatched epistles and emissaries to Egypt, Tunisia, and Morocco, calling on scholars and rulers to endorse their doctrine. Responses varied. The sultan of Morocco embraced Wahhabi condemnation of Sufi beliefs and practices, in part because powerful Sufi saints posed a challenge to his authority. The bey of Tunisia deputized a prominent scholar to compose a refutation of Wahhabi doctrine. Egypt's ulama rejected the Arabian reform movement although the pre-eminent historian of the day gave it a sympathetic account.

It was not until the late 1800s that Wahhabi clerics found like-minded counterparts outside the Saudi realm. In India and the Fertile Crescent, new currents of religious reform intersected with Wahhabi doctrine on a number of issues. In the case of India, the consolidation of British rule around 1860 spurred Muslims to ponder the causes of political decline after centuries of domination by the Mughal dynasty and earlier Muslim sultanates. The search for answers led some to retreat into a defensive posture that avoided engagement with British authorities while others reframed Islamic thought to justify cooperation. Yet other Indian Muslims embraced a campaign to purify belief and practice under the banner of reviving the Prophetic Tradition, hence they became known as the People of Tradition, or Ahli Hadith. They shared Wahhabism's goal of eradicating illegitimate innovations from ritual, especially popular customs at Sufi shrines and the graves of holy men. At the same time, Ahli Hadith scholars differed from Wahhabis on Islamic law. Whereas Wahhabi jurists hewed to the Hanbali School, Ahli Hadith scholars considered adherence to any law school an illegitimate innovation and upheld the Quran and the Prophetic Tradition as the only bases for legal rulings. Nevertheless, there was enough common ground for Wahhabi clerics to travel to India to study with Ahli Hadith scholars, laying the foundations of an enduring relationship.

The mood of reform was also taking root among religious scholars in the Arab lands. Prominent figures in Baghdad and Damascus undertook the revival of the legacy of Ibn Taymiyya, the great thirteenth- to fourteenth-century Hanbali theologian held in high regard by Wahhabi clerics. For the reformers of Baghdad and Damascus, he was a central figure in an intellectual project to return to the ways of the Pious Ancestors. But unlike the Wahhabis, the Salafis of the Fertile Crescent sought general principles for the reinterpretation of Islam to accommodate modern institutions at the same time as calling for ritual to be purified of illegitimate innovations. By 1900, the modernist Salafis were in contact with Wahhabi clerics, primarily for the sake of obtaining manuscript copies of Ibn Taymiyya's writings. Even though they did not endorse Wahhabi doctrine on belief and polytheism, their opponents accused them of spreading

Wahhabism, essentially charging them with religious deviance and disloyalty to the Ottoman sultan. The Salafis responded in two ways. They denied that they were Wahhabis and they asserted that the Arabian reformers were misunderstood due to exaggerations and distortions concocted by their Muslim opponents. Neither the Ahli Hadith movement nor the modernist Salafis gained large followings, but they began a trend to rehabilitate the reputation of Wahhabi doctrine outside Arabia.

Wahhabi outreach entered a new phase in the 1920s. The conquest of the holy cities gave Wahhabi preachers direct access to thousands of pilgrims from around the world. Abdulaziz ibn Saud understood that he was no longer just another Arabian chieftain, but was now guardian of the pilgrimage. To legitimize his standing before the Muslim world, he ensured safe passage for pilgrims and eliminated exploitation by unscrupulous guides; nevertheless, his bid for recognition faced resistance from anti-Wahhabi religious groups and regional political rivals. In India, an association of Muslim clerics called for a boycott of the pilgrimage as long as Mecca remained under Saudi-Wahhabi control. Spokesmen from the Ahli Hadith movement defended Ibn Saud's annexation of Hijaz and demonstrated support by holding public rallies in Indian towns, sending delegations to Mecca, and publishing treatises that justified the Saudis' destruction of popular holy sites as legitimate steps in the war against prohibited innovations.[1]

Saudi rule in Hijaz also opened the way for Wahhabi sympathizers there to correspond with religious reformers throughout the Muslim world. A prominent merchant in Jeddah, Muhammad Nasif, took the initiative to develop contacts with scholars and booksellers in many countries to propagate Wahhabi doctrine. The core of his network was neighboring Arab countries – Egypt, Syria, and Iraq – but its outliers stretched from North Africa to India. Nasif acted as a private individual without the backing of Ibn Saud. One of Nasif's contacts, Rashid Rida, became an influential apologist for Abdulaziz. Rashid Rida came from Ottoman Syria to settle in Cairo in the 1890s. Shortly after his arrival, he began publishing *al-Manar* (*The Lighthouse*), a religious periodical that developed a readership spanning the globe, from Java to Muslim communities in the West. *Al-Manar* became a friendly vehicle for the Saudis in their struggle with Sharif Husain of Hijaz, and Rida published the first printed collection of Wahhabi epistles and treatises, stimulating debate between defenders and critics of Wahhabism in Egyptian mosques, magazines, and bookstalls.

Transnational Islamic Organizations

Disseminating Wahhabi doctrine through print was the major development in outreach during the reign of King Abdulaziz. The next stage took place in the early 1960s, when his successors came to view religion as an instrument of foreign policy, to defend the kingdom against dynamic, and sometimes aggressive, Arab nationalist and communist movements. To balance the popularity of Egypt's President Nasser and the spread of the Baath Party, Crown Prince Faisal forged a conservative alliance rooted in open embrace of Islam as the common denominator. The Saudis looked not only to fellow conservative monarchs but also to the Muslim Brotherhood, whose members were settling the kingdom. The tacit Saudi–Muslim Brotherhood alliance bolstered Wahhabi proselytizing by providing a network of doctrinal cousins possessing a political vision better suited to the Cold War era. The institutional expression of the alliance would be the Muslim World League, founded at an international meeting in Mecca during the 1962 pilgrimage. The League's offices throughout the Muslim world provided convenient platforms for Wahhabis and the Muslim Brotherhood to proselytize. In its early years, the Muslim World League's magazines and conferences contributed to the formation of a transnational Muslim public opinion that frequently centered on political grievances and humanitarian relief for victims of floods and earthquakes.[2]

The League's activities and profile have varied according to time and place. In Bangladesh, for instance, its initial involvement arose in response to a refugee crisis caused by the expulsion of Muslims from Burma in 1978. The League sent a mission to help refugees to either resettle in Bangladesh or return to their homes. With the winding down of that crisis, the League kept open its office in Dhaka, where it worked with the Saudi embassy to dispense funds to Bangladeshi Muslim associations in the manner of a wealthy foundation supporting local projects. The League also developed a robust program of medical aid by financing and operating three hospitals. Much like Christian missionary societies that combine medical service with spiritual salvation, the League's hospitals distributed copies of the Quran, offered religious lessons, and taught public hygiene. The League also assisted poor Muslims with vocational training and small business loans.[3]

The Muslim World League's founding was one of two moments that stand out as turning points in harnessing Wahhabi outreach to Saudi foreign policy. The second came in 1979 when the Islamic Republic of Iran began to challenge Saudi Arabia's claim to religious leadership in the Muslim world. The rivalry spurred a burst in spending on missionary activity to bolster Wahhabi doctrine abroad. In dozens of countries, the kingdom now funds Islamic cultural centers, scholarships to study in Saudi religious universities, and travel expenses for pilgrims. It also supports religious schools in Muslim countries, from Africa to China, to instill Wahhabi doctrine in future prayer leaders and religious personnel, fostering an international fraternity sympathetic to the kingdom. Saudi-financed religious institutes issue thousands of free copies of the Quran, classic religious treatises, and works by contemporary Islamist writers. To reach Muslims in the United

States and the United Kingdom, the Saudis set up King Fahd Academies where Muslims imbibe the Saudi curriculum.

That Wahhabi proselytizing wins over some Muslims is evident in the adoption of its rigorous doctrine on ritual and conservative social manners. Gauging the extent of its influence, however, is difficult because of the wide variation in religious tendencies from one country to another. When Wahhabi missionaries arrive at a new place, they frequently clash with local Muslims attached to their Sufi brotherhoods and with families that resist the requirement that girls cover completely.[4] Furthermore, rival religious tendencies within Saudi Arabia use transnational institutions to gain influence in other Muslim countries at the same time that religious factions in other countries try to use Saudi resources to gain an edge over one another. The world's most populous Muslim country, Indonesia, offers a telling example for examining these dynamics.

Proselytizing in Asia

Southeast Asia and the Middle East have a long history of interaction through trade, pilgrimage, and education. One facet of that interaction is the idea that Islam in the Arab Middle East is the criterion for judging religious belief and practice in regions whose conversion to Islam took place later in history. Hence, Muslims in Southeast Asia have gravitated to religious trends radiating from the Middle East. For instance, in the early 1900s, Indonesian pupils at the Azhar seminary in Cairo picked up the modernist teachings of Egyptian scholar Muhammad Abduh, who advocated reform of education and law to bring Islam into accord with modern conditions. On returning to Indonesia, Abduh's followers set up schools and organizations to spread modernist teachings. Indonesian religious scholars devoted to customary beliefs and practices objected to the newfangled ideas arriving from the Middle East but could not keep them out. In the course of the twentieth century, the modernist line espoused by Abduh and his Indonesian disciples became well established in much of the archipelago.

Saudi Arabia's influence in Southeast Asia builds on historical ties between the holy cities and the Indies. Since early Islamic times, pilgrims from distant lands would stay in Mecca and Medina to attend the lessons of renowned scholars. Some pilgrims returned home after a year, others spent several years, and some settled permanently. In the seventeenth and eighteenth centuries, a colony of Southeast Asian Muslims, referred to as Javans, took shape in the holy cities and formed a bridge between Arabia and the Indies, with teachers and pupils in Mecca at one end, and former pupils becoming teachers in the Indies at the other.[5] The Javans embodied the bonds between their homeland and Arabia, bonds that were refreshed with the regular arrival of traders, pilgrims, and pupils year after year. As early as the 1700s, there would be echoes in Southeast Asia of religious trends in the holy cities, be they new Sufi orders or revivalist doctrines.

Muslim religious tendencies in twentieth-century Indonesia exhibit much variety, ranging from modernist to conservative to Wahhabi-style Salafism. The religious terrain is primarily shaped by Indonesian political realities, be they Dutch imperialism, Japanese occupation, or independence under a secular nationalist government. After independence from Dutch rule, secular regimes kept Islamic tendencies in check; nevertheless, Islamic activists established a connection with the Muslim World League in 1967 through an affiliate organization called the Indonesian Council for Propagating Islam. The Council became a conduit for spreading Muslim Brotherhood ideology and the ideas of the Pakistani revivalist Sayyid Abu'l Ala Maududi.[6]

The Iranian Revolution prompted a more robust phase in Saudi outreach. In an effort to buttress its religious standing in the

Muslim world, the kingdom increased financial support for the Indonesian Council, and the World Assembly of Muslim Youth (a Saudi-based transnational organization) played a conspicuous role in funding schools, mosques, medical clinics, and religious publications.[7] In 1981, the Indonesian government permitted Saudi Arabia to set up the Institute for the Study of Islam and Arabic, located in Jakarta. The Saudi embassy managed the Institute in cooperation with Imam Muhammad ibn Saud University in Riyadh. The Saudis recruited instructors from the kingdom and other Arab countries. At first, the Institute's Arabic courses enrolled Indonesian preachers to prepare them for study in Saudi Arabia. It then broadened the scope of its mission to include Arabic courses for religious pupils. The next step was the creation of a program in Islamic Law under the auspices of Imam Muhammad ibn Saud University. The Institute then became a pipeline from Indonesia to the kingdom's religious universities. Indonesian students at Saudi universities were exposed to the kingdom's religious currents of the 1980s, not only Wahhabism but also the Sahwa movement. Enthusiasm among university students for the Afghan jihad led a number of Indonesians to volunteer for the struggle against the infidels, with the result that they later returned home imbued with the militant strain of Islamic revivalism.

A decade of interaction with Wahhabi teachers, Sahwa activists, and militants spawned a Salafi current that took root among Indonesian graduates of the kingdom's religious universities. In the early 1990s, Saudi-influenced Indonesians established organizations to spread Salafi teachings. Al-Sunna Foundation, for example, drew on financial support from al-Haramain Foundation, Kuwait's Society for the Revival of the Islamic Heritage, and private donors in several Gulf countries to advance the Salafi current. It became active at Indonesian universities and issued a periodical that publishes fatwas by Saudi clerics. It also served Riyadh's foreign policy by denouncing Iran's Islamic Republic. The Ibn Baz

Islamic Center operated a kindergarten and elementary and middle schools. Another foundation created model Islamic villages that house religious students devoted to studying Wahhabi treatises.[8]

All this activity spurred the emergence of a conspicuous, dynamic current endorsing religious tendencies coming from Saudi Arabia, but with complex effects because rivalries swirling in Saudi institutions played out in Indonesia as well. One of the leading figures in promoting Wahhabi doctrine, under the banner of Salafi Islam, was Jaafar Umar Thalib, known for favoring religious purification through education and for opposing political activism as a threat to Muslim unity. He was not the only contender for Salafi leadership, and to shore up his position he accused Indonesian rivals of backing the 'Sururi' tendency when they were students at Saudi religious universities. His rivals mounted a counterattack by mobilizing Indonesian students at the Islamic University of Medina to back them and they persuaded prominent Saudi clerics to oppose Thalib. The upshot was the division of Indonesian students in the kingdom into opposing factions, with one group persuading loyalist ulama associated with Sheikh Rabi al-Madkhali and Sheikh Muhammad Aman al-Jami to issue public warnings against the Sururi 'deviation'. The Sururi allies of Thalib's enemies used their position in Saudi foundations to channel funds to them.[9]

The splintering of Indonesian Salafis into rival factions reflecting Saudi Arabia's religious politics was not a unique case. An even more complex set of players is involved in South Asia, where Saudi support for Muslim organizations comes from different sources: the Muslim World League, the Ministry of Islamic Affairs, private donors, and expatriate Indian workers residing in the kingdom. Official Saudi sponsorship takes the usual forms: paying for pilgrimages to Mecca, grants to study at Saudi religious universities, and subsidies for publishers. In recent decades, recipients of Saudi assistance have come primarily from three religious movements:

the Ahli Hadith, the Jamaati Islami and the Deobandi movement.[10] From the perspective of doctrine and historical ties, Ahli Hadith would be the preferred partner for Wahhabi ulama, but it is the smallest of the three, partly because of its members' refusal to pray behind other Sunni imams. One measure of their limited sway is the number of pupils in their network of religious schools. In 2006, pupils in Deobandi schools outnumbered those in Ahli Hadith schools 200,000 to 35,000.[11]

The ties between Saudi Arabia and Ahli Hadith have hinged on personal relationships between religious scholars. Sheikh Abdul Ghaffar Hassan was an Indo-Pakistani scholar who taught the Prophetic Tradition at the Islamic University of Medina for 15 years. During that time, he became a close associate of Sheikh Abdulaziz ibn Baz and he counted the future Sahwa Sheikh Safar al-Hawali among his pupils. The connection to Ibn Baz bolstered Saudi support for Ahli Hadith activities back in India.[12] Ahli Hadith publishers received funds to produce inexpensive editions of their books as well as cassette recordings and CDs by Indian and Pakistani authors, some of them graduates of Saudi universities. These publishers also issued Urdu translations of works by Saudi authors such as Abdulaziz ibn Baz and collections of Saudi fatwas. Much of Ahli Hadith's own literature echoes classic Wahhabi themes such as theology, performance of ritual, and the rules for dress, food, and marriage. A perennial problem for the movement is how to define Muslim relations with India's vast Hindu majority. It urges minimal interaction with Hindus in order to avoid coming under their influence and borrowing infidel ways, much as classical Wahhabi doctrine called for avoiding interaction with lapsed Muslims.[13]

Another way that Ahli Hadith authors resemble Wahhabi counterparts is their sharp criticism of other Muslims for deviating from true Islam. Targets for their polemical attacks include Indian Muslim groups such as the Barelvi Sufis and the Deobandis; some

Ahli Hadith writers go beyond denunciation for specific errors in doctrine to excommunication (takfir). Sectarian tensions with India's Shiite community in particular sharpened in the 1980s when Ahli Hadith authors published fierce condemnations of Shiites as infidels – dovetailing with the religious cold war between revolutionary Iran and Saudi Arabia. In their view, Ayatollah Khomeini was an enemy of Islam, and Shiism was part of a Jewish conspiracy to undermine Islam. At the same time, Ahli Hadith authors consistently praised Saudi Arabia as the only proper Islamic government in the world.

Historical ties and doctrinal affinity are not the only factors that shape Saudi Arabia's relationship with South Asian Muslim movements. Political circumstances have also had important effects. Before the 1980s, the Deobandi movement in India and Pakistan – a historical rival to Ahli Hadith – was critical of Wahhabi doctrine, although it shared the commitment to combating illegitimate innovations. During the Afghan war, the Saudis realized that the Deobandi movement, which was much larger than Ahli Hadith, could play an important role in the jihad against Soviet forces. For their part, Deobandi leaders saw Saudi Arabia as a source of funds, so they began to emphasize common religious enemies – Shiites and Barelvi Sufis – and to revise historical criticism of Wahhabi doctrine. Likewise, the crisis over Kuwait produced shifts in Saudi relations with South Asian Muslims. The most prominent Pakistani activist religious organization, Jamaati Islami, had benefited from Saudi largesse for decades, but that changed when it supported Saddam Husain and criticized the Saudis for requesting United States military intervention. The Saudis quickly shut off financial support for Jamaati Islam and bolstered its patronage for the loyal Ahli Hadith.[14]

Further complicating the task of assessing Saudi influence in South Asia is Ahli Hadith's character as a movement rather than a unified organization. In Pakistan alone, there are more than 15 separate Ahli Hadith groups, each one running its own network of religious schools. The main Ahli Hadith recipient of Saudi aid is Markazi Jamiat. It was established by a Pakistani graduate of the Islamic University of Medina, Ehsan Elahi Zaheer, the author of several works condemning Sufis and Shiites. In one book, he accused Shiites of being Israeli agents. The Saudi government had the book translated from Urdu into Arabic and English. In 1987, Shiite militants killed Zaheer in the bombing of a Lahore mosque. Markazi Jamiat's activism extended to support for jihad, represented by a special division, Tehrike Mujahedin, that maintained camps in Afghanistan to train young men to fight Indian forces in Kashmir.[15]

Some Ahli Hadith organizations that are not aligned with Saudi Arabia consider Markazi Jamiat's commitment to jihad deficient. For example, the Center for Preaching and Guidance, founded in 1986 by former Islamic University of Medina students, holds that jihad is the central pillar of Islam. The Center for Preaching and Guidance tapped a broad donor base in the Pakistani diaspora spanning the Middle East and Europe. For a time, Osama bin Laden was one of its donors. In addition to viewing Kashmir as a cause for jihad against Hindus, the Center attacks what it considers Hindu customs popular in Pakistani Muslim culture, such as the festival for kite-flying. The jihad section in the Center for Preaching and Guidance is a full-fledged military branch, Lashkar Taiba, set up around 1990. Over time, the scope of Lashkar's jihad expanded from a focus on Kashmir to the global scale envisioned by al-Qaeda. Its small network of religious schools that attracts pupils from Indonesia, Malaysia, and the Philippines connects it to militants in those countries.[16] Since the Center for Preaching and Guidance is part of the broader Ahli Hadith movement, it is not easy to separate from Saudi contributions to its less militant client Markazi Jamiat. And, just as it is no simple matter to untangle the cross-cutting ties between Saudi institutions and Muslim groups, the line between charity and funding for terrorism, so often laid at the Saudi doorstep, is also difficult to draw.

Pan-Islamic Causes, Charity, and Jihad

Charity is a core value in Islam. A tithe on wealth, the *zakat*, is a basic religious duty, one of the five pillars of Islam. Additional voluntary donations earn believers special merit with God. Al Saud draws legitimacy from its support for charity, both through government spending and personal donations to causes at home and abroad. Since the 1980s, Islamic charity in Saudi Arabia and the Muslim world has been the object of Western scrutiny because of its enmeshment with political causes. Critics point to instances where al-Qaeda and Islamist militant organizations used charitable organizations as cover for money laundering and arms purchases. Since Saudi Arabia is a major donor to such organizations, and terrorists have been able to tap them for funds, critics assert that the kingdom supports terrorism. Painting the relationship between fundraising and terrorism with broad strokes overlooks the substantial resources of money and volunteer labor that benefit thousands of refugees, widows, and orphans in zones of war and natural disaster. On close inspection, humanitarian and political motives and effects are difficult to separate.[17] A more exact way to put it is that individuals in the kingdom have used charitable organizations to support terrorist groups.

The kingdom's charitable activities involve government ministries and embassies, semi-official institutions with international reach, and private initiatives. The Ministry of Finance collects the zakat whereas payment of the tithe is a private matter in most other countries. Several ministries dispense charitable donations to support religious institutions, pilgrimage services, clinics, and education. Charities often work with and through government offices. For example, the Red Crescent Society, a member of the International Red Cross, concentrates on medical emergencies and ambulance services on a regular basis, but it also operates clinics during the pilgrimage in coordination with the Ministry of Pilgrimage.[18]

Since the 1970s oil boom, charities in Saudi Arabia have acquired the resources – from government budgets, royal patrons, and private donors – to become significant participants in humanitarian operations throughout the Muslim world. The mix of private and official sectors is evident in the operations of the International Islamic Relief Organization (IIRO), a non-government organization founded in 1975 to provide emergency relief for Muslims suffering the effects of natural disasters and wars. With dozens of branches around the world, its funds are disbursed through the Islamic Affairs departments of Saudi embassies. The government's energetic involvement with pan-Islamic relief has served dynastic interests, especially since the 1980s and 1990s, when rivalry with Iran and the Islamist regime in Sudan spurred competition for leadership in providing relief.[19]

Saudi foreign policy has tapped popular religious sentiment in favor of donations and volunteering to assist fellow Muslims under attack in Afghanistan, Bosnia, Chechnya, Kashmir, and elsewhere. In fact, the war in Afghanistan marked a critical moment in the development of international Muslim support for humanitarian relief. In the early 1980s, Saudi and other Islamic charities established offices in Peshawar to assist refugees, providing food, shelter, medical care, and education. The distance, cost, and hardship of working in Peshawar meant that the Afghan cause drew young men highly committed to defending Muslims against their enemies. Such men were typically activists in Islamist movements with a militant bent. Consequently, their notion of assistance to endangered fellow believers was not limited to humanitarian relief but included da`wa, calling to their vision of religious rectitude in worship and personal morality, and jihad, fighting infidel enemies. Members of the Muslim Brotherhood and Egypt's Islamic Jihad mingled with Saudi Wahhabis in the offices of charities in Peshawar and in the camps of Afghan resistance organizations. In their eyes, relief, da`wa, and jihad were inseparable components of solidarity with fellow believers. From their positions in Peshawar branch offices of Islamic charities, they were able to use funds to purchase arms and train volunteers for jihad.[20]

One of the central figures coordinating the activities of Arab volunteers and Islamic charities was Abdullah Azzam, a Muslim Brother from Jordan who had been a university instructor in Jeddah. Thanks to the relationships he developed in Saudi Arabia, he held a position in the Peshawar office of the Muslim World League and tapped funds from the Saudi Arabia Red Crescent Society for his own operation, the Services Bureau, which focused on anti-Soviet jihad. During the Afghan war, the blending of humanitarian and militant purposes caused little, if any, concern in Western government circles. During the 1990s, however, the appearance of Arab veterans of the Afghan war in other zones of conflict such as Bosnia and Chechnya altered perceptions of the intimate relationships between militants and charities. The militants were no longer fighting a cause endorsed by the United States and its allies in Europe and the Arab world as charities came to mask terrorist funding and logistics.

During the Bosnian civil war of 1992–5, a religious interpretation of the conflict gained currency in some quarters of both Western and Muslim publics. In this view, Bosnia was turning into a terrorist haven and breeding ground behind the innocent cover of humanitarian assistance to besieged Muslims. Or, the Serbs were part of a Western crusader plot to destroy Islam in Europe. Both views reduced a multidimensional conflict to a simple plot when, in fact, the Bosnian side alone had multiple factions, as did the pan-Islamic involvement. Saudi Arabia vied with Iran and Sudan for credit and influence; NGOs in Germany, the UK, Turkey, and the US supplied relief to refugees. Muslim efforts were not completely fragmented by political competition. National governments and NGOs combined efforts through the World Islamic Council for Da`wa and Relief, established in 1988 with headquarters in Cairo. The International Islamic Relief Organization took the lead in coordinating efforts for Bosnia, often seeking to spread Wahhabi doctrine along with material relief. The IIRO played an important part in supplying food and medicine to over 100,000 refugees, subsidized health care for orphans, assisted with relocation to other European countries, and contributed to postwar reconstruction.[21]

Volunteers from the Muslim Brotherhood and the Egyptian militant organization Islamic Jihad bundled military and humanitarian assistance together. Veterans of the Afghan jihad mixed with the hundreds of Muslim volunteers and sometimes crossed the line from relief to combat. The IIRO and a second Saudi charity, al-Haramain Foundation, provided funds to purchase arms and abetted the flow of foreign Muslim fighters. (Eventually, the special United Nations Committee on Osama bin Laden put more than ten branches of al-Haramain in Asia, Africa, Europe, and the United States on its list of entities associated with al-Qaeda.)[22]

Moreover, a Saudi veteran of the Afghan jihad emerged as the leader of a unit of foreign Muslims in Bosnia. Just as it was difficult to untangle official from private roles in humanitarian relief, the connection between Saudi authorities and volunteers for jihad, often dubbed terrorists in the Western press, proved elusive.[23] At the same time, Riyadh was alert to connections between dissidents at home and their allies abroad. The government provided assistance to the Bosnian army while attempting to curb what it regarded as illegitimate 'private' jihad. To that end, authorities in Jeddah closed a branch of the Islamic Benevolence Committee that it suspected of illicit activities.[24]

Saudi Influence in the West

In the light of Saudi Arabia's connections to Islamic militants, the kingdom's efforts to influence Muslims in Western countries have drawn much scrutiny and suspicion. With the increase in Muslim immigration to the West in the 1970s, Islamic organizations with headquarters in Saudi Arabia directed resources to proselytize Muslims living in Europe and North America. Islamic centers constructed on a grand scale sprouted up in Rome, London, and Madrid. The Muslim World League set up branches in the United Kingdom, France, Italy, Denmark, Austria, and other European countries as well as in the United States. The League provided grants to build mosques to serve immigrants, while the World Assembly of Muslim Youth forged firm ties with Muslim associations in European countries, particularly associations connected to the Muslim Brotherhood.[25] As a result of such efforts, Saudi Arabian religious institutions gained a toehold in the West. They did not, however, monopolize or even dominate the field because other governments whose citizens emigrated in large numbers – Turkey, Algeria, Morocco, Pakistan, and others – also vied for influence.[26]

In the United Kingdom, the Saudis wield essentially the same tools for outreach as in Muslim lands: scholarships for study at the Islamic University of Medina, training for imams serving British mosques, distributing Wahhabi publications in English translation, and so on. Mosques affiliated with the Ahli Hadith movement and frequented by South Asian Muslims prove especially receptive to the Wahhabi message, but the impact of that message is diluted in the UK, much as it is in Indonesia, because Muslims educated in Saudi universities are divided between Wahhabi loyalists and Sahwa dissidents who frequently denounce the rulers and clerics of Riyadh.[27]

Wahhabi proselytizing in the United States did not attract much attention before the 9/11 attacks. In their wake, American media spotlighted the Saudi background of the hijackers and their leader, Osama bin Laden, and dug more deeply into the kingdom's religious culture. What they found, particularly passages in Saudi schoolbooks about hating infidels, offended liberal sensibilities. One consequence of the new awareness of Wahhabism was a debate over the extent of its influence among Muslims in the United States. Critics of the kingdom claimed that its influence was pervasive, asserting that four-fifths of American mosques were under Wahhabi influence.[28] A study of Saudi efforts to spread Wahhabi teachings by distributing literature through American mosques documented the presence of many radical texts expressing extreme anti-Western views. That study was based on a survey of 15 mosques (out of around two thousand mosques in the US). Ninety percent of the publications connected to Wahhabi doctrine or Saudi funding were in Arabic, and hence incomprehensible to most Muslims living in the United States. While the study conveyed the intolerant flavor of Wahhabi doctrine, the small size of the sample made it hard to draw firm conclusions about the extent of Saudi influence.[29]

A different picture of Saudi influence in the United States emerged from a report on American mosques, published a few months before the 9/11 attacks, by a group of American Muslim organizations and multifaith academic institutes. Its survey of mosques found that about 3 percent of mosque leaders claimed to follow Salafi Islam, the term preferred by Wahhabis for their approach to Islam, while nearly three-quarters thought it proper to interpret the Quran and the Prophetic Tradition according to circumstances of time and place, a notion at odds with Wahhabi doctrine. One-fifth of mosque leaders maintained that only a literal understanding of those sources is valid, a notion that is compatible with Wahhabi doctrine. A follow-up study published in 2011 found that only 1 percent had a Wahhabi orientation.[30]

Suspicion of Saudi influence in mosques is paralleled by rumors of Saudi efforts to co-opt segments of United States higher education with large gifts from members of the ruling family. A glance at the websites of Middle East and Islamic Studies programs receiving such gifts would make a Wahhabi wonder if the millions donated for the creation of endowed chairs and academic programs could be better spent. Prince al-Waleed bin Talal, for example, made a substantial donation to establish an Islamic Studies program at Harvard University. The program, however, hardly bears a Wahhabi imprint. In 2012–13, its director was a specialist in South Asian Ismaili devotional literature, and members of its steering committee reflected the intellectual, disciplinary, and geographical diversity of the Islamic Studies field as well as Harvard's scholarly excellence.[31] The University of California, Santa Barbara, received a gift from Saudi royal family members to establish a chair in honor of King Abdulaziz. The holder of the chair, a specialist in early modern Egyptian history and Sufism, with a doctorate from Princeton University, does not fit the profile of an academic inclined to either spread or defend Saudi religious doctrine.[32] The holder of the King Faisal Chair in Islamic Thought and Culture at the University of Southern California is the author of works on Sufism and Islamic law.[33] It appears that donations to academic institutions in the United States do not purchase influence over teaching appointments or curricula, but they do support a broader understanding of Islam and Muslim societies, unlike the efforts of the Muslim World League to spread a particular religious agenda by funding institutes and studies in Saudi Arabia.

While Saudi rulers and Wahhabi clergy may wish they wielded the sort of influence over Muslims worldwide ascribed to them by their critics, the return on their investment is modest. In 2004, officials from the Ministry for Islamic Affairs gave figures on bricks-and-mortar results of spending in non-Muslim countries between 1982 and 2000: 200 seminaries, 210 Islamic centers, 1,500 mosques, and 2,000 schools. The Minister of Islamic Affairs, Sheikh Salih Al al-Sheikh, put the number of missionaries outside the kingdom at nearly four thousand. A private Saudi analyst at the time put the figure spent on outreach in roughly two decades at more than $2 billion.[34] A credulous reading of such impressive numbers might conclude that Saudi Arabia exercises massive influence in the Muslim world. Or one could cast a skeptical eye on the claims of Saudi government officials about the results of missionary efforts, much as one might second-guess any government's boast about successful achievement of national goals. Americans lament the meager return on the massive economic and political (not to mention military) resources expended to sway hearts and minds around the globe. A frugal Wahhabi might feel the same way about money sent abroad. The evidence for the popular embrace of Wahhabism is patchy, and often in the eye of the beholder. It must compete with local traditions and other foreign Muslim powers equally determined to advance their brand of religious truth. Add the effect of rivalries within the Saudi religious camp (Sahwa activist versus Wahhabi loyalist, for example), and measuring or defining influence, let alone success, becomes elusive. Moreover, the landscape of religious tendencies in any country, no matter the religion, is never static. A recent analysis of Muslim networks in Western Europe concluded that the influence of the Muslim World League and the World Assembly of Muslim Youth was waning due to the impact of the internet on how believers locate and define religious authority.[35] Finally, to believe in the efficacy of Saudi religious institutions' outreach contradicts what one hears so often from Saudis and from Westerners who deal with the Saudi government about the low organizational capacity of its public institutions. None of this is to deny that the religious institutions do their utmost to propagate Wahhabi doctrine and have succeeded at exporting it to a much greater extent than imaginable without oil money, but religious politics are contested and local interests often turn outside resources to their own purposes.

8 Conclusion

A question that Westerners commonly ask about Saudi Arabia is: Will it ever change? King Abdullah's death in January 2015 occasioned speculation about the kingdom's future direction in the light of concerns about dynastic continuity and regional turmoil. In the short term, questions about succession were quickly settled. Abdullah's half-brother Salman ibn Abdulaziz came to the throne as planned and Prince Muqrin ibn Abdulaziz moved up from deputy crown prince to crown prince.

Looking further ahead, the significant development was King Salman's announcement of Prince Muhammad ibn Nayef (b. 1959) as deputy crown prince (second in line to the throne) because it brought the country closer to the moment when royal leadership will pass from the sons of King Abdulaziz to the next generation. The secrecy shrouding consultations within Al Saud had made it difficult to discern when the transition would occur and which prince would become the first grandson of Abdulaziz to become king. Moreover, given the large number of younger princes who have occupied powerful positions in the government, the generational transition represents a potential pivot in the monarchy's domestic and foreign orientations.

Only the new king and high-ranking princes know how the decision to select Prince Muhammad was reached. Analysts point to a few factors that likely came into play. One is that he belongs to the so-called Sudairi group of princes who have been powerful players for the last half century. Another factor is that he does not have sons, therefore other princes of his generation do not worry that he will attempt to concentrate powerful positions in his own line.

Furthermore, Prince Muhammad is credited with playing an important role during the government's four-year campaign to defeat al-Qaeda in the Arabian Peninsula. His father Prince Nayef was minister of interior for many years (and briefly the crown prince). Prince Muhammad served as an assistant minister of interior for about a decade before his father's death in summer 2012. King Abdullah appointed him minister of interior, a position he retained under King Salman.

Prince Muhammad was well prepared for the government's battles against al-Qaeda militants. He undertook specialized training in anti-terrorism tactics with the FBI in the United States and with Scotland Yard in Great Britain. Part of his strategy to combat QAP was to emphasize rehabilitation rather than punishment for militants who turned themselves in to the authorities. He made it a point to personally receive militants willing to turn their backs on QAP. That personal touch nearly proved fatal: in 2009, a militant tried to assassinate the prince by pretending to surrender and then detonating a suicide bomb when he approached the prince. The blast killed the militant but the prince incurred only minor wounds.

In the short term, Prince Muhammad's primary challenge will be to deal with the threats posed by QAP, now based in Yemen, and the Islamic State in Iraq and Syria (ISIS). In one sense, the Islamic State is a familiar adversary because it is an outgrowth of al-Qaeda's branch in Iraq – al-Qaeda in Mesopotamia. In 2006, in the course fighting American forces in Iraq, the al-Qaeda branch adopted the name of the Islamic State in Iraq. The United States forged an alliance with northern Sunni tribal leaders and the combined forces regained control over northern Iraq on behalf of the national government in Baghdad. The Shiite leadership in Baghdad, however, squandered the military success of the Americans and the tribal sheikhs by pursuing a sectarian agenda that alienated the country's Sunnis and paved the way for the militants to make a comeback, thanks in part to the civil war that erupted in neighboring Syria in 2011. There, the Islamic State proclaimed itself in 2013 the Islamic State in Iraq and Syria (sometimes translated as Iraq and al-Sham, the Arabic word for geographical Syria, or Iraq and the Levant). With an increasingly strong position in Syria, ISIS exploited Sunni discontent with Baghdad and in 2014 overran Mosul and other northern Iraqi towns.

While ISIS represents a continuation of the threat posed by Al Qaeda to Al Saud, it also poses a novel challenge because of its claim to re-establish the caliphate, the historical symbol of Muslim political and religious unity that lost its last wisp of concrete expression in 1924. The self-styled caliph Abu Bakr al-Baghdadi claims that he is the only Muslim worthy of political allegiance. The clear implication of proclaiming a new caliph and demanding allegiance from all Muslims is to deny legitimacy to other Muslim rulers, including Al Saud. How much ordinary Saudis support the ISIS caliphate is impossible to determine. On the surface, it appears to be a fringe phenomenon, albeit one with sufficient attraction for religious dissidents to be alarming to the rulers. As long as ISIS can maintain control over territory in two neighboring countries, it will offer the region's Sunni Muslims an alternative political vision that threatens established monarchies from Jordan to the Gulf. The Saudi government participates in the coalition against ISIS, but in doing so, it risks its legitimacy because it is fighting alongside Western military forces against a Muslim foe. Combating ISIS influence inside the kingdom will be a major preoccupation for Al Saud, and Prince Muhammad is a natural selection to lead that effort.

As much as any individual from his generation who might eventually ascend the throne, Prince Muhammad represents continuity. King Salman's decision to appoint his young son Muhammad (b. 1980) minister of defense, chief of the royal court, and head of a new committee on economic and development policy, however, raised eyebrows among Saudi-watchers. The king's son is one of the few in his cohort not to have attended school in a Western country. Moreover, he had little government experience apart from managing his father's princely court. How other princes of the third generation (after King Abdulaziz and his sons) will respond to his sudden promotion could affect dynamics within the royal family. The ministry of defense provides him a position to build up his power, but much will depend on his performance and his relations with other princes.

In the light of the desire for dynastic stability and the threats posed by resurgent militant forces on Saudi Arabia's borders, it seems highly unlikely that Saudi Arabia's rulers will introduce major changes to the country's religious life. That does not mean, however, that change is not coming. By this point, the reader knows that how Islam is interpreted and practiced has not been stuck in the eighteenth century but has evolved and adjusted to changes in political and economic events and conditions. The guardians of Wahhabi doctrine have their own view on the question of change. They believe that by the 1700s, Muslims desperately needed to change their ways because they had reverted to idolatry. They believe that Sheikh Muhammad ibn Abd al-Wahhab's mission achieved that change, and that it was the duty of his heirs to prevent backsliding. In other words, once the Saudi emirate and its Wahhabi allies cleared Arabia of what they considered polytheism, change signified moral corruption. And yet, in spite of royal support for Wahhabi doctrine, religious life in Saudi Arabia has never been uniform or static.

The Muslims of Arabia have a long history of religious diversity that includes different Sunni legal and theological schools, Sufi orders, and Shiite communities. Religious expression differed between nomadic and settled populations. The Wahhabi mission arrived too late on the historical scene to completely efface developments during the first millennium of Islam, although it did effectively suppress public expression of other religious tendencies. Moreover, external influence proved impossible to keep at bay, and the dynasty's instinct for political survival has meant fluctuations in its support for Wahhabi purists. Consequently, the kingdom is susceptible to social and cultural flux, notwithstanding clerical efforts to establish a steady state. Time and again, the embrace of innovations – girls' education, television, satellite channels, the internet, and who knows what next – ran roughshod over prohibitions, and the religious establishment invariably played catch-up to put its imprint on the new. The latest inventions in communications media such as Facebook and Twitter certainly offer state clerics venues for cementing ties with loyalists, but they also make it possible for others to elude prohibitions on creating and consuming music and visual entertainment, as well as to argue over religion, what it allows and forbids, be it women driving or national elections.

Saudis' allegiance to Islam is not in question, but what they regard as faithful fulfillment of beliefs and duties is shifting. How firmly rooted Wahhabi doctrine remains is difficult to say. Some argue that it is losing relevance because it is preoccupied with trivial matters and is, in the end, the instrument of a dynasty that bends doctrine for the sake of *raison d'état*. In this view, willingness to comply with fatwas issued by a compromised religious establishment is fading, school students are less interested in religion courses, and many just go through the motions of conforming to official rules for worship and public behavior. Others, however, argue that Wahhabi doctrine remains very strong because, they assume, a majority of the population embraces its teachings. This view notes that schoolchildren can get teachers fired for expressing suspect views, students on scholarships to study overseas spy on one another's moral conduct, and recordings of sermons that cast liberals as hypocrites are highly popular. That assessments vary is indicative of change and uncertainty in the face of technological and generational change, economic pressures, and political stresses. How these forces will alter religious life is unpredictable, but that these forces are at work and that the role of religion in all facets of life will continue to change is certain.

Notes

Foreword

1 Stephane Lacroix, *Awakening Islam: The Politics of Religious Dissent in Contemporary Saudi Arabia*, trans. George Holoch (Cambridge, MA, 2011), p. 4.

2 Akbar Ahmed, *The Thistle and the Drone: How America's War on Terror Became a Global War on Tribal Islam* (Washington, DC, 2013), pp. 106ff.

3 'Campaign to stop misuse of Prophet's name', *Arab News*, 23 December 2013.

4 Madawi al-Rasheed, A *History of Saudi Arabia*, 2nd edn (Cambridge, 2010), pp. 163–5.

5 *New York Times*, 8 January 2014.

1. Introduction

1 Ibrahim al-Rashid (ed.), *Saudi Arabia Enters the World: Secret U.S. Documents on the Emergence of the Kingdom of Saudi Arabia as a World Power, 1936–1949, Part I* (Salisbury, NC, 1980), pp. 201–3.

2 The religious police organization is also referred to as the Committee for Ordering the Good and Forbidding the Evil, or Committee for Commanding Right and Forbidding Wrong.

2. The Establishment of the Wahhabi Tradition

1 Maribel Fierro, 'The treatises against innovations (*kutub al-bida*'')', *Der Islam* lxix/2 (1992), p. 205.

2 Fierro, 'The treatises against innovation'. On contemporary discussions of innovations, see Muhammad Al Atawneh, *Wahhabi Islam Facing the Challenges of Modernity: Dar al-Ifta' in the Modern Saudi State* (Leiden, 2010).

3 Abd Allah Salih al-Uthaymin, *Muhammad ibn Abd al-Wahhab: The Man and his Works* (London, 2009), pp. 24–5.

4 Samer Traboulsi, 'An early refutation of Muhammad ibn 'Abd al-Wahhab's reformist views', *Die Welt des Islams* xlii/3 (2002), p. 376.

5 Al-Uthaymin, *Muhammad ibn Abd al-Wahhab*, pp. 48–9.

6 Ibid., pp. 54–6.

7 Ibid., pp. 129–31.

8 Ibid., pp. 45–8; Sulaiman ibn Suhaim was the religious scholar.

9 David Commins, *The Wahhabi Mission and Saudi Arabia* (London, 2006), pp. 33–6.

10 Joseph Kostiner, *The Making of Saudi Arabia, 1916–1936: From Chieftaincy to Monarchical State* (Oxford, 1994), pp. 66–70.

11 James Piscatori, 'Managing God's guests: the pilgrimage, Saudi Arabia and the politics of legitimacy', in Paul Dresch and James Piscatori (eds), *Monarchies and Nations: Globalisation and Identity in the Arab Nations of the Gulf* (London, 2005), p. 223.

3. Wahhabism and the Modern Saudi State

1 'Saudi royal wealth: where do they get all that money?', cable from US Embassy, Riyadh, to Treasury Department, Washington, DC, 30 November 1996. Available at http://wikileaks.ch/cable/1996/11/96RIYADH4784.html (accessed 9 July 2014).

2 See Chapter 6 for details on the Muslim Brotherhood.

3 Human Rights Watch, 'Precarious justice: arbitrary detention and unfair trials in the deficient criminal justice system of Saudi Arabia', *Human Rights Watch* xx/3 (March 2008). The report offers a succinct critical overview of law, criminal procedure, and courts in addition to human rights violations. On recent reforms, see 'Saudi

Arabia: criminal justice strengthened', Human Rights Watch, 14 January 2010. Available at www.hrw.org/news/2010/01/14/saudi-arabia-criminal-justice-strengthened (accessed 9 July 2014).

4   Amnesty International's 2011 report on the death penalty ranked Saudi Arabia third in the world in the number of executions (after China and Iran) at 82, a marked increase over the previous four years. Amnesty International, *Death Sentences and Executions, 2011* (London, 2012).

5   Correspondence with Abdulaziz al-Fahad, attorney in Saudi Arabia, on the scope of the appeals process.

6   Correspondence with Abdulaziz al-Fahad.

7   Abdulaziz al-Fahad, 'Commentary: from exclusivism to accommodation: doctrinal and legal evolution of Wahhabism', *New York University Law Review* lxxix/2 (2004), pp. 485–519. The fatwa is translated on pp. 518–19.

8   Muhammad Al Atawneh, *Wahhabi Islam Facing the Challenges of Modernity: Dar al-Ifta' in the Modern Saudi State* (Leiden, 2010), p. 84 for quote, pp. 84–92 for section.

9   Ibid., p. 163.

10 Ibid., pp. 140–6.

11 Mona Al Munajjed, *Women in Saudi Arabia Today* (London, 1997), pp. 60–80.

12 Robert Lacey, *The Kingdom: Arabia and the House of Saud* (New York, 1981), pp. 366–8 on the Buraida protests.

13 Eleanor Abdella Doumato, *Getting God's Ear: Women, Islam and Healing in Saudi Arabia and the Gulf* (New York, 2000), p. 227.

14 Al Munajjed, *Women in Saudi Arabia*, pp. 60–80.

15 Delwin Roy, 'Saudi Arabian education: development policy', *Middle Eastern Studies* xxxvii/3 (1992), p. 495.

16 Malise Ruthven, *Fundamentalism: A Very Short Introduction* (Oxford, 2007), pp. 43–4.

17 'Saudi Arabia's education reforms emphasize training for jobs', *Chronicle of Higher Education* lvii/7 (8 October 2010).

18 Michaela Prokop, 'Saudi Arabia: the politics of education', *International Affairs* lxxix/1 (2003), p. 80.

19 Eleanor Abdella Doumato, 'Saudi Arabia: from Wahhabi roots to contemporary revisionism', in Eleanor Abdella Doumato and

Gregory Starrett (eds), *Teaching Islam: Textbooks and Religion in the Middle East* (Boulder, CO, 2006), p. 155.

20 Stephane Lacroix, *Awakening Islam: The Politics of Religious Dissent in Contemporary Saudi Arabia*, trans. George Holoch (Cambridge, MA, 2011), p. 46.

21 Eleanor Abdella Doumato, 'Manning the barricades: Islam according to Saudi Arabia's school texts', *Middle East Journal* lvii/2 (2003), pp. 233–5.

22 Doumato, 'Saudi Arabia: from Wahhabi roots', pp. 163–4, 171, 173.

23 Caryle Murphy, *A Kingdom's Future: Saudi Arabia through the Eyes of its Twenty-Somethings* (Washington, DC, 2013), p. 29.

24 A brief overview of Saudi higher education is in Mohammad A. Alkhazim, 'Higher education in Saudi Arabia: challenges, solutions, and opportunities missed', *Higher Education Policy* xvi/4 (2003), pp. 479–86.

25 Murphy, *A Kingdom's Future*, pp. 27–9.

26 Al Munajjed, *Women in Saudi Arabia*, pp. 60–80. Amani Hamdan, 'Women and education in Saudi Arabia: challenges and achievements', *International Education Journal* vi/1 (2005), pp. 51–2.

27 Murphy, *A Kingdom's Future*, pp. 37–8.

28 'Saudi Arabia opens largest women's university in the world', *al-Arabiyya News*, 15 May 2011. Available at http://english. alarabiya.net/articles/2011/05/15/149218.html (accessed 19 July 2014).

29 David E. Long, *The Hajj Today: A Survey of the Contemporary Pilgrimage to Makkah* (Albany, NY, 1979), pp. 11–23.

30 James Piscatori, 'Managing God's guests: the pilgrimage, Saudi Arabia and the politics of legitimacy', in Paul Dresch and James Piscatori (eds), *Monarchies and Nations: Globalisation and Identity in the Arab Nations of the Gulf* (London, 2005), pp. 224–6.

31 Ibid., pp. 229–30.

32 Ibid., pp. 226, 233–4, 242.

33 Rosie Bsheer, 'Choking Mecca in the name of beauty – and development (part 1)', *Jadaliyya*, 21 October 2010. Available at www.jadaliyya.com/pages/index/251/choking-mecca-in-the-name-of-beauty_and-developmen (accessed 9 July 2014).

34 Abdullah al-Maqati and Inad al-Otaibi, 'Youth who resisted hai'a still in custody', *Saudi Gazette*, 25 June 2011. Available at www.saudigazette.com.sa/index.cfm?method=home.regcon& contentid=20110625103766 (accessed 9 July 2014). M.D. Hamidan, 'Detained municipal surveyor was harassing schoolgirls: Haia', *Arab News*, 24 June 2011. Available at www.arabnews.com/node/381867 (accessed 9 July 2014).

35 Saudi religious police assume responsibility for monitoring a wider range of conduct than entailed in the classical notion of *hisba*: the ruler's duty to enforce public morality. See Frank Vogel, 'The public and private in Saudi Arabia: restrictions on the powers of Committees for Ordering the Good and Forbidding the Evil', *Social Research* lxx/3 (2003), pp. 749–68.

36 Abd Allah Salih al-Uthaymin, *Muhammad ibn Abd al-Wahhab: The Man and his Works* (London, 2009), pp. 146–7.

37 David Commins, *The Wahhabi Mission and Saudi Arabia* (London, 2006), pp. 94–5.

38 US Department of State, *International Religious Freedom Report, Saudi Arabia* (Washington, DC, 2010), p. 5. For a summary of the Commission's structure and duties, see Human Rights Watch, 'Precarious justice', pp. 58–9.

39 Ibid., pp. 59–60.

40 A spectrum of opinion is reflected in interviews with young Saudis in Murphy, *A Kingdom's Future*, pp. 84–6.

41 John Paul Jones, *If Olaya Street Could Talk – Saudi Arabia: The Heartland of Oil and Islam*, (Albuquerque, NM, 2007), pp. 104–5; see also pp. 196–205 for a veteran expatriate's tales of encounters with religious police.

42 Omaima Al Najjar, 'Omaima Al Najjar being investigated by the religious police', Omaima Al Najjar – Saudi Woman Speaks Out, blog, 27 December 2010. Available at http://omaimanajjar.wordpress.com/2010/12/27/omaima-al-najjar-being-investigated-by-the-religious-police (accessed 9 July 2014).

43 Al-Uthaymin, *Muhammad ibn Abd al-Wahhab*, pp. 45–7.

44 Commins, *The Wahhabi Mission*, pp. 60–1.

45 'Saudi Arabia', in World Association of Newspapers, *World Press Trends 2008*, pp. 743–7. Available at www.ihudaif.com/wp-content/

uploads/2010/01/world-association-of-newspapers-%e2%80%93-world-press-trends-2008.pdf (accessed 9 July 2014).

46 Lacroix, *Awakening Islam*, pp. 17–19. Newspapers in the Eastern Province spotlighted social and economic problems, Toby Jones, *Desert Kingdom: How Oil and Water Forged Modern Saudi Arabia* (Cambridge, MA, 2010), pp. 145–50.

4. Religion and Daily Life

1 Maggie Michael, 'Saudi women sue male guardians who stop marriage', NBCNews.com, 28 November 2010. Available at www.msnbc.msn.com/id/40407940/ns/world_news-mideast_n_africa/t/saudi-women-sue-male-guardians-who-stop-marriage/#.UQOAuWfDtk0 (accessed 9 July 2014).

2 Katherine Zoepf, 'Talk of women's rights divides Saudi Arabia', *New York Times*, 31 May 2010. Caryle Murphy, *A Kingdom's Future: Saudi Arabia through the Eyes of its Twenty-Somethings* (Washington, DC, 2013), pp. 87–8.

3 Ibid., pp. 99–104.

4 Ibid., pp. 47–8.

5 Abubaker Bagader and Ava Molnar Heinrichsdorff, *Voices of Change: Short Stories by Saudi Arabian Women Writers* (Boulder, CO, 1998), pp. 10–12.

6 Caryle Murphy, 'Child marriage case showcases deep splits in Saudi society', *Global Post*, 16 April 2009. Available at www.globalpost.com/dispatch/saudi-arabia/090416/child-marriage-case-showcases-deep-splits-saudi-society (accessed 9 July 2014).

7 Caryle Murphy, 'Child marriage reignites debate in Saudi Arabia', *The National*, 11 October 2010. Available at www.thenational.ae/news/world/middle-east/child-marriage-reignites-debate-in-saudi-arabia (accessed 9 July 2014).

8 'Single women want govt backing for polygamy', *Saudi Gazette*, 15 April 2011. Available at www.saudigazette.com.sa/index.cfm?method=home.regcon&contentid=2011041598337 (accessed 9 July 2014).

9 'One Saudi woman speaks out frankly', American Bedu, blog, 19 April 2009. Available at http://americanbedu.com/2009/04/18 (accessed 9 July 2014).

10 'Saudi Arabia: growing up in polygamy', American Bedu, blog, 4 May 2008. Available at http://americanbedu.com/2008/05/04 (accessed 9 July 2014).

11 Julie McCarthy, 'Defending and attacking polygamy in Saudi Arabia', NPR (National Public Radio), 18 July 2004. Available at www.npr.org/templates/story/story.php?storyId=3499026 (accessed 9 July 2014).

12 Muhammad Al Atawneh, *Wahhabi Islam Facing the Challenges of Modernity: Dar al-Ifta' in the Modern Saudi State* (Leiden, 2010), pp. 134–7.

13 Christopher Wilcke, 'Workplace battle continues for Saudi women', Human Rights Watch, 22 August 2012 (first published on CNN World's Global Public Square blog). Available at www.hrw.org/news/2012/08/22/workplace-battle-continues-saudi-women (accessed 9 July 2014).

14 Annemarie van Geel, 'Whither the Saudi woman? Gender mixing, empowerment and modernity', in Paul Aarts and Roel Meijer (eds), *Saudi Arabia between Conservatism, Accommodation and Reform* (The Hague, 2012), pp. 60–2.

15 Donald Cole, *Nomads of the Nomads: The Al Murrah Bedouin of the Empty Quarter* (Chicago, 1975), pp. 61–5.

16 Ibid., pp. 76–7.

17 Al Atawneh, *Wahhabi Islam*, pp. 101–7.

18 A.J. Arberry, *The Koran Interpreted* (New York, 1955), p. 337, chapter 24, verse 31.

19 Al Atawneh, *Wahhabi Islam*, p. 103.

20 Van Geel, 'Whither the Saudis woman?', pp. 64–5.

21 Amelie Le Renard, '"Only for women": women, the state and reform in Saudi Arabia', *Middle East Journal* lxii/4 (2008), p. 615.

22 Arberry, *The Koran*, p. 402, chapter 33, verse 59. Other translations render the word for veil as outer garment or cloak. The exact appearance of the apparel is unknown but the concept of modesty is evident.

23 Al Atawneh, *Wahhabi Islam*, pp. 105–6.

24 Ibid., pp. 116–18.

25 Arberry, *The Koran*, p. 490, chapter 49, verse 12.

26 'Saudi fatwa row spoils Ramadan TV season', Menassat.com, 15 September 2008. Available at http://anita4u.community-en.

menassat.com/?q=en/news-articles/4619-saudi-fatwa-row-spoils-ramadan-tv-season (accessed 19 July 2014).

27 Joshua Teitelbaum, 'Dueling for *da'wa*: state vs society on the Saudi internet', *Middle East Journal* lvi/2 (2002), pp. 224–5.

28 'Saudi Arabia', Reporters without Borders website, 2012. Available at   http://en.rsf.org/saudi-arabia-saudi-arabia-11-03-2011,39745.html (accessed 19 July 2014).

29 Teitelbaum, 'Dueling for *da'wa*', pp. 228–9.

30 Murphy, *A Kingdom's Future*, p. 18.

31 David Batty, 'Secret cinema gently subverts Saudi Arabia's puritanism', *Guardian*, 15 October 2012. Available at www.guardian.co.uk/world/2012/oct/15/saudi-secret-cinema-red-wax (accessed 9 July 2014).

32 'Saudi Arabia "may allow" cinema after three-decade ban', *Telegraph*, 21 December 2008. Available at www.telegraph.co.uk/news/worldnews/middleeast/saudiarabia/3885631/Saudi-Arabia-may-allow-cinemas-after-three-decade-ban.html (accessed 9 July 2014).

33 John Paul Jones, *If Olaya Street Could Talk – Saudi Arabia: The Heartland of Oil and Islam* (Albuquerque, NM, 2007), pp. 88–9.

34 Christopher Wilcke, '"Steps of the devil": denial of women's and girls' rights to sport in Saudi Arabia', Human Rights Watch report, New York, 15 February 2012.

35 Ian Black, 'Saudi women face gyms ban', *Guardian*, 26 April 2009. Available at www.guardian.co.uk/world/2009/apr/26/saudi-women-sports-ban?INTCMP=SRCH (accessed 9 July 2014).

36 Faiza Salih Ambah, 'Saudi women jump through many hoops for basketball team', *Christian Science Monitor*, 16 April 2008. Available at www.csmonitor.com/World/Middle-East/2008/0416/p04s01-wome.html (accessed 9 July 2014).

37 Katherine Zoepf, 'For Saudi women, biggest challenge is getting to play', *New York Times*, 17 November 2010.

38 'Saudi prince joins debate over women's sports', NBCNews.com, 23 June 2009. Available at www.msnbc.msn.com/id/31509184/ns/world_news-mideast_n_africa/t/saudi-prince-joins-debate-over-womens-sports (accessed 9 July 2014).

39 'Tendencies of Saudi tourists', *Global Travel Industry News*, 30

March 2011. Available at www.eturbonews.com/22042/tendencies-saudi-tourists (accessed 9 July 2014).

40 Rodolfo Estimo, 'Malaysia: Saudi tourists' favorite destination', *Arab News*, 10 January 2013. Available at www.arabnews.com/malaysia-saudi-tourists%E2%80%99-favorite-destination (accessed 9 July 2014).

5. Islam in Contemporary Saudi Society

1   Christopher Dickey, 'The fire that won't die out', *Newsweek*, 22 July 2002.

2   'Saudi Arabia: religious police role in school fire criticized', Human Rights Watch, 15 March 2002.

3   'Cleric sacked over Saudi school fire', *BBC News*, 25 March 2002.

4   Stephane Lacroix, *Awakening Islam: The Politics of Religious Dissent in Contemporary Saudi Arabia*, trans. George Holoch (Cambridge, MA, 2011), pp. 240–1.

5   Toby Jones, 'Seeking a "social contract" for Saudi Arabia', *Middle East Report* 228 (2003), pp. 42–8.

6   See Chapter 6 for details on the Sahwa movement.

7   International Crisis Group, 'Can Saudi Arabia reform itself?', *Middle East Report* 28 (14 July 2004), pp. 16–18.

8   Mark Thompson, 'Saudi Arabia braces for unrest', *Gulf States Newsletter*, 11 March 2011.

9   Michaela Prokop, 'Saudi Arabia: the politics of education', *International Affairs* lxxix/1 (2003), pp. 80–1. 'The Ismailis of Najran: second-class Saudi citizens', Human Rights Watch report, March 2008. Available at www.hrw.org/sites/default/files/reports/saudiarabia0908web.pdf (accessed 9 July 2014).

10 Fouad N. Ibrahim, *The Shiis of Saudi Arabia* (London, 2006), pp. 31–40.

11 On the Shiite protests and political organizations, see ibid.; and Toby Jones, *Desert Kingdom: How Oil and Water Forged Modern Saudi Arabia* (Cambridge, MA, 2010).

12 Annual summaries of conditions for Twelver Shiites and other religious minorities are contained in US Department of State, 'International religious freedom report, Saudi Arabia', (Washington, DC, annually from 2001).

13 Joseph Kostiner, *The Making of Saudi Arabia, 1916–1936: From Chieftaincy to Monarchical State* (Oxford, 1993), pp. 113–14, 156–7.

14 'The Ismailis of Najran'.

15 On the destruction of Khadija and Prophet's house, see Mai Yamani, *Cradle of Islam: Hijaz and the Quest for an Arabian Identity*, 2nd edn (London, 2009), p. 10.

16 William Ochsenwald, 'The Annexation of the Hijaz', in M. Ayoob and H. Kosebalaban (eds), *Religion and Politics in Saudi Arabia: Wahhabism and the State* (Boulder, CO, 2009), pp. 77–9.

17 Muhammad Al Atawneh, *Wahhabi Islam Facing the Challenges of Modernity: Dar al-Ifta' in the Modern Saudi State* (Leiden, 2010), p. 96.

18 'In Saudi Arabia, a resurgence of Sufism', *Washington Post*, 2 May 2006.

19 Soraya Altorki, 'Women, development, and employment in Saudi Arabia: the case of Unayzah', *Journal of Developing Societies* viii (1992), pp. 98–105. Donald P. Cole and Soraya Altorki, 'Production and trade in north central Arabia: change and development in 'Unayzah', in Martha Mundy and Basim Musallam (eds), *The Transformation of Nomadic Society in the Arab East* (Cambridge, 2000), pp. 149–53.

20 Al Atawneh, *Wahhabi Islam*, p. 101.

21 Mona Al Munajjed, *Women in Saudi Arabia Today* (London, 1997), pp. 80–99.

22 Altorki, 'Women, development, and employment, pp. 96–8.

23 Ibid., pp. 100–1. Cole and Altorki, 'Production and trade in north central Arabia', p. 157.

24 'First website offering jobs for Saudi women launched', *Saudi Gazette*, 24 June 2011. Available at www.saudigazette.com.sa/index.cfm?method=home.regcon&contentid=20110624103701 (accessed 9 July 2014).

25 Salih al-Zahrani, 'Tourism experts seek women's involvement; public disapproves', *Saudi Gazette*, 24 June 2011. Available at www.saudigazette.com.sa/index.cfm?method=home.regcon&contentid=20110624103709 (accessed 9 July 2014).

26 Amelie Le Renard, '"Only for women": women, the state and reform in Saudi Arabia', *Middle East Journal* lxii/4 (2008), pp. 625–6.

27 Stephanie Hancock, 'Saudi lingerie trade in a twist', *BBC News*, 25 February 2009. Rima al-Mukhtar, 'Lingerie shops told to honor deadline for hiring women', *Arab News*, 13 October 2011.

28 Katherine Zoepf, 'Talk of women's rights divides Saudi Arabia', *New York Times*, 31 May 2010.

29 Roel Meijer, 'Reform in Saudi Arabia: the gender-segregation debate', *Middle East Policy* xvii/4 (2010), pp. 80–100.

30 Personal communications with a Saudi economist, 6 December 2012, and with Khalid al-Dakhil, 8 December 2012. For Sheikh Abdulaziz ibn Baz's fatwa against women riding alone with a non-mahram driver, see 'Ruling concerning a woman riding with a non-mahram chauffeur', Fatwa-Online.com. Available at www.fatwa-online.com/fataawa/womensissues/mahram/0000206_47.htm (accessed 9 July 2014).

31 Ebtihal Mubarak, 'Driven', *Foreign Policy Online*, 17 June 2011.

32 For the views of some young women opposed to obtaining the right to drive, see Caryle Murphy, *A Kingdom's Future: Saudi Arabia through the Eyes of its Twenty-Somethings* (Washington, DC, 2013), pp. 93–4.

33 John Paul Jones, *If Olaya Street Could Talk – Saudi Arabia: The Heartland of Oil and Islam*, (Albuquerque, NM, 2007), p. 25.

34 'In recognition of Christmas in Saudi Arabia', American Bedu, blog, 25 December 2007. Available at http://americanbedu.com/2007/12/25/in-recognition-of-christmas (accessed 9 July 2014).

35 US Department of State, 'International religious freedom report', July–December 2010, pp. 5–6.

36 Ibid., p. 14.

37 'Saudis charge Filipinos for proselytizing', Reuters, 6 October 2010. Available at http://in.reuters.com/article/2010/10/06/idINIndia-51999620101006 (accessed 9 July 2014).

38 Jones, *If Olaya Street Could Talk*, pp. 56–7. 'Saudi Arabia: does Saudi accommodate non-Muslims during their special holidays?' American Bedu, blog, 18 August 2010. Available at http://americanbedu.com/2010/08/18 (accessed 9 July 2014).

39 'Saudi Arabia bans all things red ahead of Valentine's Day', CNN.com, 12 February 2008. Available at http://edition.cnn.com/2008/WORLD/meast/02/12/saudi.valentine (accessed 19 July 2014).

'Many celebrate Valentine's Day in secret', *Saudi Gazette*, 14 February 2010.

40 Vivienne Angeles, 'The Middle East and the Philippines: transnational linkages, labor migration, and the remaking of Philippine Islam', *Comparative Islamic Studies* vii/1–2 (2011), pp. 167–8.

6. Religious Politics

1   The discussion of the Muslim Brotherhood in Saudi Arabia is based on Stephane Lacroix, *Awakening Islam: The Politics of Religious Dissent in Contemporary Saudi Arabia*, trans. George Holoch (Cambridge, MA, 2011).

2   Ibid., pp. 49, 67.

3   Ibid., pp. 63–9.

4   On Nasir al-Din al-Albani's background and influence in Saudi Arabia, see ibid., pp. 81–9.

5   On the Salafi Group's emergence and evolution, see ibid., pp. 89–98.

6   On Saudi Arabia's support for the Afghan jihad, see Thomas Hegghammer, *Jihad in Saudi Arabia: Violence and Pan-Islamism since 1979* (Cambridge, 2010), pp. 25–30.

7   John Paul Jones, *If Olaya Street Could Talk – Saudi Arabia: The Heartland of Oil and Islam*, (Albuquerque, 2007), pp. 23–4.

8   Abdulaziz al-Fahad, 'Ornamental constitutionalism: the Saudi Basic Law of Governance', *Yale Journal of International Law* xxx (2005), pp. 375–95.

9   Lacroix, *Awakening Islam*, pp. 211–21.

10 Ibid., p. 208.

11 Hegghammer, *Jihad in Saudi Arabia*, p. 72.

12 On Osama bin Laden and al-Qaeda, see Lawrence Wright, *The Looming Tower: Al-Qaeda and the Road to 9/11* (New York, 2006).

13 Hegghammer, *Jihad in Saudi Arabia*, pp. 170–80.

14 Robert Lacey, *Inside the Kingdom: Kings, Clerics, Modernists, Terrorists, and the Struggle for Saudi Arabia* (New York, 2009), pp. 249–50.

15 F. Gregory Gause, *Saudi Arabia in the New Middle East* (New York,

2011), pp. 5–10; Joas Wagemakers, 'Arguing for change under benevolent oppression: intellectual trends and debates in Saudi Arabia', in Roel Meijer and Paul Aarts (eds), *Saudi Arabia between Conservatism, Accommodation and Reform* (The Hague, 2012), pp. 29–30.

16 Gause, *Saudi Arabia*, pp. 5–10.

17 Caryle Murphy, *A Kingdom's Future: Saudi Arabia through the Eyes of its Twenty-Somethings* (Washington, DC, 2013), pp. 21–6.

18 Ibid., p. 25.

19 Wagemakers, 'Arguing for change', pp. 13–14. Murphy, *A Kingdom's Future*, pp. 78–82.

7. The International Reach of Wahhabism

1 Yoginder Sikand, 'Wahabi/Ahle Hadith, Deobandi and Saudi connection', SunniCity.com, 14 April 2010. Available at http://sunnicity.com/2010/04/14/wahabiahle-hadith-deobandi-and-saudi-connection (accessed 9 July 2014).

2 Thomas Hegghammer, *Jihad in Saudi Arabia: Violence and Pan-Islamism since 1979* (Cambridge, 2010), pp. 18–19.

3 Nazmul Ahsan Kalimullah and Caroline Barbara Fraser, 'Islamic nongovernmental organisations in Bangladesh with reference to three case studies', *Islamic Quarterly* xxxiv/2 (1990), pp. 78–89.

4 Michaela Prokop, 'Saudi Arabia: the politics of education', *International Affairs* lxxix/1 (2003), pp. 83–5.

5 Fred von der Mehden, *Two Worlds of Islam: Interaction between Southeast Asia and the Middle East* (Gainesville, FL, 1993), pp. 3–14.

6 Noorhaidi Hasan, *Laskar Jihad: Islam, Militancy and the Quest for Identity in Post-New Order Indonesia* (Ithaca, NY, 2006), p. 33.

7 The World Assembly of Muslim Youth is dominated by the Saudi Muslim Brotherhood's Hijazi network. Stephane Lacroix, *Awakening Islam: The Politics of Religious Dissent in Contemporary Saudi Arabia*, trans. George Holoch (Cambridge, MA, 2011), p. 67.

8 Hasan, *Laskar Jihad*, pp. 32–50.

9 Noorhaidi Hasan, 'Ambivalent doctrines and conflicts in the Salafi

movement in Indonesia', in Roel Meijer (ed.), *Global Salafism: Islam's New Religious Movement* (New York, 2009), pp. 174–82.
10 Sikand, 'Wahabi/Ahle Hadith, Deobandi'.
11 Mariam Abou Zahab, 'Salafism in Pakistan: the Ahl-e Hadith movement', in Meijer (ed.), *Global Salafism*, p. 132.
12 Ibid., p. 130.
13 Sikand, 'Wahabi/Ahle Hadith, Deobandi'.
14 Abou Zahab, 'Salafism in Pakistan', p. 130.
15 Ibid., p. 131.
16 Ibid., pp. 133–40.
17 Hegghammer, *Jihad in Saudi Arabia*, pp. 26–8, 124–8.
18 Millard Burr and Robert O. Collins, *Alms for Jihad: Charity and Terrorism in the Islamic World* (Cambridge, 2006), pp. 27, 31.
19 Ibid., p. 27.
20 Hegghammer, *Jihad in Saudi Arabia*, pp. 25–48.
21 Jonathan Benthall and Jerome Bellion-Jourdan, *The Charitable Crescent: Politics of Aid in the Muslim World* (London, 2003), pp. 128–32.
22 UN Security Council Committee pursuant to resolutions 1267 (1999) and 1989 (2011) concerning Al-Qaida and associated individuals and entities. Available at www.un.org/sc/committees/1267/NSQE10304E.shtml (accessed 9 July 2014).
23 Benthall and Bellion-Jourdan, *Charitable Crescent*, pp. 134–9.
24 Hegghammer, *Jihad in Saudi Arabia*, pp. 32–6.
25 Pew Forum, 'Muslim networks and movements in Western Europe', Pew Forum on Religion and Public Life, 15 September 2010. Available at www.pewforum.org/Muslim/Muslim-Networks-and-Movements-in-Western-Europe.aspx (accessed 9 July 2014).
26 Philip Jenkins, *God's Continent: Christianity, Islam, and Europe's Religious Crisis* (Oxford, 2007), pp. 134–5.
27 Jonathan Birt, 'Wahhabism in the United Kingdom', in Madawi al-Rasheed (ed.), *Transnational Connections and the Arab Gulf* (London, 2005), pp. 168–84. Sadek Hamid, 'The development of British Salafism', *ISIM Review* xxi (Spring 2008), pp. 10–11.
28 Stephen Schwartz, 'Wahhabism and Islam in the U.S.', *National Review Online*, 30 June 2003. Available at www.nationalreview.com/articles/207366/wahhabism-islam-u-s/stephen-schwartz# (accessed 9 July 2014).

29   Freedom House, 'Saudi publications on hate ideology invade American mosques' (Washington, DC, 2005), pp. 2–3. Available at www.freedomhouse.org/sites/default/files/inline_images/Saudi% 20Publications%20on%20Hate%20Ideology%20Invade%20 American%20Mosques.pdf (accessed 19 July 2014). On the estimated number of mosques in the United States, see Kathleen E. Foley, 'The American mosque: behind the controversy', Institute for Social Policy and Understanding and the British Council, Policy Brief (June 2012), pp. 5–6. Available at www.ispu.org/pdfs/ISPU_Brief_Foley.revised.2.pdf (accessed 19 July 2014).

30   Ihsan Bagby, Paul M. Perl, and Bryan T. Froehle, 'The mosque in America: a national portrait. A report from the mosque study project', Council on American–Islamic Relations, 2001, pp. 4, 27–30. Available at http://higginsctc.org/terrorism/Masjid_Study_Project_2000_Report.pdf (accessed 19 July 2014). Ihsan Bagby, 'The American mosque 2011: basic characteristics of the American mosque: attitudes of mosque leaders', Council on American–Islamic Relations Report 1 (2011), p. 18. Available at http://faithcommunitiestoday.org/sites/faithcommunitiestoday.org/files/The%20American%20Mosque%202011%20web.pdf (accessed 19 July 2014).

31   'Program steering committee', Harvard University, the Prince Alwaleed bin Talal Islamic Studies Program. Available at www.islamicstudies.harvard.edu/program-oversight (accessed 9 July 2014).

32   'Professor Adam Sabra', faculty profile, University of California, Santa Barbara, Department of History. Available at www.history.ucsb.edu/people/person.php?account_id=372&first_name=Adam&last_name=Sabra (accessed 9 July 2014).

33   'Professor Sherman Jackson', faculty profile, University of Southern California, School of Religion, Professor Sherman Jackson. Available at http://dornsife.usc.edu/cf/faculty-and-staff/faculty.cfm?pid=1038031 (accessed 9 July 2014).

34   David B. Ottaway, 'U.S. eyes money trails of Saudi-backed charities', *Washington Post*, 19 August 2004.

35   Pew Forum 'Muslim networks and movements in Western Europe'.

Select Bibliography

Abou Zahab, Mariam, 'Salafism in Pakistan: Yhe Ahl-e Hadith Movement', in Roel Meijer (ed.), *Global Salafism: Islam's New Religious Movement*, New York, 2009, pp. 126–42.

Al Atawneh, Muhammad, *Wahhabi Islam Facing the Challenges of Modernity: Dar al-Ifta' in the Modern Saudi State*, Leiden, 2010.

Al-Fahad, Abdulaziz, 'Commentary: from exclusivism to accommodation: doctrinal and legal evolution of Wahhabism', *New York University Law Review* lxxix/2 (2004), pp. 485–519.

Al-Fahad, Abdulaziz, 'Ornamental constitutionalism: the Saudi Basic Law of Governance', *Yale Journal of International Law* xxx (2005), pp. 375–96.

Alkhazim, Mohammad A., 'Higher education in Saudi Arabia: challenges, solutions, and opportunities missed', *Higher Education Policy* xvi/4 (2003), pp. 479–86.

Al-Mukhtar, Rima, 'Lingerie shops told to honor deadline for hiring women', *Arab News*, 13 October 2011.

AlMunajjed, Mona, *Women in Saudi Arabia Today*, London, 1997.

Al Najjar, Omaima, 'Omaima Al Najjar being investigated by the religious police', Omaima Al Najjar – Saudi Woman Speaks Out, blog, 27 December 2010. Available at http://omaimanajjar.wordpress.com/2010/12/27/omaima-al-najjar-being-investigated-by-the-religious-police (accessed 9 July 2014).

Al-Rashid, Ibrahim (ed.), *Saudi Arabia Enters the World: Secret U.S. Documents on the Emergence of the Kingdom of Saudi Arabia as a World Power, 1936–1949, Part I*, Salisbury, NC, 1980.

Altorki, Soraya, 'Women, development, and employment in Saudi Arabia: the case of Unayzah', *Journal of Developing Societies* viii (1992), pp. 96–110.

Ambah, Faiza Salih, 'Saudi Women Jump through Many Hoops for Basketball Team', *Christian Science Monitor*, 16 April 2008. Available at www.csmonitor.com/World/Middle-East/2008/0416/p04s01-wome.html (accessed 9 July 2014).

Amnesty International, *Death Sentences and Executions 2011*, London, 2012.

Angeles, Vivienne, 'The Middle East and the Philippines: transnational linkages, labor migration, and the remaking of Philippine Islam', *Comparative Islamic Studies* vii/1–2 (2011), pp. 157–81.

Arberry, A.J., *The Koran Interpreted*, New York, 1955.

Bagader, Abubaker, Ava Heinrichsdorff, and Deborah Akers, *Voices of Change: Short Stories by Saudi Arabian Women Writers*, Boulder, CO, 1998.

Bagby, Ihsan, Paul M. Perl, and Bryan T. Froehle, *The American Mosque 2011: Basic Characteristics of the American Mosque: Attitudes of Mosque Leaders*, Report Number 1, n.p., 2012.

Bagby, Ihsan, Paul M. Perl, and Bryan T. Froehle, 'The mosque in America: a national portrait. A report from the mosque study project', Council of American–Islamic Relations, 2001. Available at http://higginsctc.org/terrorism/Masjid_Study_Project_2000_Report.pdf (accessed 19 July 2014).

BBC News, 'Cleric Sacked over Saudi school fire', *BBC News*, 25 March 2002.

Benthall, Jonathan and Jerome Bellion-Jourdan, *The Charitable Crescent: Politics of Aid in the Muslim World*, London, 2003.

Birt, Jonathan, 'Wahhabism in the United Kingdom', in Madawi Al-Rasheed (ed.), *Transnational Connections and the Arab Gulf*, London, 2005, pp. 168–84.

Black, Ian, 'Saudi Women Face Gyms Ban', *Guardian*, 26 April 2009. Available at www.guardian.co.uk/world/2009/apr/26/saudi-women-sports-ban?INTCMP=SRCH (accessed 9 July 2014).

Bsheer, Rosie, 'Choking Mecca in the name of beauty – and development (Part 1)', *Jadaliyya*, 21 October 2010. Available at www.jadaliyya.com/pages/index/251/choking-mecca-in-the-name-of-beauty_and-developmen (accessed 9 July 2014).

Burr, Millard and Robert O. Collins, *Alms for Jihad: Charity and Terrorism in the Islamic World*, Cambridge, 2006.

Cole, Donald P., *Nomads of the Nomads: The Al Murrah Bedouin of the Empty Quarter*, Chicago, 1975.

Cole, Donald P. and Soraya Altorki, 'Production and Trade in North Central Arabia: Change and Development in "Unayzah"', in Martha Mundy and Basim Musallam (eds), *The Transformation of Nomadic Society in the Arab East*, Cambridge, 2000, pp. 149–53.

Commins, David, *The Wahhabi Mission and Saudi Arabia*, London, 2006.

Dickey, Christopher, 'The fire that won't die out', *Newsweek*, 22 July 2002.

Doumato, Eleanor Abdella, *Getting God's Ear: Women, Islam and Healing in Saudi Arabia and the Gulf*, New York, 2000.

Doumato, Eleanor Abdella, 'Manning the barricades: Islam according to Saudi Arabia's school texts', *Middle East Journal* lvii/2 (2003), pp. 230–47.

Doumato, Eleanor Abdella, 'Saudi Arabia: from "Wahhabi" roots to contemporary revivalism', in Eleanor A. Doumato and Gregory Starrett (eds), *Teaching Islam: Textbooks and Religion in the Middle East*, Boulder, CO, 2007, p. 155.

Estimo, Rodolfo, 'Malaysia: Saudi tourists' favorite destination', *Arab News*, 10 January 2013. Available at www.arabnews.com/malaysia-saudi-tourists%E2%80%99-favorite-destination (accessed 9 July 2014).

Freedom House, 'Saudi publications on hate ideology invade American mosques', Washington, DC, 2005. Available at www.freedomhouse.org/sites/default/files/inline_images/Saudi%20Publications%20on%20Hate%20Ideology%20Invade%20American%20Mosques.pdf (accessed 19 July 2014).

Fierro, Maribel, 'The treatises against innovations (*kutub al-bida'*)', *Der Islam* lxix/2 (1992), pp. 204–46.

'First website offering jobs for Saudi women launched', *Saudi Gazette*, 24 June 2011. Available at www.saudigazette.com.sa/index.cfm?method=home.regcon&contentid=20110624103701 (accessed 9 July 2014).

Foley, Kathleen E., 'The American mosque: behind the controversy', Institute for Social Policy and Understanding and the British Council, Policy Brief (June 2012). Available at www.ispu.org/pdfs/ISPU_Brief_Foley.revised.2.pdf (accessed 19 July 2014).

Gause, F. Gregory, *Saudi Arabia in the New Middle East*, New York, 2011.

Hamdan, Amani, 'Women and education in Saudi Arabia: challenges and achievements', *International Education Journal* vi/1 (2005), pp. 42–64.

Hamid, Sadek, 'The development of British Salafism', *ISIM Review* xxi (Spring 2008), p. 10.

Hamidan, M.D., 'Detained municipal surveyor was harassing schoolgirls: Haia', *Arab News*, 24 June 2011. Available at www.arabnews.com/node/381867 (accessed 9 July 2014).

Hancock, Stephanie, 'Saudi lingerie trade in a twist', *BBC News*, 25 February 2009.

Hasan, Noorhaidi, *Laskar Jihad: Islam, Militancy and the Quest for Identity in Post-New Order Indonesia*, Ithaca, NY, 2006.

Hasan, Noorhaidi, 'Ambivalent doctrines and conflicts in the Salafi movement in Indonesia', in Roel Meijer (ed.), *Global Salafism: Islam's New Religious Movement*, New York, 2009, pp. 174–82.

Hegghammer, Thomas, *Jihad in Saudi Arabia: Violence and Pan-Islamism since 1979*, Cambridge, 2010.

Human Rights Watch, 'Precarious justice: arbitrary detention and unfair trials in the deficient criminal justice system of Saudi Arabia', *Human Rights Watch* xx/3 (March 2008).

Ibrahim, Fouad N., *The Shiis of Saudi Arabia*, London, 2006.

'In recognition of Christmas in Saudi Arabia', American Bedu, blog, 25 December 2007. Available at http://americanbedu.com/2007/12/25/in-recognition-of-christmas (accessed 9 July 2014).

'In Saudi Arabia, a resurgence of Sufism', *Washington Post*, 2 May 2006.

International Crisis Group, 'Can Saudi Arabia reform itself?' *Middle East Report* 28 (14 July 2004).

'The Ismailis of Najran: second-class Saudi citizens', Human Rights Watch report, March 2008. Available at www.hrw.org/sites/default/files/reports/saudiarabia0908web.pdf (accessed 9 July 2014).

Jenkins, Philip, *God's Continent: Christianity, Islam, and Europe's Religious Crisis*, Oxford, 2007.

Jones, John Paul, *If Olaya Street Could Talk – Saudi Arabia: The Heartland of Oil and Islam*, Albuquerque, NM, 2007.

Jones, Toby, *Desert Kingdom: How Oil and Water Forged Modern Saudi Arabia*, Cambridge, MA, 2010.

Jones, Toby, 'Seeking a "Social Contract" for Saudi Arabia', *Middle East Report* 228 (2003), pp. 42–8.

Kalimullah, Nazmul Ahsan and Caroline Barbara Fraser, 'Islamic nongovernmental organisations in Bangladesh with reference to three case studies', *Islamic Quarterly* xxxiv/2 (1990), pp. 71–92.

Kostiner, Joseph, *The Making of Saudi Arabia, 1916–1936: From Chieftaincy to Monarchical State*, Oxford, 1994.

Lacey, Robert, *Inside the Kingdom: Kings, Clerics, Modernists, Terrorists, and the Struggle for Saudi Arabia*, New York, 2009.

Lacey, Robert, *The Kingdom: Arabia and the House of Saud*, New York, 1981.

Lacroix, Stéphane, *Awakening Islam: The Politics of Religious Dissent in Contemporary Saudi Arabia*, Cambridge, MA, 2011.

Le Renard, Amelie, '"Only for women": women, the state and reform in Saudi Arabia', *Middle East Journal* lxii/4 (2008), pp. 610–29.

Long, David E., *The Hajj Today: A Survey of the Contemporary Pilgrimage to Makkah*, Albany, NY, 1979.

'Many celebrate Valentine's Day in secret', *Saudi Gazette*, 14 February 2010.

McCarthy, Julie, 'Defending and attacking polygamy in Saudi Arabia', NPR (National Public Radio), 18 July 2004. Available at www.npr.org/templates/story/story.php?storyId=3499026 (accessed 9 July 2014).

Meijer, Roel, 'Reform in Saudi Arabia: the gender-segregation debate', *Middle East Policy* xvii/4 (2010), pp. 80–100.

Michael, Maggie, 'Saudi women sue male guardians who stop marriage', NBCNews.com, 28 November 2010. Available at www.msnbc.msn.com/id/40407940/ns/world_news-mideast_n_africa/t/saudi-women-sue-male-guardians-who-stop-marriage/#.UQOAuWfDtk0 (accessed 9 July 2014).

Mubarak, Ebtihal, 'Driven', *Foreign Policy Online*, 17 June 2011.

Murphy, Caryle, *A Kingdom's Future: Saudi Arabia through the Eyes of its Twenty-Somethings*, Washington, DC, 2013.

Murphy, Caryle, 'Child marriage case showcases deep splits in Saudi society', *Global Post*, 16 April 2009. Available at www.globalpost.

com/dispatch/saudi-arabia/090416/child-marriage-case-showcases-deep-splits-saudi-society (accessed 9 July 2014).

Murphy, Caryle, 'Child marriage reignites debate in Saudi Arabia', *The National*, 11 October 2010. Available at www.thenational.ae/news/world/middle-east/child-marriage-reignites-debate-in-saudi-arabia (accessed 9 July 2014).

Ochsenwald, William, 'The annexation of the Hijaz', in M. Ayoob and H. Kosebalaban (eds), *Religion and Politics in Saudi Arabia: Wahhabism and the State*, Boulder, CO, 2009, pp. 77–9.

'One Saudi woman speaks out frankly', American Bedu, blog, 27 December 2010. Available at http://americanbedu.com/27 December 2010 (accessed 9 July 2014).

Ottaway, David B., 'U.S. eyes money trails of Saudi-backed charities', *Washington Post*, 19 August 2004.

Pew Forum, 'Muslim Networks and Movements in Western Europe', Pew Forum on Religion and Public Life, 15 September 2010. Available at www.pewforum.org/Muslim/Muslim-Networks-and-Movements-in-Western-Europe.aspx (accessed 9 July 2014).

Piscatori, James, 'Managing God's guests: the pilgrimage, Saudi Arabia and the politics of legitimacy', in Paul Dresch and James Piscatori (eds), *Monarchies and Nations: Globalisation and Identity in the Arab Nations of the Gulf*, London, 2005, pp. 222–46.

Prokop, Michaela, 'Saudi Arabia: the politics of education', *International Affairs* lxxix/1 (2003), pp. 77–89.

Roy, Delwin, 'Saudi Arabian education: development policy', *Middle Eastern Studies* xxxvii/3 (1992), pp. 477–508.

'Ruling concerning a woman riding with a non-mahram chauffeur', Fatwa-Online.com. Available at www.fatwa-online.com/fataawa/womensissues/mahram/0000206_47.htm (accessed 4 July 2014).

'Saudi Arabia', Reporters without Borders website, 2012. Available at http://en.rsf.org/report-saudi-arabia,146.html (accessed 9 July 2014)

'Saudi Arabia bans all things red ahead of Valentine's Day', CNN.com, 12 February 2008. Available at http://edition.cnn.com/2008/WORLD/meast/02/12/saudi.valentine (accessed 19 July 2014).

'Saudi Arabia: criminal justice strengthened', Human Rights Watch, 14 January 2010. Available at www.hrw.org/news/2010/01/14/saudiarabia-criminal-justice-strengthened (accessed 9 July 2014).

'Saudi Arabia: does Saudi accommodate non-Muslims during their special holidays?' American Bedu, blog, 18 August 2010. Available at http://americanbedu.com/2010/08/18 (accessed 9 July 2014).

'Saudi Arabia: economic weakness led to unemployment rate hike', *G20 Statistical Update*, International Labour Office, April 2010.

'Saudi Arabia: growing up in polygamy', American Bedu, blog, 4 May 2008. Available at http://americanbedu.com/2008/05/04 (accessed 9 July 2014).

'Saudi Arabia "may allow" cinema after three-decade ban', *Telegraph*, 21 December 2008. Available at www.telegraph.co.uk/news/worldnews/middleeast/saudiarabia/3885631/Saudi-Arabia-may-allow-cinemas-after-three-decade-ban.html (accessed 9 July 2014).

'Saudi Arabia opens largest women's university in the world', *Al Arabiyya News*, 15 May 2011. Available at http://english.alarabiya.net/articles/2011/05/15/149218.html (accessed 9 July 2014).

'Saudi Arabia: religious police role in school fire criticized', Human Rights Watch Report, 15 March 2002.

'Saudi Arabia's education reforms emphasize training for jobs', *Chronicle of Higher Education* lvii/7 (8 October 2010).

'Saudi fatwa row spoils Ramadan TV season', Menassat.com, 15 September 2008. Available at www.menassat.com/?q=en/news-articles/4619-saudi-fatwa-row-spoils-ramadan-tv-season (accessed 9 July 2014).

'Saudi prince joins debate over women's sports', NBCNews.com, 23 June 2009. Available at www.msnbc.msn.com/id/31509184/ns/world_news-mideast_n_africa/t/saudi-prince-joins-debate-over-womens-sports (accessed 9 July 2014).

'Saudi royal wealth: where do they get all that money?', cable from US Embassy, Riyadh, to Treasury Department, Washington, DC, 30 November 1996. Available at http://wikileaks.ch/cable/1996/11/96RIYADH4784.html (accessed 9 July 2014).

'Saudis charge Filipinos for proselytizing', Reuters, 6 October 2010. Available at http://in.reuters.com/article/2010/10/06/idINIndia-51999620101006 (accessed 9 July 2014).

Schwartz, Stephen, 'Wahhabism and Islam in the U.S.', *National Review Online*, 30 June 2003. Available at www.nationalreview.com/articles/207366/wahhabism-islam-u-s/stephen-schwartz# (accessed 9 July 2014).

'Secret cinema gently subverts Saudi Arabia's puritanism', *Guardian*, 15 October 2012. Available at www.guardian.co.uk/world/2012/oct/15/saudi-secret-cinema-red-wax (accessed 9 July 2014).

Sikand, Yoginder, 'Wahabi, Ahle Hadith, Deobandi and Saudi Connection', *SunniNews*, 14 April 2010. Available at http://sunninews.wordpress.com/2010/04/14/wahabiahle-hadith-deobandi-and-saudi-connection (accessed 9 July 2014).

'Single women want govt backing for polygamy', *Saudi Gazette*, 15 April 2011. Available at www.saudigazette.com.sa/index.cfm?method=home.regcon&contentid=2011041598337 (accessed 9 July 2014).

Teitelbaum, Joshua, 'Dueling for *da'wa*: state vs society on the Saudi internet', *Middle East Journal* lvi/2 (2002), pp. 222–39.

'Tendencies of Saudi tourists', *Global Travel Industry News*, 30 March 2011. Available at www.eturbonews.com/22042/tendencies-saudi-tourists (accessed 9 July 2014).

'Program steering committee', Harvard University, the Prince Alwaleed bin Talal Islamic Studies Program. Available at www.islamicstudies.harvard.edu/program-oversight (accessed 9 July 2014).

Thompson, Mark, 'Saudi Arabia braces for unrest', *Gulf States Newsletter*, 11 March 2011.

'Tourism experts seek women's involvement; public disapproves', *Saudi Gazette*, 24 June 2011. Available at www.saudigazette.com.sa/index.cfm?method=home.regcon&contentid=20110624103709 (accessed 9 July 2014).

Traboulsi, Samer, 'An early refutation of Muhammad ibn 'Abd al-Wahhab's reformist views', *Die Welt des Islams* xlii/3 (2002), pp. 373–415.

UN Security Council Committee pursuant to resolutions 1267 (1999) and 1989 (2011) concerning Al-Qaida and associated individuals and entities. Available at www.un.org/sc/committees/1267/NSQE10304E.shtml (accessed 9 July 2014).

US Department of State, 'International religious freedom report, Saudi Arabia', Washington, DC, 2010.

Uthaymin, Abd Allah Salih al-, *Muhammad ibn Abd al-Wahhab: The Man and his Works*, London, 2009.

Van Geel, Annemarie, 'Whither the Saudi woman? Gender mixing, empowerment and modernity', in Paul Aarts and Roel Meijer (eds), *Saudi Arabia between Conservatism, Accommodation and Reform*, The Hague, 2012, pp. 57–78.

Vogel, Frank, 'The public and private in Saudi Arabia: restrictions on the powers of Committees for Ordering the Good and Forbidding the Evil', *Social Research* lxx/3 (2003), pp. 749–68.

Von der Mehden, Fred, *Two Worlds of Islam: Interaction between Southeast Asia and the Middle East*, Gainesville, FL, 1993.

Wagemakers, Joas, 'Arguing for change under benevolent oppression: intellectual trends and debates in Saudi Arabia', in Paul Aarts and Roel Meijer (eds), *Saudi Arabia between Conservatism, Accommodation and Reform*, The Hague, 2012, pp. 13–32.

Wilcke, Christopher, '"Steps of the devil": denial of women's and girls' rights to sport in Saudi Arabia', Human Rights Watch (New York, 2012).

Wilcke, Christopher, 'Workplace battle continues for Saudi women', Human Rights Watch, 22 August 2012 (first published on CNN World's Global Public Square blog). Available at www.hrw.org/news/2012/08/22/workplace-battle-continues-saudi-women (accessed 9 July 2014).

World Association of Newspapers, 'Saudi Arabia', *World Press Trends 2008*, pp. 743–7. Available at www.ihudaif.com/wp-content/uploads/2010/01/world-association-of-newspapers-%e2%80%93-world-press-trends-2008.pdf (accessed 9 July 2014).

Wright, Lawrence, *The Looming Tower: Al-Qaeda and the Road to 9/11*, New York, 2006.

Yamani, Mai, *Cradle of Islam: Hijaz and the Quest for an Arabian Identity*, London, 2009.

'Youth who resisted hai'a still in custody', *Saudi Gazette*, 25 June 2011. Available at www.saudigazette.com.sa/index.cfm?method=home.regcon&contentid=20110625103766 (accessed 9 July 2014).

Zoepf, Katherine, 'For Saudi women, biggest challenge is getting to play', *New York Times*, 17 November 2010.

Zoepf, Katherine, 'Talk of women's rights divides Saudi Arabia', *New York Times*, 31 May 2010.

Suggestions for Further Reading

The number and quality of books about religion in Saudi Arabia has increased in recent years, due in part to the government's decision to allow foreign scholars to carry out research inside the kingdom. Nevertheless, there are not yet many books in English by Saudi authors that combine an insider's familiarity with an ear for the global audience.

For an introduction to the history of Saudi Arabia, the most comprehensive overview is Alexei Vassiliev, *The History of Saudi Arabia* (London, 1998); a superb compact account is Madawi al-Rasheed, *A History of Saudi Arabia*, 2nd edn, (Cambridge, 2010). The life and ideas of Wahhabism's founder is the focus of Abd Allah Salih al-'Uthaymin, *Muhammad Ibn 'Abd al-Wahhab: The Man and his Works* (London, 2009). The historical evolution of the Wahhabi movement and its alliance with the Saudi dynasty is treated in David Commins, *The Wahhabi Mission and Saudi Arabia*, 2nd edn, (London, 2009).

For studies of religion and politics in recent decades, a fine overview is Robert Lacey, *Inside the Kingdom: Kings, Clerics, Modernists, Terrorists, and the Struggle for Saudi Arabia* (New York, 2009). The impact of modern Islamic revivalist currents, in particular the Muslim Brotherhood, is the subject of Stephane Lacroix's deeply researched *Awakening Islam: The Politics of Religious Dissent in Contemporary Saudi Arabia*, trans. George Holoch (Cambridge, MA, 2011). Thomas Hegghammer, *Jihad in Saudi Arabia: Violence and Pan-Islamism since 1979* (Cambridge, 2010) provides dispassionate analysis of the kingdom's support for Muslim causes abroad and al-Qaeda's terrorist campaign. Fouad Ibrahim, *The Shiis of Saudi Arabia* (London, 2006) provides an insider's perspective on the country's largest religious minority.

General accounts of the role of religion in contemporary society are few. There are two commendable studies of religion, women and gender: Eleanor Abdella Doumato, *Getting God's Ear: Women, Islam and Healing in Saudi Arabia and the Gulf* (New York, 2000), and Madawi al-Rasheed, *A Most Masculine State: Gender, Politics and Religion in Saudi Arabia* (Cambridge, 2013). Caryle Murphy, *A Kingdom's Future: Saudi Arabia through the Eyes of its Twenty-Somethings* (Washington, DC, 2013) canvasses the range of opinions and aspirations held by educated young Saudis. Social manners and religious customs of the upper crust from Hijaz are the focus of Mai Yamani, *Cradle of Islam: Hijaz and the Quest for Identity in Saudi Arabia*, 2nd edn, (London, 2009). Hamza Bogary, *The Sheltered Quarter: A Tale of a Boyhood in Mecca* (Austin, TX, 1991) is a marvelous Saudi coming-of-age novella that imparts the flavor of religion in daily life in Mecca before the oil boom. An expatriate's view of Saudi interactions with American residents during the 1960s and 1970s is the colorful account by John Paul Jones, *If Olaya Street Could Talk – Saudi Arabia: The Heartland of Oil and Islam* (Albuquerque, NM, 2007).

Index